Books are to be returned on or before
the last date below

A Game of Two Halves

Professional football is one of the most popular television genres worldwide, attracting the support of millions of fans and the sponsorship of powerful companies. In *A Game of Two Halves*, Cornel Sandvoss considers the relationship between football and television, football's links with transnational capitalism and the importance of football fandom in forming social and cultural identities around the globe, to present the phenomenon of football as a reflection of postmodern culture and globalization.

Analysing the social, economic and technological premises of football fandom through ethnographic audience research, Cornel Sandvoss explores the motivations and pleasures of football fans, the intense bond formed between supporters and their clubs, the implications of football consumption for political discourse and citizenship, football as a factor of cultural globalization and the pivotal role of football and television in a postmodern cultural order.

Cornel Sandvoss is Lecturer in the School of Media and Cultural Production at De Montfort University, Leicester, specializing in the sociology of media, culture and technology.

I.M. MARSH LIBRARY LIVERPOOL L17 6BD

D0242183

Comedia
Series Editor: David Morley

Comedia titles available from Routledge:

The Dynasty Years
Hollywood television and critical media studies
Jostein Gripsrud

Family Television
Cultural power and domestic leisure
David Morley

A Game of Two Halves
Football, television and globalization
Cornel Sandvoss

Hiding in the Light
On images and things
Dick Hebdige

Home Territories
Media, mobility and identity
David Morley

Impossible Bodies
Femininity and masculinity at the movies
Chris Hoimlund

The Known World of Broadcast News
Stanley Baran and Roger Wallis

Migrancy, Culture, Identity
Iain Chambers

The Photographic Image in Digital Culture
Edited by Martin Lister

The Place of Media Power
Pilgrims and witnesses of the media age
Nick Couldry

Spectacular Bodies
Gender, genre and the action cinema
Yvonne Tasker

Stuart Hall
Critical dialogues in cultural studies
Edited by Kuan-Lising Chen and David Morley

A Game of Two Halves

Football, television and globalization

Cornel Sandvoss

Routledge
Taylor & Francis Group

LONDON AND NEW YORK

First published 2003
by Routledge
11 New Fetter Lane, London EC4P 4EE

Simultaneously published in the USA and Canada
by Routledge
29 West 35th Street, New York, NY 10001

Routledge is an imprint of the Taylor & Francis Group

© 2003 Cornel Sandvoss

Typeset in Galliard by The Running Head Limited, Cambridge
Printed and bound in Great Britain by MPG Books Ltd, Bodmin

All rights reserved. No part of this book may be reprinted or reproduced or
utilized in any form or by any electronic, mechanical, or other means, now
known or hereafter invented, including photocopying and recording, or in
any information storage or retrieval system, without permission in writing
from the publishers.

British Library Cataloguing in Publication Data
A catalogue record for this book is available from the British Library

Library of Congress Cataloging in Publication Data
Sandvoss, Cornel.
    A game of two halves: football, television and globalization / Cornel Sandvoss.
    p. cm.
    1. Soccer—Social aspects. 2. Television and sports. I. Title.
    GV943.9.S64527 2003
    796.334'04—dc21   2003005294

ISBN 0–415–31484–4 (hbk)
ISBN 0–415–31485–2 (pbk)

In Liebe und Gedenken an Walter Laue (1916–2002)

Contents

Acknowledgements

I am indebted to a long list of people and institutions for their help and support with this project.

On the academic front I would like to thank David Morley for his most valuable feedback and his tremendous help as series editor in ensuring the publication of this book, my former PhD supervisor Roger Silverstone for his support and reassuring assessment of my research into football fan cultures, and John Tomlinson for his insightful comments on the thesis arising out of this research.

I would also like to acknowledge and thank a number of institutions, governmental organizations and research bodies who have financially supported my research. These include the British Council, the Foreign and Commonwealth Office, the Deutsche Akademische Austauschdienst and the Department of Sociology at the London School of Economics.

I am indebted to my family and many friends. My parents, Waltraud and Ulrich Sandvoss, and my grandparents, Walter and Ilsa Laue, have supported me as much as possible during most difficult times for themselves. Lisa Pinsley made useful comments on many drafts of my work and undertook the laborious task of helping to adjust my syntax to the English language. I am also grateful to a long list of friends for accompanying and sharing many of their interesting observations with me during different stages of my research. In naming some of them I run the risk of omitting others. Nevertheless, those I am particularly indebted to include: Andreas Meyer, Christina Hermann, Vivi Theodoropoulou, Susanne Munzert and Tanya Horeck.

In the course of my fieldwork numerous organizations and individuals have supported my study. I particularly would like to thank Stefan Thomé from the Fan-Projekt Leverkusen for his immense support of my research and James Edwards of the Chelsea Independent Supporters Association for his helpful advice and support during my fieldwork. I am equally grateful to Jürgen von Einem of Bayer AG for his open and valuable thoughts on the economics of contemporary football. I am also indebted to Colin Hutchinson and Chelsea Football Club as well as Kevin Payne and DC United for assisting my research. I would like to thank the many other clubs that were happy and quick to help, in particular Nottingham Forest, Charlton Athletic, Aston Villa, Sheffield

Wednesday, Middlesbrough FC, Leicester City, Borussia Mönchengladbach, VfL Bochum, Eintracht Frankfurt, Borussia Dortmund, Fortuna Köln, TSV 1860 Munich, New York Metro Stars, as well as SC Freiburg, Bayern München, Hansa Rostock, 1.FC Kaiserslautern, 1.FC Nürnberg, VfB Stuttgart, Manchester United, Southampton FC and Coventry City. My thanks also go to Andreas Thiemann of *SAT.1*, Keith Cooper, former Director of Communications at FIFA, and the Kölner Zentralarchiv für Sozialforschung for their support of my study.

Last, but not least, I would like to deeply thank all participants and interviewees who have dedicated many hours of their time to my project and shared many illuminating experiences, observations, impressions and reflections. Without their help this book would not have been possible.

Chapter 1

Introduction

Football and modernity

The day I commenced the research for this book in August 1998 I arrived at the BayArena, home of German first division side Bayer Leverkusen. The name of the ground had been changed at the beginning of the season to promote the team's sponsor and owner – the pharmaceutical multinational Bayer. I had bought a season ticket for the largest section of the recently redeveloped ground named 'Family Street'. Nothing in the crowd savoured of the scenes of football-related violence and hooliganism that had come to sum up the public image of the sport in the years before and after the Heysel disaster in which 39 fans were killed in 1985.[1] Even the overt display of masculinity and sexist chauvinism so often associated with football fandom seemed strangely lacking. Indeed, the spectators in 'Family Street' accurately reflected its name. Families, fathers with their sons and daughters, mothers and their children slowly took up their seats, protected from the warm August sunshine by the ground's glass roofing, and avidly followed the pre-game entertainment on newly installed giant video screens. And in contrast to the 1980s, when the term 'rushing' referred to the practice of rival fan groups storming sections of the ground occupied by fans of the opposing team, there was very a different 'rush' at the BayArena. At half time hordes of fans, often driven by their children, fought their way to a newly built onsite McDonald's restaurant. It was here, under the golden arches of McDonald's, that my research began.

As spectator football is subject to dramatic transformations, it has become increasingly popular. Football fandom now crosses age, gender, class and geographic divides. Even in the United States, where 'eleven men in funny shorts' have traditionally evoked more irritation than enthusiasm, officials of the newly founded professional soccer league now proudly state that soccer's popularity has overtaken traditional North American sports such as ice hockey.[2] If the first day of my research had indicated football's commercial nature, the last day of my fieldwork, which I spent among an enthusiastic crowd of DC United fans at Washington's RFK Stadium – 43 games, 17 stadia, and 15 months later – powerfully illustrated the global state of the game. Yet what are the premises of the global presence and appeal of professional football clubs? How do football clubs form the ground for the fandom of millions of supporters from different social, cultural and geographic backgrounds? What role do they come to play in the everyday life of their audiences? To investigate the reasons for football's outstanding popularity, and the social and cultural consequences of its unrivalled standing within popular culture, is the aim of this book.

The rise and fall of cultural practices such as football fandom is not coincidental, nor can they be explained by looking at such practices in isolation from their historical framing. Rather they are powerful reflections of historical, social and economic conditions. With this conviction at heart, the following investigation seeks to explore the context of football fandom in the modern era – in particular focusing on the role of television as the single most important factor behind the transformation of football in the past 50 years. Football fandom is not only a remarkable phenomenon of (post-)modern life, but also a signifier of its very essence. This book serves as a case study of those macro transformations crucial to the changing nature of football fandom today: consumption-based identity formation and narcissism, globalization and rationalization. As such, I hope this book presents readers not only with a new perspective on football fandom – which in part also translates to other (team) sports – but also provides another piece in the puzzle of understanding modernity.

The empirical basis of this discussion and its theoretical abstraction derives from 15 months of qualitative research I conducted in the United Kingdom, Germany and the United States. During this period I focused on two selected clubs – Chelsea Football Club and TSV Bayer 04 Leverkusen – and their fans around the world, as well as fans of other clubs within the respective regions of these clubs. In addition I also interviewed a number of fans in the newly founded Major League Soccer in the United States, here focusing on fans of Washington-based DC United. In total I interviewed 89 fans and conducted 44 participant observations. A discussion of my methodology can be found in the Appendix.

In its methodological and theoretical framing, this book is thus closer to audience studies and the sociology of consumption than most academic work on football and its fans to date. Following the growing attention to violence among spectators, the study of hooliganism has long been the core concern of academic investigations of football fans. Stuart Hall's exploration (1979) of the interrelation between hooliganism and its media coverage aside, approaches to football hooliganism ranging from Ian Taylor's influential analysis (1971) in which he identifies hooliganism as a response to social control, to various recent accounts of spectator violence (Murphy *et al.* 1990; Dunning 1994; Giulianotti *et al.* 1994; Kerr 1994; Roversi 1994; see also Giulianotti 2000) are largely criminological,[3] and hence are of limited value in the analysis of fandom as broader social phenomenon.[4] A second strain of research focusing on spectator football consists of the various studies of the political economy of the game. Arnold (1991), Alan Tomlinson (1991), King (1998) and Lee (1998) explore the political economy of football in Britain, with other work focusing on the institutional basis of local football cultures in Europe (Gehrmann 1988; Horak 1994; Lanfranchi 1994a, 1994b) and around the world (Vamplew 1994; Mason 1995; Bar-On 1997; Leite Lopes 1997; Nkwi and Vidacs 1997; Tuastad 1997; Colombijn 1999). In addition recent work has explored aspects of the global interconnectivities of contemporary sport and football (Harvey and Houle 1994; Rowe *et al.* 1994; Williams 1994a; Blake 1995; Tomlinson 1996; Miller *et al.* 2001). Finally an increasing body of work has been dedicated to the symbiosis between sports and the media (Klatell and Marcus 1988; Barnett 1990).[5] In contrast to recent historical trends in media and communications research most of these studies privilege textual (Colley and Davies 1982; O'Connor and Boyle 1993; Maguire *et al.* 1999) and institutional analysis (Sugden and Tomlinson 1998) over audience research. Their focus lies with the text (football) and its production rather than the audience (fans).

While providing a useful background for my discussion the methodological basis of such work limits its benefit for our understanding of football fandom. As Rose and Friedman (1994: 34) argue, 'it would be simplistic to assume that any spectator who derives pleasures from television sports spectatorship is unproblematically taking up the hegemonic values of television sport'. The above studies, whether focusing on media texts or institutions, have little to say about fans themselves, on what grounds their fandom is constructed and what role football occupies in their lifeworld. In order to answer such questions we have, as Jhally (1989) argues, to progress beyond mere institutional and textual analysis.[6] What is needed is an exploration of the cultural, social and economic framing of football as well as its macro premises that manifest themselves in the everyday life of fans. Before we can engage in the detailed analysis of contemporary football fandom, it is, however, important to identify the historical framing of spectator football as well as of the media that have entered a symbiotic relationship with football. Their historical condition constitutes the basis for understanding their contemporary condition. Let me therefore briefly summarize the historical background of the rise of football and television.

Excursus 1: Association football and modernity

Life in the Middle Ages was marked by an acute lack of mobility for the vast majority of the population. Yet, despite frequent hardships, crop failures, epidemics and other incalculable threats, most members of medieval agricultural societies had considerable amounts of free time at their disposal. One form of entertainment that evolved in this condition of limited mobility yet substantial spare time was the practice of 'folk football'. Organized on a local level involving a vast number of participants, folk football first emerged in medieval England (Schulze-Marmeling 1992), although its precise time and place of origin remain contested.[7] Further evidence of the proliferation of folk football can be found in the various highway acts and other legal initiatives that sought to ban football. Both Guttmann (1994: 7) and Marples (1954: 28) refer to the ban enforced by the Mayor of London in 1314 as the first written documentation of football.

The authorities' dislike of folk football is hardly surprising. The game was marked by an almost complete absence of rules and regulations. Neither the space of competition nor the number of participants was defined while the length of a game was, if at all, determined by sunset. Victory was secured by carrying the ball into the opponents' village or half of town. The violent conduct of folk football often caused homicides and injuries (Elias and Dunning 1986; Holt 1989: 36–7). Accordingly, the geographer John Bale (1993: 13) has interpreted early folk football as a mass participation event blurring distinctions between actor and spectator reminiscent of the tradition of carnival – a point also made by Schulze-Marmeling (1992) who emphasizes the 'subversiveness' of the game. The carnivalesque element of football in the Middle Ages as a temporary inversion of the social order thus reflects the lack of physical and social mobility in the feudal societies of medieval Europe.

With the turn of the seventeenth century the established balance between work and leisure came under the pressure of various economic, social and cultural transformations. The growing number of puritans targeted Sunday afternoon amusement and sports and successfully introduced the sad Sabbath (Marples 1954). Puritanism also prepared the ground for amateurism and related ideas of sporting 'fairness' and 'honesty' as 'play ethic became the ultimate mirror image of Protestant work ethic' (Brailsford 1991: 26; see also Overman 1997). The spread of the Protestant work ethic in turn prepared the ground for the dramatic economic, social and cultural transformations that were both the premise and the consequence of rational industrialism and industrial modernity. While the introduction of industrial technologies of production did not result in the immediate disappearance of workers' freedom (Thompson 1974), most of the population were increasingly deprived of actual spaces of leisure. Cunningham observes how in the later eighteenth century,

> The wealthy tried, successfully in many instances, to appropriate . . . public spaces for their own exclusive use, to privatise them. At the same time . . . they frowned on and became suspicious of public gatherings of the lower orders for whatever purpose. The result was that leisure became increasingly class-bound. The leisure class retreated to the home or to those fenced-off private enclosures . . . and those excluded sought new patrons in publicans . . . leisure became class-bound and impenetrable for those outside the class in question.
>
> (Cunningham 1980: 76)

Through the proliferation of private property and the measurement of space, the lower classes were thus forced into the requirements of capitalistic rationalization. The pressures from the new forces of capitalist regimentation through privatization and changing work patterns thereby eroded the basis of the unregulated leisure activity of folk football and eventually led to its near complete extinction by the 1830s (Vamplew 1987). The unregulated practice of folk football could no longer be accommodated in the emerging patterns of industrial life. Instead, driven by middle-class utilitarians concerned about the precarious leisure situation of the working classes and their supposed resulting moral decline, new forms of 'rational recreation' (Cunningham 1980: 76) incorporated the principles of rationalization and industrial production that had dramatically transformed the patterns of work and leisure. Unsurprisingly, many of the new forms of rational recreation originated in one of the earliest rational, bureaucratized institutions of modernity: public schools.

The first known reference to football at public schools was made as early as 1519 by William Horman, then headmaster of Eton (Marples 1954); however, the modern form of the game did not evolve at public schools until between 1750 and 1840 (Dunning 1971: 134). During this period football emerged as a suitable vehicle to exercise authority and control over often rebellious upper-class pupils (Taylor 1992), an observation that has attracted particular attention within figurational sociology, which has interpreted modern sport as a manifestation of what Norbert Elias (1986a, 1986b, 1994) has famously called the 'civilizing process'. The transformation of the medieval ball-kicking practice into modern football at public schools was part of the bourgeois struggle for emancipation and capitalist hegemony, and is thus reflective of what figurational sociologists have described as processes of pacification, privatization, commercialization and individualization (Maguire 1992). Dunning's and Elias's work reminds us that the technological innovations of previous centuries, especially the introduction of the mechanical measurement of space and time (cf. Giddens 1990), were necessary premises for the development of modern football, but they were not sufficient premises in themselves. The rise of football was as much an expression of the attempts of an enlightened middle class to establish new social and cultural values of rationalism as it was a reflection of technological change. If we understand technologies as (rational) systems of organization as Simpson (1995) suggests, the crucial technological advance in the proliferation of modern football was born of the institutional network of public schools and universities: in 1842 representatives of 14 colleges who had played various different ball games at public schools met in Cambridge and agreed on a common set of rules (Guttmann 1994). These rules, updated by an ad hoc committee in 1863, still form the code of rules of contemporary Association football or, as it has become known in North America, soccer. The interlocal network of the upper classes in early modernity thus led to the standardization of the game that made its future supra-local and transnational diffusion possible. In this sense the Protestant work ethic, the industrial restructuring of work and leisure practices, and technological change constituted the central premises for the rise of the modern leisure practice of football.

Clock-regulated labour in the age of laissez-faire capitalism had left workers without leisure time and recreational opportunities (Riordan 1993). However, by the mid-nineteenth century – as processes of industrial production became increasingly complex and diversified leading to a growing need for skilled, less easily replaceable workers – the working classes successfully campaigned for free Saturday afternoons, shorter working hours and increased real wages (Brailsford 1991). Still newly emerging leisure practices bore little if any resemblance to pre-industrial times. The overall amount of leisure time had been reduced and in contrast to the Middle Ages work and leisure were now sharply demarcated. As former spaces of leisure had been commodified by the upper and middle classes at the end of the eighteenth and the beginning of the nineteenth centuries, the working classes were forced to take up new leisure practices. They soon found a new pastime that reflected the needs of the new patterns of everyday life in industrial society: spectator sport.

Participation in sports remained a minority activity throughout the nineteenth century (Vamplew 1987). However, spectator sports offered an alternative form of entertainment. As much as working life had been rationalized in the eighteenth and nineteenth centuries, the division between players and spectators – fuelled by the same underlying principles of rationalization and Taylorization – now led to rationalization and commercialization of leisure. One of the first professional English clubs, Aston Villa, introduced gate money in 1874 and by the late 1870s crowds of 20,000 were commonplace. Two decades later an average of 50,000 attended league games (Guttmann 1986). In addition to the introduction of the half-Saturday, another important premise in the rise of spectator sport was technological change. The rationalization of everyday life in the late nineteenth century including areas such as transport and housing resulted in the need for new, domestic technologies. New urban leisure markets emerged, as the share of the urban population in England rose from 50.1 per cent in 1851 to 77.0 per cent in 1901 (Vamplew 1987: 13). The rise of professional football was further embedded in the introduction of a nationwide railway system in England (Jones 1988: 44). Improved public transport enabled thousands of spectators to gather in a particular space. Football stadia evolved soon after the introduction of gate money had created both the need to fence off non-paying spectators as well as the financial means to improve facilities and stands. Together public transport and the public stadium (even if admission was charged) constituted the first mass medium of modern sport.

Association football quickly spread throughout the British Isles (Wagg 1995a), with standardization and bureaucratization providing the crucial premises in the supra-local adoption of football. Moreover, Britain's commitment to free trade and its role as core industrial power of the time ensured the quick diffusion of the game by British tradesmen, colonials and emigrants throughout the world (Birley 1995). Football, following the path of modern industrialism, spread from England and Wales to Europe (Duke 1995; Lanfranchi 1995; Wagg 1995b), North America (Waldstein and Wagg 1995) and South America (Guttmann 1994; Del Burgo 1995), and eventually the African continent (Stuart 1995). Accounts of the diffusion of the game to different parts of the world underline the intrinsic interrelation between football and industrial modernity. As more and more regions became integrated into the emerging capitalist global economy

(Pohl 1989) the leisure practice of football – standardized in its rules and rationalized in its demands on time and space – constituted the cultural equivalent to the changing processes of industrial production.

The rise of football as a form of mass leisure thus reflected the dramatic transformations of modern work and leisure. Yet the role of football's agency in the proliferation of industrialism and capitalism remains controversial. In his neo-Marxist analysis Brohm (1978) identifies sport as a manifestation of bourgeois industrial society. To Brohm, 'the vertical hierarchical structure of sport models the social structure of bureaucratic capitalism, with its system of competitive selection, promotion, hierarchy and social advancement' (Brohm 1978: 49). Thus sport and recreation have served to reproduce structures of (capitalist) domination (Jarvie and Maguire 1993). In contrast, Guttmann (1986) employs a Weberian rather than Marxist framework. He identifies modern sport as the consequence of quantification, specialization and the quest for records (Guttmann 1979). Thus Guttmann argues that modern sport is based upon bureaucratization and rationalization rather than capitalism in itself, although this distinction remains, of course, problematic. Either way, we can safely conclude that the transformation of unregulated mass participation folk football into the rationalized, institutionalized and bureaucratized practice of Association football reflected the modern and rationalized conditions of production and consumption in industrial societies – regardless of whether we emphasize the role of capitalism or of industrialism in this process. Hence football is rooted in the industrial system of modernity organized on the basis of what Weber (1921) has termed *Zweckrationalität* (formal rationality).[8]

Excursus 2: television and modern everyday life

At the turn of the twentieth century, centralized, urban leisure started to compete with more decentralized forms of consumption aided by the rise of new technologies such as the telegraph and railways (Ingham and Beamish 1993). New communication technologies helped to establish the national dimension of sport by enabling sports results to be communicated instantly over vast distances. Radio reporting was immediate and, crucially, national rather than local. When Preston North End won the FA Cup in 1938, many listeners in Britain could for the first time follow the event on their radio sets simultaneously.[9] Thus mass communication crucially contributed to the social and territorial diffusion of football. In a similar vein Lever and Wheeler (1993) outline the impact of mass media on modern sports in the United States:

> One catalyst for changing cultural values was the emerging system of mass communications. Along with the technology of the industrial revolution that produced the steamboats, railroads, and mass transit that moved people to leisure events, the rapidly evolving technology of mass media brought the drama and the excitement of sporting events to the people . . . the mass

media, more than anything else, were responsible for promoting organized sport from a relatively minor element of culture into a full-blown social institution.

(Lever and Wheeler 1993: 126)

It is important to remember that both spectator sports and the mass media grew out of the same rationalization imperative of modern industrialism. As Clarke and Clarke (1982) remind us, media effects on sport must not be understood as external corruption, but instead express a deep and telling symbiosis. While the growth of consumer capitalism had created centralized forms of urban leisure, it was simultaneously eroding their premises through its emphasis on the private and domestic nature of consumption. As Margaret Marsh (1990) argues, as early as the late nineteenth century domestic ideology began to see urban life in a more critical light and followed a new suburban ideal. Suburban living, in turn, constructed forms of 'domesticity [which] were increasingly accompanied, and at times replaced, by a consumer mentality' (Spigel 1992: 17). This new suburban, decentralized consumer mentality in many quarters of the industrialized world was dependent on technological and organizational rationalization allowing for decentralization. According to Silverstone (1994: 54), the at first gradual and then increasingly rapid movement to the suburbs in Britain from the late 1880s onwards 'was facilitated by communication technologies such as the car, the telephone, the radio'. In turn these communication technologies guaranteed a form of decentralized mobility, as 'individuals within private homes were free to come and go as they pleased, as well as . . . increasingly free to bring the world into their living room' (Silverstone 1994: 54). This ability, based on the use of physical and virtual media of mass transportation, promoted the decentralization of consumption and leisure. Radio allowed listeners to consume football matches separated from their inner-city context, in which the grounds of football clubs were situated. Geographical place was thus increasingly supplanted by flexible and hybrid spaces of decentralized consumption. Raymond Williams has famously summarized this impact of broadcast technology on modern living under the term of 'mobile privatization':

By the end of the 1920s the radio industry had become a major sector of industrial production, within a rapid general expansion of the new kinds of machines which were eventually to be called 'consumer durables' . . . Socially, this complex is characterised by the two apparently paradoxical yet deeply connected tendencies of modern urban industrial living: on the one hand mobility, on the other hand the more apparently self-sufficient family home. The earlier period of public technology . . . was being replaced by a kind of technology . . . which served an at once mobile and home-centred way of living: a form of *mobile privatization*.

(Williams 1974: 26, original emphasis)

By the time television first appeared on the scene in the mid- to late 1930s the patterns of 'mobile privatization' were already established. Television was part of a second generation of mass media that reinforced the structures of decentralized, private and mobile suburban life. As Silverstone (1994: 62) argues, 'the space for television had been created by a social and cultural fabric already prepared'. This social and cultural fabric was in turn an expression of the ever more central role of rationalized mass consumption in capitalist societies. Thus the social, cultural and economic premises of the rise of television were interrelated with those of the rise of modern football. Both expressed the need for structured and standardized consumption practices that could be incorporated into the patterns of everyday life shaped by rational industrial production.

These standardized practices of mass consumption reflected in the rise of television and radio were epitomized in the economic regime of Fordism. As Harvey (1990) reminds us, Fordist production techniques in combination with Keynesian economic policies prepared the ground for the modern mass demand for consumer products. With its powerful labour movements, Fordism persistently restructured and reshaped the working day and leisure time. The needs of a modern, universal leisure market were exemplified by the Fordist eight hour day (Rojek 1995). Regular Fordist work and leisure patterns led to the manifestation of the weekend as a place of consumption for the Victorian wage-earner, combining 'both social identity and privacy' (Cross 1997: 120). The establishment of half-Saturdays had been a crucial premise for the rise of professional football in England. Now, the extended leisure time of the Fordist weekend became the focal point of the consumption of mediated sports. This is underlined by the rise of Saturday afternoon sports magazines on American and British television (Goldlust 1987; Whannel 1991). Such magazines, many of which were among the longest-running television programmes of their age, and the designation of Saturday afternoons as a regular space of sports consumption, reflected what Harvey (1990: 156) labels 'the relatively stable aesthetics of Fordist modernism'.

Fordism, suburbanization and mass consumption thus constituted a triangle whereby both television and football were soon firmly integrated into the everyday life of millions of viewers. Television incorporated the stable and cyclical sports calendar into its schedules and thus reproduced and reinforced the temporal organization of Fordist leisure practices. As the consumption of spectator sport increasingly shifted to the domestic, magazines such as the BBC's *Grandstand* and *Sports Special* or ITV's *World of Sport* engraved set routines into the everyday life of the audience. With the number of households owning television sets rapidly increasing,[10] television offered instant access to Saturday afternoon sporting action. It could be watched from around the country, no admission was charged and an unlimited number of seats was available. Thus television sport constituted a quantum leap in the rationalization process of modern leisure: it bridged time and distance, dislocating consumption practices from the local context of events. In this sense football on television both reflected and promoted the underlying structural premises of industrialism and rationalization, forces that had enabled the formation of modern football a century before. As much as football mirrored the arrival of industrial mass labour and urbanization, television constituted a dynamic force in the transformation from production-oriented industrialism towards Fordist, suburban consumerism.

For the subsequent discussion of football fandom it is important to bear in mind that the popularity of football was based upon its ability to be integrated into clearly defined spaces and times of leisure in early and high industrial society. At the same time, the historical foundations of football and television can only partially explain their popularity. Beyond the structural foundations of their consumption, questions such as how excitement and pleasure are constituted in the viewing of football cannot be answered from a macro perspective alone. The socio-historical premises of football tell us little about why the game has given rise to the set of cultural practices I summarize as fandom here. In order to answer such questions, we also need to look at the audiences, spectators and supporters of football.

My argument in the following is divided into three parts. Having established the interrelation between spectator football, mass media and industrial modernity, I first turn to the relationship between football fandom and consumption. In Chapter 2 I develop a definition of football fandom as an act of consumption and communication in light of Bourdieu's analysis of consumption. Chapter 3 further pursues the relationship between fans and their object of fandom, identifying football fandom as a space of projection and self-reflection.

Moving from the micro to the macro foundations of football fandom, the second part of my argument is dedicated to the cultural, social and economic conditions of football and fandom. Chapter 4 analyses the impact of cultural universalization on football fandom, arguing that the cultural proliferation of football furthers the structural transformation of the public sphere and allows political participation and the construction of identity and citizenship through the participation of fans in discourses surrounding contemporary football. Drawing on such themes, Chapter 5 investigates football fandom in light of processes of (cultural) globalization. Following an outline of the economic premises of the globalization of football, I analyse the interrelation between football fandom and cultural globalization, localization and deterritorialization.

The changing regimes of rationalized production and – through television – distribution of football provide the backdrop to the final part of this book, conceptualizing professional football as postmodern cultural form. Chapter 6 illustrates the application of formal rational regimes – summarized under the heading of 'McDonaldization' – in the production of football and assesses the implications of the growing rationalization of contemporary football. On this basis I discuss the growing contentlessness of football clubs as objects of fandom, the changing dynamics between place and space and the resulting transformations of the landscapes of football. Returning to the symbiosis between football and television, Chapter 7 analyses the role of the televisual representation of football as means of rationalization contributing to the semiotic openness of football, which in turn provides the *conditio sine qua non* of football fandom as mass cultural phenomenon. I further discuss the modes of televisual representation and their reading by fans in light of the postmodern frameworks of hyperreality and simulation. The postmodern discourses concluding my argument serve as a reminder of the limits to the appropriation of increasingly rationalized football by football fans.

Part I

Football fandom and consumption

> I remember in high school, already I was pretty old. I suddenly asked myself at one point, why do I care if my high school team wins the football game? I mean, I don't know anybody on the team, you know? I mean, they have nothing to do with me. I mean, why I am cheering for my team? . . . It doesn't make sense. But the point is, it does make sense: it's a way of building up irrational attitudes of submission to authority, and group cohesion behind leadership elements – in fact, it's training in irrational jingoism.
>
> (Noam Chomsky in *Manufacturing Consent*, Channel 4, 1995)

Chomsky's famous assessment of the authoritarian nature of modern team sports has long haunted sports fans concerned with the political correctness of their fandom. Moreover, Chomsky not only paints a gloomy picture of the political consequences of team sports, he raises the all-important question in sports fandom: why am I cheering for 'my' team? For all his wit, Chomsky himself is unable to answer this question. Regardless of whether he correctly assesses the social and political implications of team sports, the suspicion that they serve authoritarian, hegemonic interests on the macro level is a poor explanation for the pleasures experienced by fans on the micro level. If we aim to understand what the motivations of football fans are, we first need to understand the personal, immediate social benefits of football fandom. It is this endeavour with which I want to begin my exploration of modern football.

While the study of fans and fandom has attracted increasing academic attention in recent years (Fiske 1992; Jenkins 1992; Hills 2002), only a small body of largely quantitative research has focused on sports fans (Wann *et al.* 2001). Most work on fandom has explored fans of genres such as film (Stacey 1994), music (Thornton 1995; Cavicchi 1997) or science fiction (Bacon-Smith 1992). As these texts vary across genres, so do fan practices. The analysis of football fandom thus differs with regard to the actual object of fandom from previous studies of fandom in other cultural and textual areas. However, further aspects distinguish the study of football fandom here from other work. Many fan studies have focused on small, often subcultural groups of readers, listeners or viewers. Given football's immense popularity and large following, this narrow definition of fandom is unsuitable for the exploration of football. Furthermore, in contrast to psychoanalytic approaches to fandom in areas such as film and 'cult' television in particular, this investigation is sociological in its method as much as in its direction, as the interest and focus of this book expands beyond the level of the individual and its relation to the external world through the lens of the self, exploring the cultural practice of football – of which fandom constitutes an important aspect – rather than fandom in and for itself. We should therefore bear in mind that my findings are based on a particular case, and that while a broader and unified theory of fandom is desirable, such an enterprise is outside the scale and scope of this book.

In the following chapter I therefore define football fandom, and examine the everyday life context of fandom. I argue that football fandom is best analysed within a framework of consumption and its accompanying theories, most notably Pierre Bourdieu's social critique (1984) of the judgement of taste. Pursuing the discussion of fandom and consumption further, Chapter 3 analyses the processes and mechanisms through which the relationship between object of fandom (the football club) and football fans is constituted and maintained as football clubs become spaces of identification and self-reflection.

Chapter 2

Fan practices and consumption

Having outlined the history of Association football, I now want to turn attention to the micro level of contemporary football: the audience, spectator, supporters and fans. Etymologically the word 'fan', as well as its academic derivative 'fandom', derive from the word *fanaticus*, the Latin word for a member and devotee of a temple. The word 'fan' (initially 'fann' or 'phan') emerged as an abbreviation of the word 'fanatic' in the United States at the end of the nineteenth century. The *Oxford English Dictionary* (1989) defines 'fan' as follows:

> A fanatic; in modern English [orig. US]: a keen and regular spectator of a [professional] sport, orig. of baseball; a regular supporter of a [professional] sports team; hence, a keen follower of a specified hobby or amusement, and gen. an enthusiast for a particular person or thing.

Three aspects are worth noting here. Firstly, fans are spectators. This may seem banal, but it is worth remembering that fans are clearly located on one side of the Taylorist participant/spectator divide that underlies much of modern (mass mediated) entertainment. Secondly, historically the word 'fan' refers to a sports enthusiast. Today those with a particularly high interest in various aspects of popular culture such as science fiction television programmes, comics or popular music are described as fans, in everyday conversations as much as in academic discourses. Regrettably, most studies of fandom have treated the phenomenon as if it only exists within the genre under investigation. The many investigations of, for instance, science fiction fandom are void of any reference to the existence of fandom in other cultural spheres such as sport. While the practices of football fandom differ from those of music, film or science fiction fandom, they all constitute particular forms of interaction between fan and fan text. By (fan) 'text', I describe all forms of semiotic structures, whether linguistic or not, consumed by fans and audiences. Alongside traditional print texts, this includes, for instance, the televisual representation of football with its different verbal and visual levels as well as unmediated experiences. While these texts are different to fandom in other genres, the study of sports fandom nevertheless offers many insights applicable to other forms of fandom, given the historical origin of fandom in modern professional sports, and I will therefore outline the key parallels and contrasts between football fandom and other genres below. In this context a final point is worth noting concerning the *OED* definition of 'fan'. The first sports spectators referred to as fans were not followers of Association football, nor were they to be found in Europe. Instead fans were first talked about in baseball, a sport that was professional from its very beginning, promoted by a sports goods manufacturer[1] in a country that was quicker to develop markets of mass consumption than any other industrializing nation. This origin of fandom suggests the need to explore the interrelation between fans and mass consumption in further depth.

Recent accounts of fandom in the field of cultural studies have stressed the often negative and hostile representation of fan culture in the mass media. Jenkins (1992: 13) recognizes a 'stereotypical conception of the fan as emotionally unstable, socially maladjusted and dangerously out of sync with reality'. Jenson (1992: 13) refers to the image of a fan as 'an obsessed loner, suffering from a disease or isolation or a frenzied crowd member . . . in either case, the fan is seen as being irrational, out of control and prey to a number of forces'. In contrast to such accounts of fans of pop stars, television shows and films, the portrayal of football fans in the media, especially the tabloid newspapers, has been more ambiguous, shifting between an emphasis on violent fans' behaviour on the one hand, and active encouragement of fan practices and support for (national) teams on the other, celebrating football fandom as ranging between patriotic duty and legitimized chauvinism.

Whatever the public portrayal of fandom, however, fans across all genres seem happy to define themselves as fans (cf. Jenkins 1992; Jenson 1992); an observation that is confirmed by my own findings. Although my respondents were drawn from diverse consumption contexts (organized fans, regular ground visitors, television viewers) they all considered themselves fans, including those who followed football exclusively through the media.[2] In this sense, football fans also depart from common conceptualizations of television fandom. Both Jenkins's (1992) and Bacon-Smith's studies (1986) of fans are based upon a narrower understanding of fandom in which fans are set apart from other viewers. This position is also reflected in Fiske's definition of fandom:

> Fandom . . . selects from the repertoire of mass-produced and mass-distributed entertainment certain performers, narratives or genres and takes them into the culture of a self-selected fraction of people. They are reworked into a pleasurable, intensely signifying popular culture, that is both similar to, yet significantly different from, the culture of more 'normal' popular audiences.
>
> (Fiske 1992: 30)

According to the self-categorization of my interviewees, however, many football fans seem less easily distinguishable from what Fiske would call the 'normal' audiences of football. This narrow definition of fandom includes only a small number of all those who considered themselves fans in my study. The keenness with which football audiences label themselves as fans, however, leaves little room for doubt concerning the adequacy of the label 'fan' for such spectators. If large parts of the audience consider themselves fans, the question arises of whether it is useful to position football fans in contrast to, rather than within, existing research on audiences. Instead, I sought to identify the categories that, according to the fans themselves, constituted fandom. Once participants had identified themselves as fans, I asked them what they thought defined them as a fan. From this question a dynamic definition based upon a series of different practices, rather than a static definition based on a pre-given relationship, emerged:

> I spend a lot of time going to football and talking about football, thinking about football.
>
> (Samuel, Chelsea supporter)

> I am always looking on the teletext. I went to Stamford Bridge when I was a kid, but I haven't been since. But I always follow them daily in the papers as well.
>
> (Brendon, Chelsea fan)

> I think I am a fanatical fan, because I have been going [there] for ten years. I am a season-ticket holder. That I pass as a fanatical fan.
>
> (Vicky, Chelsea supporter)

> I think the fact that I had season tickets for two years, plus the fact that I am very enthusiastic when attending football matches, makes me a fan.
>
> (Derrek, DC United fan)

> I watch all the games on TV and go to games as much as possible.
>
> (Bob, DC United fan)

> Having an insatiable appetite for news and info on my team plus seeing them live or on TV as often as I can.
>
> (Stan, Chelsea fan)

While different fans identify different practices (reading the newspaper, watching their team on television, being a season-ticket holder or attending all home games), they all explain their fandom in terms of a *series of acts of consumption*, often media consumption. In other words, fans are consumers. This fundamental assumption has often been overlooked in research on football fans, where fans and 'new consumers' have been constructed either in opposition to each other or as marking the recent transformations of professional football (see for example King 1998). The observation that fandom is constituted by a series of acts of consumption is, of course, no sufficient definition in itself. It allows us neither to grasp the particularity of fandom, nor distinguish it from other sections of the audience. Two additions have to be made with regard to the regularity and the deliberateness of fan consumption. As cited above, the *OED* defines a fan as a 'keen and *regular* spectator' (emphasis added). The consumption practices of fans are indeed more structured than those of other members of the football audience. Participants in my study followed football regularly and incorporated league and cup schedules firmly into the fabric of their everyday life:

> *A*: We go to every home game.
> *Question*: Do you go to away games, too?
> *A*: As often as possible, I guess 14, 15 games.
> (Hilmar, Bayer Leverkusen fan)

> Last season I managed to go to all games.
> (Sandro, Bayer Leverkusen fan)

> If Chelsea are playing I will move other events to accommodate the match . . . So, yeah, it is quite rare that I miss something completely . . . I know well in advance when they are playing.
> (Dan, Chelsea supporter)

Watching and consuming football therefore structure fans' leisure and sometimes even their work lives.

> *Thorsten*: I arrange my concerts according to the match schedule.
> *Simon*: Yes, I just dropped out of a school trip.
> (Thorsten and Simon, Bayer Leverkusen fans)

> It gives me a fixed structure. At the beginning of the season I make a calendar with all the dates of the games from the first to fourth division I can go to.
> (Thilo, Preußen Köln fan)

> It all starts with planning my holidays . . . Now I plan the holidays in a way that I take into account the vacations of the children, but I also have a little calendar lying next to it, with away games on days I have to work and I might take that day off.
> (Manfred, Bayer Leverkusen fan)

Equally, those who followed football exclusively through the media engaged in regular consumption patterns:

> Usually, since I have Premiere,[3] I watch football every Saturday from 15:30 to 20:00.
> (Moritz, Bayern München fan)

To be honest, I can't say when I have missed *ran*[4] the last time.

(Wojtek, Bayern München fan)

The regular viewing and reading of fan texts constitutes an intrinsic aspect of fandom. Fiske (1989b: 146–7) has argued in this context that 'fans are excessive readers . . . being a fan involves active, enthusiastic, partisan, participatory engagement with the text'. Indeed, many fans I observed in pubs and stadia were 'enthusiastic', 'participatory' and especially 'partisan' in their reading of the text. However, to claim that all fans are participatory and active on all occasions misconstrues the complex role of fandom in everyday life. Sometimes fans are not enthusiastic or participatory. Viewers of an early-round cup game against little-known opposition, even if their club is winning, are anything but enthusiastic. Sometimes, when their team loses, fans seek to disengage from the text. Yet what qualifies them as fans is the regularity of the reading of such texts. The accounts of fans in my study thus confirm Thompson's position (1995: 222), that 'there is not a clear-cut dividing line between a fan and a non-fan'. As there is no consistent intrinsic difference between consumption by fans and by non-fans, it is all the more important to assess the context and meaning of these consumption practices.

Football, distinction and consumption

Analysing football fandom we therefore need to identify the underlying structures of consumption processes. Silverstone (1994: 109) has summarized the main themes emerging from the study of consumption as commodification, symbolization, articulation and globalization/fragmentation. While I return to some of these themes in the following chapters, it is the notion of *articulation* that is particularly relevant in football fandom. Fans, as Fiske (1989a: 7) argues, 'draw sharp and intolerant lines between what, or who, they are fans of and what they are not'. In other words, fandom is a matter of taste. Pierre Bourdieu, in *Distinction* (1984), has famously explored processes and patterns of taste in modern societies, and his enlightening analysis of taste also has much to offer for our understanding of (football) fandom. Bourdieu (1984: 2) defines consumption as 'a stage in a process of communication, that is, an act of deciphering, decoding, which presupposes practical or explicit mastery of a cipher or code'. On the basis of this understanding of consumption as communication, Bourdieu develops the model of the habitus, which in turn is based on his detailed, multi-dimensional model of class. He moves away from a Marxist, means-of-production oriented notion of class, introducing further variables such as social and cultural capital, the latter interrelated with educational capital. Thus Bourdieu is able to develop a detailed mapping of consumption preferences among different social groups. Juxtaposing economic and cultural capital, Bourdieu distinguishes between the consumption patterns of, for example, higher-education teachers and private-sector executives. He argues:

The division into classes performed by sociology leads to the common root of classifiable practices which agents produce and of the classificatory judgements they make of other agents' practices and their own. The habitus is both the generative principle of objectively classifiable judgements and the system of classification (*principium divisionis*) of these practices.

(Bourdieu 1984: 169–70)

On this basis Bourdieu concludes that

the habitus is not only a structuring structure, which organizes practices and the perception of practice, but also a structured structure: the principle of division into logical classes which organizes the perception of the social world is itself the product of internalization of the division into social classes.

(Bourdieu 1984: 170)

Hence taste is a forced choice. In turn, consumption affirms distinction. The habitus forms the articulation of each individual's social positioning. It 'functions as a sort of social orientation, a "sense of one's place"' (Bourdieu 1984: 465). Examining the consumption of cultural goods, Bourdieu (1984: 281) concludes that 'what is at stake is indeed "personality", in other words the quality of the person, which is affirmed in the capacity to appropriate an object of quality'. Although Bourdieu does not use the term in this context, what is at stake is also a question of identity. Consumption, which is structured by the habitus, not only articulates one's social positioning but also informs one's identity. Identity formation through consumption is, however, far from voluntary. It operates beyond the control of the consumer: 'The schemes of the habitus, the primary forms of classification, owe their specific efficacy to the fact that they function below the level of consciousness and language, beyond the reach of introspective scrutiny or control by the will' (Bourdieu 1984: 466). Hence, consumption and taste are not associated with choice and freedom in Bourdieu's work – they are the expression and reaffirmation of rigid structures of class and hegemony, although it is not the working classes in Bourdieu's model but the petty bourgeoisie that emerges as most entrapped in a system of rational domination.

At first sight it may seem difficult to see how Bourdieu's rigid model can serve to explain a practice as socially and culturally universal and diverse as football fandom. In a Germany-wide survey commissioned by the Bertelsmann subsidary UFA in 1998, spectator football emerged as univocally popular across different demographic groups.[5] The average popularity score of football remained almost unchanged among different income groups:[6] members of low and average income households ranked their interest in football 2.3, high income households 2.4. Respondents with low, average and higher education all ranked their football interest 2.4. Similarly, in my own research I encountered participants from all social and educational classes,[7] confirming two central objections of Bourdieu's critics: Bourdieu's misunderstanding of the nature of (a) class (Gans 1966;

DiMaggio 1979; Honneth 1986; Lewis 1987) and (b) commodities (Grossberg 1985; Frow 1987; Fenster 1991). All these objections assume that Bourdieu, through his misconception of either of these two dimensions (or both, for that matter), comes to underestimate individual choice or at least the spaces of appropriation in which consumers operate (although Bourdieu does acknowledge the latter).

Two different aspects have been raised in relation to class. The first position follows the lines of George Lewis's argument (1987) that *Distinction* merely reflects the specific socio-cultural condition of French society in the mid- and late 1960s.[8] In a more recent study Peterson and Kern (1996) argue that high- and low-brow taste have lost their specific social positions and connotations in the United States:

> Rising levels of living, broader education, and presentation of arts via the media have made aesthetic taste more accessible to wider segments of the population . . . While snobbish exclusion was an effective marker of status in a relatively homogeneous and circumscribed WASP-ish world that could enforce its dominance over all others by force if necessary, omnivorous inclusion seems better adapted to an increasingly global world managed by those who make their way, in part, by showing respect for the cultural expressions of others.
>
> (Peterson and Kern 1996: 905–6)

However, Peterson and Kern admit that they are outlining a tendency rather than a concluded process. In other words, while the interrelation between class and taste becomes increasingly blurred, it nevertheless exists. The question is to what extent class structures – and in turn is structured by – football fandom. Peterson and Kern's study has one significant problem in common with Bourdieu's work. It rests upon a quantitative rather than a qualitative base. Yet the evidence of my research suggests that the connection between class and taste in football fandom is more complex than can be accounted for through quantitative data alone. In contrast to the universal popularity of football among groups with varying economic and educational capital, qualitative data reveals that football is still associated with particular social groups and cultural and social settings. As the following interviewee recalls,

> I think the first interest in football probably was when I was a kid. Football wasn't exactly encouraged, it was not exactly part of the whole sort of scene and when I was at school it was not played and quite, as I said, discouraged. But I definitely remember watching things like the World Cup and stuff. At the boarding school, we were able to stay up sometimes and watch the World Cup games, so I suppose my first memories are really obvious things like England v. Argentina in 1986.
>
> (Emil, Chelsea fan)

This account indicates that smaller sections of society who still have an uneasy relationship with what has been perceived as a working-class sport are over-looked in broadly structured surveys. It also demonstrates how a particular socio-cultural heritage (in other words social and cultural capital) is overcome by social networks and the mass media, particularly television. Television, no doubt, has popularized football across all classes. Yet an unspecified object of consumption such as 'football' is too broad a category to use when considering the often subtle difference in taste and consumption so important to Bourdieu's analysis. The crucial questions are *what* is consumed, and *how* it is consumed. Consequently, we need to ask whether different clubs recruit their support from specific clusters within a multi-dimensional model of class. Respondents in the UFA study (1998) were asked which clubs they sympathized with. In Table 2.1, clubs are organized according to the popularity they enjoy in relation to the educational capital of respondents and in Table 2.2 (on page 24) according to the economic capital of respondents.

There are two ways of reading such data. On the one hand, all clubs recruit sympathizers from all groups. However, on closer examination similar patterns emerge as in, for example, Bourdieu's investigations of Parisian cinema audiences in relation to economic and educational capital (Bourdieu 1984: 271). SC Freiburg, for instance, a club from the university town of Freiburg, known for its collective work ethic and short-passing game, enjoys a particularly high popularity among respondents with high educational capital.[9] In contrast, Cologne-based club 1.FC Köln is moderately popular among those with lower education, but loses almost a third of its popularity among those with high educational capital. In terms of economic capital the popularity of clubs such as TSV 1860 München and VfB Stuttgart increases among groups with higher income, while for instance Werder Bremen attracts more sympathy from respondents with low income. Some of these variations arise out of the differentiation in income structures between structurally weak regions, such as the North Sea coast and East Germany, in contrast to service and industry centres in southern Germany with lower unemployment, such as Munich and Stuttgart. However, given the more even distribution of educational capital among regions in Germany, such an explanation alone is not sufficient.

Processes of distinction and thus communication in football fandom are even more evident as we turn to how football clubs are consumed by different fans. Concerning the ranking of films among occupational groups Bourdieu (1984) points out that not only are different films varyingly popular, but different occupational groups also consume the same films in different ways. This underlines another observation of Bourdieu's about sport (here in the sense of physical exercise rather than professional spectator sport):

> Because agents apprehend objects through the schemes of perception and appreciation of their habitus it would be naive to suppose that all practitioners of the same sport (or even any other practice) confer the same meaning

Table 2.1 Sympathy potential of Bundesliga clubs according to educational degree

Volksschule*	%	Mittlere Reife†	%	Abitur‡	%
I.FC Kaiserslautern	34	Schalke 04	28	Schalke 04	34
Karlsruher SC	29	Hansa Rostock	27	I.FC Kaiserslautern	31
Schalke 04	26	I.FC Kaiserslautern	26	Hansa Rostock	30
Borussia Dortmund	25	Karlsruher SC	26	Karlsruher SC	29
Hansa Rostock	25	Borussia Dortmund	24	Borussia Dortmund	26
TSV 1860 München	24	Arminia Bielefeld	22	TSV 1860 München	22
FC Bayern München	21	TSV 1860 München	22	SC Freiburg	20
Werder Bremen	21	FC Bayern München	20	VfB Stuttgart	19
Hamburger SV	20	Bayer 04 Leverkusen	19	FC Bayern München	18
Hertha BSC Berlin	19	VfB Stuttgart	19	MSV Duisburg	18
VfL Bochum	19	SC Freiburg	18	Arminia Bielefeld	18
MSV Duisburg	19	Hamburger SV	17	Werder Bremen	17
I.FC Köln	18	Borussia M'gladbach	17	Borussia M'gladbach	17
Arminia Bielefeld	18	Werder Bremen	16	VfL Wolfsburg	17
Borussia M'gladbach	18	VfL Wolfsburg	16	VfL Bochum	16
Bayer 04 Leverkusen	17	Hertha BSC Berlin	15	Bayer 04 Leverkusen	15
VfB Stuttgart	17	I.FC Köln	15	Hertha BSC Berlin	14
SC Freiburg	16	VfL Bochum	14	Hamburger SV	14
VfL Wolfsburg	14	MSV Duisburg	14	I.FC Köln	13
I.FC Nürnberg	11	I.FC Nürnberg	14	I.FC Nürnberg	12
Eintracht Frankfurt	7	Eintracht Frankfurt	9	Eintracht Frankfurt	11

Source: UFA Fußballstudie; n = 2033, respondents expressing sympathy for a club (multiple choices possible).

Notes
* *Volksschule:* minimum of 9 years of schooling.
† *Mittlere Reife:* minimum of 10 years of schooling.
‡ *Abitur:* minimum of 13 years of schooling.

on their practice or even, strictly speaking, that they are practising the same practice.

(Bourdieu 1984: 211)

This observation is verified by my observations of football fans. Class differences are less likely to be articulated through the support of a particular club than in the way such support manifests itself in different practices. Compare the two following accounts of a 34-year-old unemployed job-seeker and a retired engineer:

I need this [supporting Bayer] as an outlet, when I have accumulated two weeks of frustration. I am much calmer during the football season. I just

Table 2.2 Sympathy potential of Bundesliga clubs according to economic capital

< DM 2,999*	%	DM 3,000–DM 4,999*	%	> DM 5,000*	%
1.FC Kaiserslautern	37	1.FC Kaiserslautern	35	TSV 1860 München	26
Hansa Rostock	34	Karlsruher SC	35	1.FC Kaiserslautern	24
Schalke 04	30	Schalke 04	33	Karlsruher SC	22
Borussia Dortmund	27	Hansa Rostock	32	MSV Duisburg	21
Werder Bremen	24	TSV 1860 München	31	VfB Stuttgart	21
Karlsruher SC	24	Borussia Dortmund	29	FC Bayern München	19
FC Bayern München	22	FC Bayern München	24	Arminia Bielefeld	19
Hamburger SV	21	Hamburger SV	24	Borussia M'gladbach	19
Hertha BSC Berlin	20	SC Freiburg	23	Hansa Rostock	19
Arminia Bielefeld	20	Arminia Bielefeld	22	Schalke 04	19
TSV 1860 München	20	Borussia M'gladbach	22	1.FC Köln	18
MSV Duisburg	18	Werder Bremen	21	Bayer 04 Leverkusen	18
VfL Bochum	17	1.FC Köln	21	VfL Bochum	17
SC Freiburg	17	Bayer 04 Leverkusen	21	Borussia Dortmund	17
1.FC Köln	16	VfB Stuttgart	19	VfL Wolfsburg	17
Bayer 04 Leverkusen	16	Hertha BSC Berlin	18	SC Freiburg	16
Borussia M'gladbach	16	VfL Wolfsburg	18	1.FC Nürnberg	15
VfB Stuttgart	16	MSV Duisburg	17	Hertha BSC Berlin	14
VfL Wolfsburg	15	VfL Bochum	16	Werder Bremen	14
1.FC Nürnberg	13	1.FC Nürnberg	14	Hamburger SV	12
Eintracht Frankfurt	6	Eintracht Frankfurt	10	Eintracht Frankfurt	10

Source: UFA Fußballstudie; n = 2033, respondents expressing sympathy for a club (multiple choices possible).

Note
* Average monthly household income.

shout it all out. I shout 'you arsehole', 'you wanker' and when the game is over, I can go home and feel much better.

(Chris, Bayer Leverkusen fan)

It [supporting Bayer] is part of my leisure time. I play chess, I worked for the local energy services and I founded a sports club there. We have played football there for years. I played tennis, passionately. They also have a very good basketball team [Bayer]. My wife and I have season tickets there . . . Apart from that, there are other leisure activities, sometimes we go to the theatre . . . I would say, football is only one component of all this.

(Mr Perschul, Bayer Leverkusen fan)

The consumption practices expressing the fandom of these two interviewees differ as much as the content of their fandom. They express the different structure and fabric of their respective everyday lives, the rewards and frustrations of different life situations and their socio-cultural framing. However, in this respect, they also substantiate some of the criticism directed at Bourdieu's work: this distinction does not find its modus operandi in class alone, even if we understand class as a multi-dimensional system composed of social, cultural and economic capital as Bourdieu does. Other factors equally determine the habitus of football fans. In a study of social networks and day-to-day conversations in Toronto security firms, Bonnie Erickson (1996) rejects Bourdieu's notion of class as the crucial distinction in consumption:

> If we look at class alone, sport is a relatively classless genre useful in coordinating ties between classes . . . But, if we turn from class to other forms of inequality, we see that sports knowledge contributes to domination in these even while it contributes to coordination between classes . . . Sport talk can link the male majorities in all classes but excludes women, which may be one more reason for its popularity in a very macho industry.
>
> (Erickson 1996: 244–5)

It should be noted that Erickson's methodology is questionable, as she ignores a crucial dimension of Bourdieu's argument. She concentrates on one industry, in which naturally similarities in cultural and social capital generate similar tastes, so her claim that 'sports knowledge is nearly classless' (Erickson 1996: 244) stands on thin empirical ice. Nevertheless, her findings about gender clearly indicate the need to examine the importance of lines of division beyond class. In my conversations with fans, spectator football emerged as a still predominantly male domain, reflecting a history of signifying practices. Equally, the UFA study quoted above (1998) points to a clear gender discrepancy in the popularity of football (1.8 among males in contrast to 2.9 among females). A total of 77 per cent of all male respondents were either very interested or interested in football, outnumbering females with equal interest two to one. While television as domestic medium potentially erodes the boundaries of football as a male domain, gender remains the most significant line of division and discrimination in football fandom. 'In situ football' particularly is numerically (and my participant observations suggest also culturally) dominated by men.[10] The female respondents in this book only speak for the growing minority of females who have not been put off by the often overtly masculine nature of fandom. Nevertheless, female fans still feel under particular scrutiny:

> I realize this quite often when people, when they hear that I am a fan, ask: 'What, you are a football fan, as a woman?' I hear that very often.
>
> (Sabine, Borussia Mönchengladbach fan)

While the majority of male interviewees said they were happy with the increasing number of female fans, a minority voiced their open discontent:

If a woman or girl stands next to me and she shouts, but builds a completely different form of enthusiasm, and then also criticizes you, because you are pissed, I don't feel free at all then. I feel inhibited.

(Thorsten, Bayer Leverkusen fan)

Clearly, the issues articulated in fandom run deeper than just class position. Social, cultural and economic capital alone cannot explain the different practices in football fandom. It is worth noting that Thorsten quoted above is of comparatively high educational capital, having just graduated from a German grammar school. What is at stake is not only class positions, but questions of identity and identification in the consumption practices that constitute football fandom. Gender is only one line of distinction that emerged in the course of my research. Other dimensions articulated through fandom include age and geographical location. These observations underline Silverstone's critique of Bourdieu's model:

> For Bourdieu class remains the single most powerful determinant of consumption behaviour and status . . . For all its subtlety and sensitivity, *Distinction* has little to say about variations, transformations and oppositions within, especially, working-class culture; little to say about other dimensions of social differentiation which can be articulated in consumption (difference of religion, ethnicity, gender); little to say about the prior coding of products in and through consumption; and little to say, in Daniel Miller's (1987: 155) terms, about 'the actual brilliance often displayed in the art of living in modern society by people of all classes'.
>
> (Silverstone 1994: 116)

These are the limitations of Bourdieu's concept of consumption we have to bear in mind. Two conclusions are nevertheless important to my argument. Firstly, football fandom offers a space for the articulation of difference through different practices of fandom, that manifest themselves in varying forms of participation and readings of the industrially pre-structured texts of spectator football. Secondly, such differences express more than just class positions. They articulate age, gender, ethnicity. Yet the conflicting positions on gender roles in football fandom suggest – and this is where fandom departs from the normal processes of consumption as they are investigated by Bourdieu – that football fandom articulates more than structured social and cultural positions as part of a largely unconscious habitus. Football fandom articulates conscious aspects of the self: values and opinions, fantasies and self-reflections. In short, while the habitus articulates who we are, values, beliefs and self-reflection express who we think we are.

Chapter 3

Fandom, identity and self-reflection

Football fandom as a form of consumption allows football fans to engage in a process which is aimed at communicating essential coordinates of the self, including class and gender positions, and related value and belief systems. In this sense, football fandom creates a space used by fans for the *articulation* and *reflection* of self. To borrow and invert Marshall McLuhan's useful phrase (1964), football fandom constitutes an 'extension of self'. My hypothesis is the following. Football fans – through consumption in a supermediated world – communicate a projection of themselves. The main object of consumption in football fandom and hence the crucial, if not exclusive, vehicle for this act of articulation (and projection) is the football club, as fans as consumers of performances constitute an audience engaged with a text. Hence the questions I want to pursue are: how are such texts read by their audiences? and how do such readings enable processes of self-reflection and projection?

Wolfgang Iser (1978), drawing on previous work within semiotics and German literature studies, famously argued that texts are polysemic, in other words that texts, as Stuart Hall (1980) later put it, are encoded as well as decoded. Yet, while emphasizing the space for divergent readings, Iser reminds us that such possibilities are not endless. Many studies of media audiences confirm Iser's position, acknowledging the significance of both text and audiences' reading (Morley 1980; Fiske 1987; Livingstone 1998). The increasingly influential notion of an 'active audience' appropriating texts to different ends is of particular importance to the study of football fans. Fans are more involved in terms of regularity and intensity in the reading of the texts constituting their fandom than other audiences. Their regular consumption of football is accompanied by often diametrically opposed readings of football texts among different fan groups. While this might be less surprising between supporters of different teams, opposing readings also emerge among fans of the same team. Compare the following extracts from interviews with two Chelsea fans, one a comparatively affluent businesswoman in her 40s from Surrey (Karen), the other a 30-year-old fan writer and freelance journalist living in Brixton (John):

> I think Chelsea stand for success. We have so many brilliant players. We also have a very successful past, winning the FA Cup and the European

Cup-Winners' Cup in 1970–71. There were some dire years in between, but today the main attribute of the club is success, fortunately.

(Karen, Chelsea fan)

Nobody could ever give [success] as a reason for supporting Chelsea, because Chelsea have never been successful. Chelsea have always been almost successful, and fucked it up, which is possibly why a lot of people support Chelsea . . . There are people who have been almost successful in their life who support Chelsea. They have all the right attributes, but never quite succeed. When Chelsea won the League in 1955, they won it with the fewest number of points that any champions ever managed to get. I think they went on a six-match run without a win in their League championship-winning season, which is unheard of. Whatever, our most successful period was really in the '60s and the early '70s, when we kept building very talented, very successful young squads and then dismantling them and then building another one. And you could only keep doing it for so long before the thing collapsed. So maybe that reflects Chelsea fans' lives.

(John, Chelsea fan)

The diametric opposition between these two accounts is remarkable. Both accounts tell us more about the reader (the fan) than about the text (the club). Both interviewees describe the foundations of their own fandom, which in turn reflects their self-images – a process that John acknowledges. Fandom in this sense functions as a representation of self. While varying personality structures are no simple imprint of socio-demographic factors, the parallels between the interviewees' divergent readings and their socio-economic backgrounds are impossible to overlook.[1] The affluent and in her own view successful business-woman follows Chelsea for what she believes the club and she have in common: success. Later in the interview she stresses the cosmopolitan flair surrounding Chelsea, a quality for which she would like to be known herself. For the freelance writer, in contrast, economic success has not materialized in comparable terms. As a university graduate of high educational and cultural capital, he has pursued goals that have come with much less monetary gain. As the achievement of quantifiable goals within a given set of rules – in other words productivity – is rewarded in capitalist societies through money and capital, trophies and cups are sport's equivalent recognition system of conformist achievements.[2] Not surprisingly, then, in his eyes the club he supports has likewise failed to convert the talent of its players into actual trophies. Much as his professional life has not been geared towards financial rewards, the team he supports has failed to achieve such rationally verified success manifested in trophies.

It is the very structure of football clubs (and, for that matter, other sports teams) that produces polysemic narratives that allow for such diverse readings. Both interviewees cited above could put forward good arguments for their respective cases.[3] Moreover, these are only two of the manifold interpretations that can be constructed around Chelsea FC or indeed any other football club. Football audiences read and appropriate hybrid semiotic structures composed of players and managers, tradition and history, board members and fans, stadia and landscapes and their diverse representation in different media. Different components of this plurality matter for different fans. The themes of failure and underachievement, for instance, are recurring motives in the description of clubs, especially among males in their 30s and 40s:

> Well, . . . there is a lot of flair, but it hasn't always been like that. When I started to go . . . they had a wonderful team, Peter Osgood, . . . and all those names. We were really living on memories for a long time, not playing any football at all until recently. So adjectives to the club would be 'an exciting, but not a great team'. They couldn't really win that many competitions over the years . . . They are inconsistent. They have always been inconsistent till now. They could win at Manchester United one week and then next week lose at home to Leicester or something like that.
>
> (Will, 32, male Chelsea fan)

> *Samuel*: [Chelsea is] successful, glamorous, erm, annoying.
> *Question*: In what sense are they annoying?
> *Samuel*: No matter how good a team they have, they never win enough matches. Inconsistency, that's what makes them annoying. It has always been this way, I think.
>
> (Samuel, 41, male Chelsea fan)

The clustering of this interpretation within a particular age group indicates how clubs function as a space of self-reflection. The club reflects important issues of its fans' lifeworlds. In talking about their football club many middle-aged male participants expressed a sense of disillusionment with their own working life. The club's failure to achieve ultimate success reflects their realization that economic goals set by themselves and/or by their socio-cultural environment may remain elusive. In this sense, their fandom is based on the team's failure. As Michael, a 37-year-old Chelsea fan, stated, 'I have always said, when we win the Premier League, I will stop watching Chelsea.' Without having to take this account quite literally, its underlying logic is clear. The ultimate success of the club remains fantastic. Its fulfilment would mean a symbolic victory, a victory that cannot be mirrored in the fan's life. The motive of underachievement is equally prominent in the case of other clubs regardless of their actual success. During my participant observation, one Bayer Leverkusen fan entertained others on the train by singing a song about his unfulfilled years as a Bayer fan, asking the audience to plant flowers on his grave if Bayer ever were to win the championship. Thus he inextricably links the fortunes of his object of fandom to his own life. As long as he lives Bayer will not succeed. These readings are unaffected by the actual success of clubs. One of my interviewees stressed the motive of underachievement and failure in his fandom despite supporting Real Madrid, the most successful club team in the world:

> I think there is a problem with Real Madrid . . ., you expect them to win everything, that they have got to beat all the contenders all the time. So, I think, it is essentially 'potential unfulfilled' for the last ten years.
>
> (Manuel, Real Madrid fan)

This example illustrates how certain motives in the reading of clubs recur among the fans of different clubs. The processes of appropriation, then, are determined by the individual, social, cultural and economic position of the fan rather than the actual semiotic condition of football clubs. Football clubs function as poly-semic spaces of reflection and projection.

Football clubs as spaces of projection

These processes are further exemplified by a number of Chelsea FC fans, who constructed their fandom in relation to the cultural and ethnic composition of the team.[4] Fans that consider themselves cosmopolitan and internationally minded describe the club in light of its multinational squad:

> It works out I am about one eighth Italian. I get slaughtered by my friends for it, but I have got no feelings for England, the national squad. I couldn't care. That's that. [Chelsea] are made up of so many nationalities, so that's good for me . . . I like the fact that we have got Danish, we have got Finnish players, we have got everyone in there. So that's what I like, it is a good mix from all the countries.
>
> (Brendon, Chelsea fan, geography student)

> I am pro-European and I always have been . . . I think [Chelsea] has broken down a lot of the sort of barriers and the prejudices that there were. A lot of them were bigots and racists and all the rest of it and yet, now, they are solidly behind the team . . . And you hear they are very defensive about the Italians or whatever, because it is an attack on Chelsea as opposed to an attack on an Italian or Romanian or whatever.
>
> (Dan, Chelsea fan, lawyer)

> My family had affinities to the Mediterranean, we are Mediterranean . . . Both my parents would be Barcelona fans, and now my mum is a huge Internazionale fan, she loves Ronaldo and she lives in Portugal, so she sees more games than I do . . . When people criticize the fact we have a lot of foreign players, I was brought up with kids that had families in Spain, black kids, white kids. That makes perfect sense, it just reflects the area, I think

. . . It just reflects where it is, makes perfect sense to me. And I love that, I love that cosmopolitan feeling, I think it is nonsense not to have that.

(Ally, Chelsea fan, teacher)

These statements reflect the lifestyle and habitus of fans with cosmopolitan attitudes expressed through their fandom. For the young geography student alienated by English nationalism, the lawyer who considers himself European, the teacher of Mediterranean descent growing up in East London, their Chelsea fandom reflects their own, cosmopolitan heritage and beliefs. But so it does for other fans holding opposed, even racist, views:

We are at Chelsea, all the supporters from my age were right-wing. I don't make any excuses about it, we were right-wing. We didn't like blacks at Chelsea. This and we didn't like the IRA . . . We never ever wanted black players at Chelsea, never ever wanted one. We were the last white team in London ever, we were just singing, 'we are the white team'. We didn't want one. When we had the first one ever, we booed him off the pitch . . . To be honest, everybody is right-wing, I still think people are now, but now they have got blacks, they play for Chelsea, we try just to see the shirt.

(Benny, Chelsea fan, office worker)

To this fan the same club that represents cosmopolitanism to the fans quoted above is a symbol of his racist beliefs. Those aspects not compliant with his ideological position are ignored in his reading of the club ('they have got blacks, they play for Chelsea, we try just to see the shirt') in the same way as cosmopolitanly inclined interviewees ignored those aspects of the club's history that were alien to their values and beliefs. What emerges from these accounts is the ability of fans to appropriate the club as text according to their social, cultural and ideological position formed through inter-personal as well as intra-personal factors. Racism, for instance, cannot be assumed to be a simple reflection of class position.

My argument then is the following: fandom has to be analysed as a form of consumption and hence as a form of communication. Football fandom constitutes a particular form of consumption in that what is articulated, is articulated consciously. In contrast to Bourdieu's unconscious habitus reflecting a particular class position, the habitus in football fandom consciously reflects particular values and beliefs. Football fandom is thus based on the duality of *identity* and *identification/self-reflection*. Several observations confirm this point. Firstly, the awareness with which football texts are consumed by football fans underlines the importance fandom has to their lives. Many football fans consider their fandom as an integral part of their personality. Indeed, to some of my interviewees support for their club was so personal that they had difficulty talking about their fandom:

LIVERPOOL JOHN MOORES UNIVERSITY
LEARNING SERVICES

It's difficult, it is very difficult. It is just very personal to me. What other people think about it isn't important to me . . . I was there when there were only 6,000 people there, week in and week out. Now I see 30,000 and they are not real supporters. They are here because it's fashionable. It's very personal, to me. It's the club I was brought up with. This is my life, basically.

(Michael, Chelsea fan)

The claims and assumptions made in this statement are by now familiar to us: the interviewee sees the club and himself as inseparably intertwined. The club is, to return to the phrase introduced above, an extension of himself. He is engaged in what Thompson (1995) has described as 'mediated quasi-interaction'. The interviewee makes sense of the club only in relation to himself ('the club I was brought up with'), expresses his fear of this part of himself being taken away and therefore disputes the right of others to have a similarly personal relationship to the club ('they are not real supporters'). How deeply fandom and personality are interrelated is also evident when fans position their fandom in relation to their immediate social environment. Some interviewees claimed that football is more important to them than their respective partners:

I feel a lot more than I let out. I feel more things . . . because if, I know, if it comes to choosing between my wife and football, Chelsea, there would only be one winner.

(Benny, Chelsea fan)

Thomas: It would be difficult if I had a girlfriend and I loved her and she wouldn't want me to go to matches that often, but I would consider it.
Harald: No, I thought about that, that doesn't work. Either she would accept my enthusiasm or it doesn't work.

(Harald and Thomas, Bayer Leverkusen fans)

Few fans made as extreme claims as Benny or Harald, yet many try to explain the intensity of their relation to their object of fandom by using their family as a point of reference. The intensity of their fandom is often actively acknowledged by fans' immediate social environment:

[My friends] put up with me and their interest has increased as I bug them. Most of my family understands my devotion and follows enough to be knowledgeable. In our wedding vows she surprised me by throwing in 'love and cherish . . . even during the World Cup!'. I can only hope my newborn will capture my love of the game.

(Ben, DC United fan)

Similarly, to many fans it is of crucial significance that they share their fandom with those closest to them:

[Chelsea] was always more a private thing, something with my dad. And now, where we both have season tickets, it is something we do together, like me and my dad . . . so it is always something I have done within the family.

(Catherine, Chelsea fan)

Either way, whether seen as rivalling or being part of family life, fandom surfaces as an essential part of the self.

Secondly, the importance of identification (rather than socially, culturally and economically determined identity) and self-reflection in the construction of fandom is evident in the ways particular clubs become the focus of attention for fans. Geographical and social proximity to certain clubs plays a significant role, especially for those attending games regularly:

My mum was a big Chelsea fan. We were a London-based family, although my dad is from the North originally, but anyway, she went out with a Chelsea player before she met my dad. But when I was a kid, she used to take me down to Stamford Bridge. And when she had some shopping to do she would leave me there and come back and watch the rest of the game with me and stuff like that.

(Ally, Chelsea fan)

It was something that was laid into my cradle. I have always been going to the ground here and I was born here and I stand by it.

(Carl, Bayer Leverkusen fan)

Actually, I have been a Leverkusen fan . . . all my life. As a little boy, well, as long as I can remember, my dad used to take me to the ground.

(Hilmar, Bayer Leverkusen fan)

In these cases the fandom of Chelsea FC or Bayer Leverkusen reflects certain forms of inherited social and cultural capital, in combination with geographical location, which to a certain degree is determined by the former two. Yet in other cases – and notably those when first contact with football is made through the media – the initial reasons for supporting a particular team are largely independent of geographic factors:

I remember, as a child I used to have the *Shoot* magazine, which is a weekly football magazine, and whether I just liked the colour . . . it wasn't a million miles away, it was London. Although I am not really sure whether I was that conscious at that age as to where they were. I had no sense of geographical location. I don't know what defining moments switched me on to Chelsea.

(Dan, Chelsea fan)

As random a category as the club's colours is often quoted as initial motivation to follow a particular team among such fans. In the following account the editor of a Chelsea fanzine confirms this observation:

> What made me a fan of Chelsea? I guess it was just the colours they play. I liked their strip, so I picked Chelsea at the beginning of the game. We just ran a questionnaire in some pages and there was this question, 'Why do you support Chelsea?'. And a lot of people have written in, 'because they played in blue'. And a lot of others use idiosyncratic reasons, and fewer people than expected have been ticking because my mum and dad did.
>
> (James Edwards, editor of the *Chelsea Independent*, personal interview)

Colour preferences are, of course, a coincidental personal preference. Football audiences developing into fans at a later stage of their adolescence or adulthood often utilize the plenitude of available fan texts through the mass media to choose particular clubs in accordance with their own *Weltanschauung*, value systems and lifestyles:

> My husband and I actually moved to North Kensington, off Portobello Road, five years ago, first time we moved here. And about a year later I said – I didn't know anything about football really – I just said, 'What football team should we go for?'. And he said, 'Well, Chelsea.' And he said he never really followed it – he is British Australian, I met him in Australia – he said that in Australia when people asked him, he would just say Chelsea, because that was all he knew really. And then I said to a friend, I suppose I go for Chelsea, and I asked him as well: 'Who should I go for, I live in North Kensington?' And they said, 'yeah, Chelsea' . . . Yes, I feel very much part of it . . . we moved here, the other place was a bit cheaper, but I had really an identification with north Kensington, and with Mark Hughes, a huge identification with him and I am going to like Poyet and Flo, it is hard to explain. I feel my personality fits in well with Chelsea somehow. Out of the London teams I feel that Chelsea fits me most, more than Arsenal or Tottenham or any of the other teams.
>
> (Alexandra, Chelsea fan)

I wasn't born in a city or town. I grew up some 100 km from here, in Heinsberg. There I went through all phases of a football fan who hasn't got a club in his own locality. First I collected football cards, wrote to clubs for signatures. In the beginning I also wanted other clubs to win, Bayern München, Borussia Mönchengladbach . . . But then I decided to look for a club who hadn't won a competition yet and that treated its supporters fairly. So I wrote to all Bundesliga clubs and waited for an answer. Bayer 04 answered in the most positive fashion and they hadn't won a trophy yet. I wanted to be there when they win something for the first time. And that is how it all started.

(Richard, Bayer Leverkusen fan)

The choice of object of fandom thus becomes a conscious choice mixing social and cultural lines of identification (and hence self-reflection) with geographical proximity. The different reasons for the support of a particular club, however, did not result in different degrees of fandom. Fans who started following a team for the colour of their shirts were as likely to be committed followers of a team as those born in the vicinity of the same club. To all these fans, regardless of the origins of their fandom, clubs serve as spaces of self-projection.

'We', 'they' and the reflection of self

Football fans' use of clubs as spaces of self-projection is further verified on a linguistic level. Speaking about the club they support, in other words the object of their fandom, all football fans interviewed frequently employed the first person plural 'we':

. . . *we* have two Brazilian internationals . . .

(Hilmar, Bayer Leverkusen fan, emphasis added)

. . . *we* were still in the second division at that time . . .

(Chris, Bayer Leverkusen fan, emphasis added)

. . . *we* lost in the semi-final . . .

(Roman, Chelsea fan, emphasis added)

The use of the pronoun 'we' reveals the relationship between fan and club. The club is not considered as the *object* of fandom but as forming a unit with the fan. Often this includes notions of community in which 'we' simultaneously refers to the club and fellow fans supporting the team.

The club is known for being the most popular club in Argentina. There is this thing that *we* are half of the country plus one, to say that *we* are the majority.

(Pablo, Boca Juniors fan, emphasis added)

Yet even those fans who claimed not to have any bond, let alone identification with fellow fans, talked about the club they followed in terms of 'we':

I don't have an affinity with other Chelsea fans; I am a strange Chelsea fan, obviously, because I go to football but I don't feel anything particular

for any Chelsea fans . . . *Our* main rivalry now is with Manchester United, it
is just purely jealousy, *we* haven't won a league game against them since . . .
(Will, Chelsea fan, emphasis added)

Such statements disclose the processes of identification, and therefore appropriation, that take place between the fan and the club. In the eyes of fans, they and
the club form a single entity. In this context the distinction Hills draws (1999)
between fans of cultural texts and cultural icons is worth pursuing. Football fans,
being fans of a text (and for that matter other fans focusing on a particular text
such as fans of other team sports), engage in different practices than fans of particular icons (such as singers, music bands, actors or even royalty). The
difference is manifested linguistically in the use of the first person pronoun 'we'
and the third person pronoun 'they', 'he' or 'she' (in the case of single performers).[5] In contrast to football fandom, fans of a particular band or singer are
unlikely to refer to their favourite group in terms of 'we'. The following extracts
from the Crafts *et al.* interview collection *My Music* (1993) illustrates the linguistic terms music fans use in discussing their object of fandom. In the following
extract a friend interviews a fan of the American band the Grateful Dead:

> *Question*: Would you call them your favourite band?
> *A*: Yeah, because *they*'re like the only band I listen to really. I mean Joni's
> not a band, *she* is a singer.
> (Crafts *et al.* 1993: 61, emphasis added)

Music fans implicitly acknowledge their awareness of the distance between themselves as audience and the performer.[6] As Miller and McHoul observe,

> very few forms of identification outside team sports permit 'we'. For instance
> even the most loyal fan of, say, the Rolling Stones, will not say 'We played
> well tonight' after a particularly successful gig. It will always be a referential
> 'they'. Sports may be unique in this respect. They effectively up the ante for
> pronominal distinction among supporters.
> (Miller and McHoul 1998: 88)

Indeed, when fans of icons such as actors or musicians articulate their belief in a
special bond between themselves and the icon, they are often portrayed as
lunatics and psychopaths (Jenson 1992). We also have to distinguish between
fans of different sports. Fans of individual sport stars do not use the pronoun
'we' when referring to their idols. Sport icons such as Jesse Owens, Muhammad
Ali or Boris Becker all have attracted a broad fan base. Yet their fans do not refer,
for example, to the day 'when we won Wimbledon'. The distance between fan
and object expressed in the use of language is no indication of the intensity of
fandom. Rather, the difference between textual fandom (such as that of football
fans) and iconic fandom (such as that of music fans) is that football fans articu-

late who they think they are while music fans articulate who they would like to be (while consumers simply articulate who they are). Drawing on Sacks (1995), McHoul and Miller's distinction between listed and categorized 'we' points to a similar conclusion. A 'listed we' refers to a clearly defined group of people. In the case of a 'categorized we', 'we' comes to represent wider social categories. The 'we' football fans use, as Miller and McHoul (1998: 85–6) demonstrate, is a categorized 'we'. Through the use of a categorized 'we', fans articulate their image of themselves, in other words their projection of self.

The contrast between fans of football clubs, on the one hand, and fans of other texts and icons, on the other, helps to clarify my argument. Stacey (1994) divides fan identification in the case of female cinema audiences in 1940s Britain into five categories: devotion, adoration, worship, inspiration, and transcendence and aspiration. All these fan activities express a desire to be the object of fandom – or more precisely to be like the object of fandom (the star/icon) – and therefore implicitly acknowledge not being so. A similar case can be made about fans of cultural icons such as pop stars. Consider, for instance, the case of Madonna fans (for a further analysis of Madonna fandom see Fiske 1989a, 1989b). They might dress like Madonna or take part in video competitions remaking Madonna clips (Fiske 1989b). By doing so they articulate their fantasies, their desires. They articulate who they would like to be. They select aspects of the outside world as represented by the icon and seek to integrate into their lifeworld the values and concepts their favourite icon represents. Football fans engage in the reverse process. As club and fan are interpreted as a single entity by fans, they project their own values onto the club. In other words, when football fans talk about their club, they naturally speak about their image of themselves. They project who they believe themselves to be onto the club:

> We don't play beautifully, but we like to see our players have guts.
>
> (Pablo, Boca Juniors fan, emphasis added)

In contrast to Madonna fans, who state that '*she*'s not ashamed to be pretty' or '*she* is sexy, but *she* doesn't need men' (quoted in Fiske 1989a: 99–100, emphasis added), this football fan does not acknowledge any divide between spectator and performer. He supports Boca Juniors not because they have guts (something he desires), but because they represent his own guts (something he believes himself to possess already). Identification with the club makes the club the fan's symbolic representative in the outside world. Remember the Chelsea fan who holds openly racist views and who sees Chelsea as the 'white club'. Remember the businesswoman who thinks that Chelsea represents success or those fans with liberal views and cosmopolitan backgrounds who emphasize Chelsea's cosmopolitanism. Or consider the reasons this industrial worker, who throughout the interview articulated traditional aspiring working-class values such as discipline, hard work and obedience, identifies for supporting Bayer Leverkusen:

I realized if I were to live somewhere else, I still wouldn't be interested in football. It has got to do with Bayer and its fans, because they are on a totally different level. If I go to away games and see other fans, they are the lowest of the low. For example, 1.FC Köln [Bayer's local rival], the kind of fans they have, I could never identify with. We are lucky, we got into Bayer. They are all my age group. No vandalism or something like that. We all sit down calmly and enjoy the game, and I like that.

(Manfred, Bayer Leverkusen fan)

My participant observations at home and away games of Bayer Leverkusen, as well as an interview conducted with the head of a special police unit in Leverkusen, confirm that Bayer Leverkusen fans are as much or as little prone to violence and vandalism as supporters of most other clubs. Here, as well as in the examples quoted before, football clubs function as a space of projection for fans' image of self. In identifying with their object of fandom, fans define its signification value. Consider the example of a Chelsea fan living in South Africa, who remembers how he became a Chelsea fan more than three decades ago:

I was reading the sports pages and came across the results or fixtures of English soccer and noticed the word Chelsea amongst the teams. There is a suburb close to where I lived which was called Chelsea. Who Chelsea were, where they played, who played for them, I didn't know, but I decided that, because I knew the Chelsea nearby, I would support the team.

(Jerrell, Chelsea fan)

Amazingly, football fans can base their fandom on as little as the seven letters of the name of a football club in a newspaper. This demonstrates how little the actual initial historical and cultural referentiality of a football club (its denotation and connotations) can bear relevance to the fan. The club provides the space for something else: a projection of self through which the fan and the club form a unit in which clubs come to function as an extension of self of the fan. The way in which fans see their own values and socio-cultural position represented by their club is also verified by football fans' sometimes fierce opposition to change, if transformations threaten fans' ability to maintain the bond with their club, something to which I will turn in the final chapter.

Football fandom and narcissism

It is worth pursuing the notion of fandom as an extension of self further. Marshall McLuhan in his frequently critiqued yet still informative study of modern electronic mass media has argued that electronic media function as an extension of modern man:

During the mechanical ages we had extended our bodies in space. Today, after more than a century of electric technology, we have extended our central nervous system itself into a global embrace, abolishing both space and time as far as our planet is concerned.

(McLuhan 1964: 3)

In order to adopt McLuhan's parable of the extension of self to football fandom, some additions and comments are required. Media (whether electronic media such as television or simple physical media such as the football stadium) function as an extension of the world to ourselves and vice versa. In fandom we extend ourselves back into the world through the way we consume and appropriate mass media (and their content). It is not only the media as technological structure but also their consumption that constitutes an extension of self. In this sense football clubs are transformed into symbolic representatives in the everyday life of fans. Football clubs become a signifier and an extension of fans in their respective lifeworlds. Yet clubs are spaces not only for projection, but also of reflection. In the cases cited above, the club functions as both screen and mirror at the same time, throwing back the fan's self-projection.

The object of fandom is therefore a reflection of the fan. What fans are fascinated by is their own image, an extension of themselves.[7] McLuhan (1964) illustrates the relationship between extension and self-reflection using the myth of Narcissus. Narcissus, the extraordinarily beautiful adolescent, is punished by the gods after one of his suitors kills himself in unfulfilled love. Narcissus falls in love with his own image while drinking from a river and seeing his reflection in the water. Unable to fulfil his actual desire, McLuhan writes, Narcissus kills himself.[8] McLuhan (1964) stresses two aspects which have often been overlooked in the discussion of the myth. Firstly, he emphasizes the fact that Narcissus falls in love with his own image rather than himself:

[T]he point of this myth is the fact that men at once become fascinated by any extension of themselves . . . the wisdom of the Narcissus myth does not convey any idea that Narcissus fell in love with anything he regarded himself. Obviously, he would have had very different feelings about the image had he known it was an extension of himself.

(McLuhan 1964: 42)

This observation is crucial to the interpretation of football fandom as an extension of self. Previously, I have argued that fandom is based upon a conscious habitus, that fans are more aware, although not necessarily more in control, of the patterns of consumption that articulate their fandom. The notion of fandom as an extension of self implies that fandom is based on the fan's projection onto the club. In this sense, fans build a strong emotional bond with their favourite club as their extension, not as themselves. While their fandom is based upon the reflection of themselves, they do not recognize it. The underlying principle of football fandom lies in the fact that in McLuhan's words (1964: 42) 'men at once become fascinated by any extension of themselves'. Hence, as fans are not aware that they are attracted by their own reflection, the interrelation between fan and object is communicated between object and subject rather than the latter merely being informed by the former:

> [T]he youth Narcissus mistook his own reflection in the water for another person. The extension of himself by mirror numbed his perceptions until he became the servo-mechanism of his own extended or repeated image.
>
> (McLuhan 1964: 41)

This interpretation helps to explain a seemingly paradoxical situation. Although I argue that fans are essentially attracted by their own reflection mirrored by the club, they are not unaffected by the external transformations their object of fandom undergoes. To some degree, fans incorporate these transformations into their reflection of self. Manfred emphasized ideals of disciplined, hard, honest work several times in the course of the interview. Speaking about Bayern München he stated, 'they aren't a football club for me any longer, they are only about money, that's got nothing to do with football'. However, later in the interview it became clear that his strong feelings against the commercialization of sport were slowly eroded by his own fandom of Bayer Leverkusen:

> Commercialization is a must. Without all that money we couldn't buy the good players, I accept that. It starts with merchandizing activities and bill-board advertisements and ends in a stock market flotation. These are necessary decisions, this is politics.
>
> (Manfred, Bayer Leverkusen fan)

Much like the water of the river that blurs Narcissus' image as his tears fall into the water, football clubs as semiotic spaces of projection and reflection are no neutral medium of reflection. The image of self, projected onto the club, is reflected through the signification value of the club. While polysemy is a premise that enables a recognizable self-reflection, the rudimentary semiotic structure of the object of fandom thus remains of significance. To this extent, Manfred becomes a 'servo-mechanism of his own extended or repeated image'. Football fandom as an extension of self therefore functions as an antenna to the outside world through which macro changes are incorporated into the fabric of everyday life. Yet, and this is the point McLuhan underlines, it does so through the filter of the self and an inevitable simultaneously arising numbness. Thus fans are not aware that they focus on a reflection of themselves. McLuhan argues that the very name Narcissus derives from the Greek word ναρκωση (narcosis), numbness:

> In the physical stress of superstimulation of various kinds, the central nervous system acts to protect itself by a strategy of amputation or isolation of the offending organ, sense, or function . . . Such amplification is bearable by the

nervous system only through numbness or blocking of perception. This is the sense of the Narcissus myth. The young man's image is a self-amputation or extension induced by irritating pressures. As counter-irritant, the image produces a generalized numbness or shock that forbids self-recognition.

(McLuhan 1964: 41)

However, seeking to explain how fandom functions as a narcissistic extension of the fan without fans recognizing their own projection or reflection raises a further predicament. On the one hand, football fandom constitutes an interface between internal information (reflection of self) and external information (macro transformations). On the other hand, McLuhan (1964: 41) argues that at the end of this process Narcissus 'was numb. He had adapted to his extension of himself and had become a closed system'. Similarly, Richard Sennett argues (1992: 324) that in narcissism 'is the danger of projection, a reaction to the world as though reality could be comprehended through images of the self . . . erasing the line between self and other means that nothing new, nothing "other," ever enters the self'. In fandom, then, as the above fan interviews demonstrate, information and numbness arising out of its narcissistic elements are simultaneous processes. The very process of appropriation and reading of fan texts is constituted through elements of information as well as numbness, yet neither is reached fully. Consider, for instance, the example of Benny, who holds racists views. In looking at his favourite club he sees his own racist beliefs:

> Aston Villa on Saturday, they were singing to Chelsea, 'En-ger-land, En-ger-land', they are an English team? [Ugo] Ehiogu, [not understandable], West Indian, Jamaica, where did they get England from? Okay, part of the old empire, but at least Vialli and Zola come from the same continent as me. They have players from all over the world and that annoys me. We don't . . . I love Vialli, I love, Zola, I love the boys, I want them for ever. Desailly . . . he is the best bargain, including Gullit, we ever had.
>
> (Benny, Chelsea fan)

On the one hand his fandom represents an enclosed system. He is able to project his own racism onto the club, which in his eyes is superior to clubs like Aston Villa fielding players of Afro-Caribbean descent. He is anaesthetized towards certain semiotic codes of his object of fandom. He is unable to negotiate within his self-reflection developments such as the Bosman ruling, the signing of ever more foreign players and the new cosmopolitan self-understanding of the decreasingly racist Chelsea crowd. However, these transformations are not blocked out completely, and he also seeks to appropriate such information. Vialli and Zola are 'at least from the same continent' and Marcel Desailly, a black player, is judged by his performance. Thereby the fan text as distorting mirror of self not only affects the image of the fan but also affects his or her sense of self and respective *Weltanschauung*. This determining influence of the text encapsulating the reflection of self over the fan as point of origin of the projection is highlighted in McLuhan's assumption that Narcissus falls under the spell of his own reflection and becomes 'the servo-mechanism of his own extended or repeated image'. Fandom, much like taste in Bourdieu's work, then, is this structuring as well as structured process of communication.

A final dimension in the interpretation of the Narcissus myth that McLuhan does not elaborate further is the notion that in order to fulfil the narcissistic potential of their fandom, football fans seek an audience of their own. According to Abercrombie and Longhurst (1998: 88–96), Narcissus finds his most persistent lover in the nymph Echo, who is only able to repeat what others have said before, thus repeating Narcissus' last words after his death (1998: 89). In this sense, Abercrombie and Longhurst (1998: 92–3) understand audienceship (and fandom as a particular form of it) as a form of social interaction:

> Although the self is central, that does not mean that everything else is obliterated. On the contrary, an *active* audience of other, and individual, selves is required, although it is an audience whose purpose is to reflect the central self. Indeed, for the proper functioning of narcissism, the audience has to be imagined as contributing to the narcissist's image of him- or herself.
>
> (Abercrombie and Longhurst 1998: 92–3, original emphasis)

Consequently Abercrombie and Longhurst analyse media consumption, and thus fan activity, as performance. Like Goffman (1959), they conceptualize everyday life as a stage for different performances of the self. In contrast to Goffman, who understands performance as a feature of all human societies, Abercrombie and Longhurst claim such narcissistic performances to be an intrinsic feature of modern media consumption, of what they label 'diffused audiences'. Diffused audiences are constituted through the everyday life consumption of decentralized, domestic media such as television and thus woven into day-to-day routines, blurring borders between private and public:

> The essential feature of this audience-experience is that, in contemporary society, everyone becomes an audience all the time. Being a member of an audience is no longer an exceptional event, nor even an everyday event. Rather it is constitutive of everyday life.
>
> (Abercrombie and Longhurst 1998: 68–9)

The accounts of fans cited here have illustrated how fans incorporate media and thus spectacle into the fabric of their everyday lives to a constitutive degree. Indeed many fans show awareness of how their performance as a fan is perceived by others. In the following extract, two fans discuss the degree to which they themselves succeed in becoming performers on a mass mediated stage:

Harald: All right, I like to watch all the surroundings [on television].

Thomas: I watched the game on DSF yesterday again and what do they show? Two brain-dead people standing around somewhere, who applaud. But they didn't show our choreography.

Harald: Against Monaco you could see the choreography, but that was coincidence.

(Harald and Thomas, Bayer Leverkusen fans)

The importance the televisual representation of their own performance bears for these fans confirms Abercrombie and Longhurst's claims:

Spectacle does not work to create the diffused audience without the simultaneous development of the narcissistic society. The notion of a narcissistic society embodies the idea that people act as if they are being looked at, as if they are at the centre of the attention of a real or imaginary audience.

(Abercrombie and Longhurst 1998: 88)

Part of their notion of the 'diffused audience' is drawn from and corresponds with the work of the situationalist Guy Debord (1994) concerning spectacle and modernity: 'The whole life of those societies in which modern conditions of production prevail, presents itself as an immense accumulation of spectacles. All that was once directly lived has become mere representation' (Debord 1994: 12). Spectacle in Debord's argument (1994: 29) has thus 'colonized' all sections of social life. Abercrombie and Longhurst do not assess the implications of the increasing representation and spectacularization of societies beyond attesting the constitution of diffused audiences. Their limited focus coincides with their omission of another aspect of the Narcissus myth: Echo, whose love is rejected by Narcissus, melts and her bones turn into stones and rock. It is only her voice, the remainder and reminder of her inability to meaningfully engage with the self-centred Narcissus, that persists. This may seem a minor addition, but it underlines the importance of reflecting upon the cultural, economic and social conditions of communication and self-reflection of football fans and their audiences. For Debord (1994) the foundations of the spectacular, represented nature of modern societies are found in the nature of capitalism itself. Earlier, I have identified interrelated forces such as industrialism and formal rationality as crucial premises for the rise of football. Either way, the investigation of the micro level of fandom in this chapter has demonstrated that we cannot understand football fandom as a contemporary cultural phenomenon in isolation from the prevailing macro foundation of contemporary life. It is these forces I want to turn to now.

Summary to Part I

Football fandom is based on a series of (intrinsically modern) consumption practices. Analysing fans as consumers, I have located football fandom within the cycle of industrial production and consumption. Drawing on Bourdieu's model (1984) of taste and habitus I have argued that football fans essentially communicate through their fandom. Yet, as the accounts of the interviewees in Part I illustrate, the consumption practices of football fans, reflective of their habitus, do not articulate their objective cultural, social and economic position, but their subjective understanding of this position. Fans are able to appropriate clubs (which are either mass mediated or directly experienced texts) as spaces of projection for their values and *Weltanschauungen* and, hence, as spaces of self-reflection. Consequently, and this is crucial for my further analysis, football fandom is dependent upon the textual openness of clubs, in other words the polysemic nature of the fan text. While Bourdieu correctly assesses acts of consumption as structured and structuring structure, consumption in football fandom also involves more direct modes of identification. I have illustrated how football fans employ clubs as an extension of their selves. This is exemplified by fans' use of 'we' when speaking about their club.

While football fans are often conscious of their use of 'we', they are unable to recognize their self-projection onto the club. I have thus analysed football fandom as an extension of self in light of the Narcissus myth. Drawing on McLuhan's interpretation of narcissism and electronic media, we have seen how football fans negotiate a reading of the club composed both of their projection and of the external signification value of the club, thus also being subject to the influence of their distorted mirror image. In other words, it is not only the fan who has the ability to appropriate the text, but to some degree the text that has the ability to appropriate the fan. What is important, then, is that we understand football fandom as a two-way process that integrates both self-reflection (as in the Narcissus myth) and communication (as in Bourdieu's model of consumption). Yet for the time being I have merely demonstrated that objects of football fandom such as teams and clubs function as spaces of self-reflection and that fans seek to communicate through their consumption. Yet, as the discussion of 'diffused audiences' and the reference to Debord's work (1994) demonstrate, important questions concerning the social, cultural and economic premises and implications of football fandom remain unanswered. It is such questions I want to pursue in the remainder of this book.

Part II

The social and cultural diffusion of football

Do I support a London football team? I do. I support Manchester United.
(Caprice Bourret, model)

It is probably in itself a sign of the contemporary condition of professional football that its current social, cultural and geographical proliferation and transformation is so adequately reflected in the reaction of California-born and UK-based model and celebrity Caprice Bourret to the question of whether she supported a London-based football club. A long way from the sport's roots in masculine working-class culture the addressee of the question alone illustrates the cultural diffusion of contemporary football: every celebrity, male or female, and regardless of their origin, is expected to relate to the semiotic system of spectator football. Football culture is popular culture and vice versa. At the same time the game has crossed not only the semiotic boundaries between genres of popular culture but equally geographical frontiers. Bourret's notion of Manchester United as a London team, rather than being an expression of a profound lack of knowledge, instead hints at the changing nature of the experience of locality in contemporary football. In its televisual omnipresence and its large fan base, a club such as Manchester United is indeed a team from London, as much as from anywhere else.

In the second part of this book I want to further explore the profound implications of the social, cultural and geographical diffusion of spectator football. I thus move from the level of the individual – and the focus on projection and self-reflection – to the space in which fans interact with the macro framing of their practices and activities: the social and the cultural realm of professional football. These transformations in turn reflect and shape football fandom as an act of identity-building self-reflection. As such, the rationalizing forces of modern industrialism and capitalism, which I previously identified as the *conditio sine qua non* of the rise of Association football, constitute the driving force of the transformations of the relation between football and fans. Under the pressure of macro transformations of the social, cultural and economic order, football has expanded along the axes of social and cultural space as well as territorial place. It has become increasingly universal as well as global. Many of the dramatic changes in contemporary football are therefore reflected as well as initiated in a range of different areas of contemporary life and accredited to different processes and forces. Particular academic attention has been paid to those trans-formations summarized under the headings of globalization or postmodernity. Both terms describe and analyse similar processes with often identical roots. While neither term presents us with a coherent theory of contemporary social and cultural change, both highlight the increasing degree of social connectivity and the growing intertextuality in cultural spheres. In the following I will focus on the expansion of cultural texts in professional football across social and cul-tural divides and analyse how spectator football and its fandom have shaped and been shaped by cultural and social, technological and economic change. Yet, while the discussion of growing cultural universality and intertextuality is often subsumed under the themes of globalization and postmodernity, I want to explore this particular aspect of contemporary football in its own right, last but not least given its blurring of the borders between the public and the private and its subsequent consequences for the organization of cultural and social and polit-ical discourses, before turning to aspects of cultural globalization in the following chapter.

Chapter 4

The politics of football
Fandom and the public sphere

In the previous chapter I have illustrated the degree to which football fans communicate their cultural and social position through their fandom. Yet, through this articulation of social and cultural determinants and their respective *Weltanschauungen*, football consumption constitutes an act of public as well as political communication. Some of the above examples, such as the racist fan to whom Chelsea FC was the 'white' club, or those fans who saw their fandom as part of a pro-cosmopolitan stance, are cases in point. In other cases interviewees expressed positions and attitudes that in turn formed the background to political discourses within football fandom. In the following extract Emil, a public-school graduate from West London, describes how he thinks that attending games at Chelsea's ground at Fulham Road reflects his lifestyle:

> It is very close to my house and is part of that area. And I suppose in some respect the type of players that are playing there, that also reflects the cosmopolitan area.
>
> (Emil, Chelsea fan)

While the geographical, cultural and political position of the interviewee are reflected in this account, the quote also indicates how football has become a vehicle of self-reflection and articulation for diverse sections of society. This cultural and social universalization of football should be understood as a dual process. Firstly, football recruits audiences across diverse social groups. Secondly, football informs and is informed by other cultural genres and areas of everyday life. The growing intertextuality within and between different genres has been repeatedly noted in recent studies of (post-)modern cultural systems (Harvey 1990; Jameson 1991). Football is no exception to such tendencies. The transformation of former England striker Gary Lineker into a BBC sports presenter seems an almost traditional career move today. The Hollywood acting career of Vinnie Jones, the former *enfant terrible* of British football, indicates how the star system of professional football and the film universe have intersected. The regional fame of celebrity chef and former Glasgow Rangers youth player Gordon Ramsay highlights the even more unlikely crossover between football and *nouvelle cuisine*.[1] The most common genre interrelation, however, has evolved between football and popular music. Redhead (1991) has portrayed how new forms of football fandom and rave culture informed each other in the late 1980s and the early 1990s. In addition to such a markedly subcultural cross-over, players such as John Barnes (with New Order), Glenn Hoddle and Andy Cole have made studio recordings, as have most professional clubs throughout Europe. While the artistic merits of such productions may be doubted, their cultural significance is undisputed. There are few more illustrative examples of the erosion of the structural boundaries of popular culture – that in Marx's famous words 'all that is solid melts into air, all that is holy is profaned' (Marx and Engels 1952: 25) – than the duet of German record international Lothar Matthäus with American gay icons Village People in the run-up to the 1994 World Cup. Another example of this cross-over between pop music and football is the marriage of England midfielder David Beckham and former girl-band celebrity Victoria Adams. In England Beckham now commands an unrivalled status as pop phenomenon and has even received book-length academic attention (Cashmore 2002).

Beyond these most striking cases, there is a long list of genres, public areas and sections of what Appadurai (1990: 296) terms the 'mediascape' that have been infiltrated by football. The success of Nick Hornby's (1992) *Fever Pitch*, a fan's autobiography, has established football-centred fiction as a growing genre of contemporary literature, as much as it launched Hornby on a career as one of the best-selling contemporary novelists. Sport has become the theme of various television quiz shows (for example the BBC's *A Question of Sport*) and comedy programmes such as *SAT.1*'s spin-off *Ran Fun*, or the BBC's *They Think It's All Over* and *Fantasy Football League*, hosted by Frank Skinner and David Baddiel, who themselves successfully recorded the official England song in the run-up to the 1996 European Championship. These cross-over tendencies have been acknowledged repeatedly in the contemporary literature on sport. Rowe (1999: 158), for example, links Real's analysis (1996) of the symbiosis between the Olympic Games and television to Jameson's analysis (1991) of the cultural logic of late capitalism and foresees the complete collapse of all division between texts. While Rowe correctly points out that this collapse has not yet fully taken place, the examples discussed above indicate how the divisions between texts of different genres are rapidly eroded. However, while the interrelation between football and other entertainment genres has been discussed extensively elsewhere (cf. Redhead 1991, 1993, 1997) with rather straightforward conclusions, the analysis of the political implications of the cultural universalization of football has attracted little attention hitherto.

The everyday politics of football

Despite a lack of academic investigations in this respect, the everyday discourses and actions of football fans suggest that fandom is political in both its content and its implications, even though negotiated outside the traditional spheres of political discourse. Interestingly, a large number of respondents were, when asked about the role of politics in football, quick to state that they neither saw nor desired a link between football and politics:

> I don't think football should have any political implications.
>
> (Karen, Chelsea fan)

> For me it is only leisure. I find in England it is associated as a working-class sport. I don't get into the sort of football discussions in England . . . I don't enjoy living that discourse. For me it is an interest that goes beyond class divisions or national interests. It is just sport.
>
> (Rudolfo, Colo-Colo fan)

Note the opposition of Rudolfo to football being associated with the working class, which he is not part of and which would disqualify him as a fan. As fans seek spaces of self-projection, a politicization of football in general or of a particular club possibly endangers fans' identification with the club, as the semiotic structure of the club threatens to be externally determined. Similar fears mark other fans' statements. Fans, even though this is not necessarily a conscious process, wish their clubs to remain neutral, blank spaces of self-projection. What is opposed by such fans then is foremost 'party politics' and political agendas introduced from the outside. Nonetheless, their everyday politics, their values and *Weltanschauungen* are communicated and integrated in a discursive process with the outside world through football fandom as extension of self. This is well illustrated in the following conversation between two Bayer Leverkusen fans who at first reject the politicization of football, only to set their own political agenda in the subsequent discussion:

> *Thomas*: Football is not political, no way.
> *Harald*: Football and politics don't have anything to do with each other and should remain separate.
> *Thomas*: No Bayer fan would have voted for the CDU [German conservative party] only because Daum [the team's manager] said he would leave the country if the Social Democrats and the Greens won the elections.
> *Harald*: There are clubs that really insist that football and politics are linked such as St Pauli or so. They can be Nazi or ultra left-wing. I want to watch a football game, it is not a party conference.
> *Thomas*: But right-wing slogans really upset me, though . . .
> *Harald*: . . . yes, sure . . .
> *Thomas*: . . . if Bayer fans scream 'Uh, uh, uh' if a coloured player has the ball, although we have got coloured players ourselves – not to mention that it would be bigoted anyway – then this is really idiotic.

Harald: Yes, also those people that do not cheer when Emerson [Brazilian international] scores, that is totally disrespectful.

Thomas: It is the same when they go on about the Dutch who play for Schalke and Eric Meijer plays for us and everyone cheers for him. But the next moment they shout '*Scheiß Holländer*' if one of Schalke's Dutch players has the ball.

Harald: It's ridiculous. I don't like the Dutch particularly, but Eric plays here and all right then.

Thomas: I don't have any problem with any nationality.

Harald: These are personal things you experience.

Thomas: There are enough nice Dutch people and there are Germans that aren't all nice – enough of them!

(Harald and Thomas, Bayer Leverkusen fans)

Having initially agreed that football and politics should represent separate realms, Harald and Thomas subsequently discuss political themes such as racism and nationalism in relation to football and their own fandom. While we have previously observed the dialogue between fan and object of fandom, the dialogical shaping of the object of fandom is particularly evident in relation to politics. This process of two-way information is, however, a complex one. Thomas points out that no one would have voted for a conservative party because of the team manager's political preferences. The team manager is thus placed outside the fan text. He is excluded from the 'we' that constitutes the space of self-projection in the interviewee's fandom. If, however, political themes emerge inside the object of fandom that cannot be displaced, fans incorporate such discourses through their distorted reflection. Harald claims that he doesn't 'like the Dutch particularly', but he is nevertheless prepared to subordinate his own beliefs to the fan text ('Eric plays here and all right then'). The separation of football and politics is, of course, in itself political, drawing on liberal ideas seeking to separate leisure and politics, the public and the private and ideas of standardized, unhindered competition, mirroring key ideologies of capitalism. Yet it is precisely this divide between sport and politics that is being blurred.

During the period of my research a long list of issues of everyday politics emerged (and many more have since). Crucial questions of contemporary life were discussed as frequently in sports broadcasts and the sports pages of newspapers as anywhere else. England manager Glenn Hoddle's comments on reincarnation, in which he implied that mental and physical disability were a punishment of sins in a previous life, triggered a discourse about the rights of disabled people, the limits of religious beliefs and the role of faith healers. Sports media monitored closely the life of Premier League striker Stan Collymore, touching on issues such as domestic violence and depression. The coverage surrounding England players Tony Adams and Paul Merson fed the ongoing discourse on alcohol and drug abuse. Racism and xenophobia were reccurring aspects of the coverage of tabloid newspapers and other media. Paul Gascoigne's infamous mimed flute playing as a symbol of Unionism inciting the largely Catholic following of Glasgow Celtic during an Old Firm clash as well as pictures of former Scotland goalkeeper Andy Goram waving the flag of the Ulster Volunteer Force paramilitaries revived the ongoing discourse on sectarianism and political violence in Scottish football. Equally fans themselves often read football texts in accordance with their political convictions:

> *Pascal*: Some teams I can't stand at all. The *Löwen* [TSV 1860 München], for example, I don't know, I don't like Bavarians particularly, and Bayern München is more than enough for me. And Hansa Rostock, but perhaps that is just, with Rostock, you just associate particular things. That is probably very ignorant.
>
> *Question*: What things?
>
> *Pascal*: I don't know, Rostock, it is just like that since these confrontations [racist riots against asylum seekers in Rostock-Lichtenhagen in 1991]. Or Hertha BSC, I was really happy that Berlin didn't have a team in the Bundesliga. I have to say that in my case there is also a very strong element of *Schadenfreude*. If I say that I don't have an actual favourite team at the moment, then there are still some teams, where I am happy when they lose. For example, if Bayern doesn't win the championship.
>
> (Pascal, football fan)

Pascal associates teams from Rostock, Berlin and Munich with particular political subtexts, such as racism and political violence, the move from the *Bonner Republik* of post-war West Germany to a reunified Germany that redefines its political ambitions, and political conservatism, a conservatism which has its traditional home in Germany's south and Bavaria. His case thus illustrates a reverse process in which politics shape football fandom as much as vice versa.

Even a fully fledged war featured widely across various sports media. When NATO commenced air strikes against Yugoslavia in spring 1999, Serb players across Europe declared their unwillingness to play for western European teams as long as the hostilities continued. Supporting Yugoslav players became an issue of politics, a statement of values and beliefs. During this time the following words on the Kosovo conflict were printed in Charlton Athletic's matchday programme preceding a game with Chelsea. They were written by Sasa Ilic, the team's Yugoslav goalkeeper:

> I have a number of close relatives and friends living in Yugoslavia who have been affected by the NATO bombing campaign and I fear for their safety . . . Some fellow Yugoslavian professional footballers playing around the world have chosen not to play for their clubs in protest at the NATO bombing, a decision which I support and understand. However, in my position I feel that choosing to play for Charlton Athletic I will make a greater contribution to remaining in the public eye. I implore NATO to

stop the bombing and ask the politicians on all sides to do everything
humanly possible to bring about a satisfactory solution to the present crisis.

(*Valley Review*, 3 April 1999: 53)

The political themes discussed in the niche media of football such as matchday
programmes and fanzines collected during my fieldwork ranged from the Kosovo
war to organized crime (*When Saturday Comes*, May 1999: 10) and child abuse.
In the wake of proceedings against the Southampton manager David Jones (who
lost his job but was subsequently acquitted), discourses on child abuse and
paedophilia also overshadowed Chelsea's campaign, when first-team coach
Graham Rix was imprisoned for sexual relations with a minor. What is important
in all these cases is that not only did these incidents occur in relation to football,
but they are negotiated within the sphere of fandom and club affiliations. In the
month following Rix's conviction the cover, the editorial and the lead article of
Chelsea's largest fanzine were dedicated to discussion of the case:

> The club knows Graham is now a convicted paedophile . . . It is almost as if
> Chelsea are wilfully ignoring the seriousness of Graham's crime. This is not
> your run of the mill footballer in a drink driving incident. If Chelsea are
> serious about attracting families they cannot just present Graham his job
> back as if nothing had happened.
>
> (*Chelsea Independent*, no. 101, April 1999)

For many Chelsea fans, this child abuse case and the question of how it should
be dealt with quickly became a crucial dimension in the construction of their
fandom. During a phone conversation with a potential interviewee, one fan
expressed his concern over the incident:

> I would like to ask you something. What do you think about the Rix story?
> . . . If the allegations are true, they should sack him. We must not have
> someone like that at the club.
>
> (Phone conversation, no in-depth interview followed)

Such statements illustrate how fans seek to externalize and project their values onto the club. The categorized 'we' of this fan does not provide a semiotic space for
the sex offender Rix. Thus the fan wishes Rix to be removed from the club. If we
understand the object of fandom (the club) as a text, then fans not only negotiate the meaning of this text, they also define its boundaries in that they exclude
segments of the text that do not correspond with their sought appropriation.

Fandom and the public sphere

The debates about the war in Yugoslavia, about sex offenders, or concerning
racist violence in particular regions and cities are all political to varying degrees

and cannot all easily be allocated to the legislative and executive channels of indirect democracies. However, they are all forms of public discourse. In light of the political nature of the discourses within contemporary football, it is worth recalling Jürgen Habermas's work on what he has defined as the 'public sphere':

> By 'the public sphere' we mean first of all a realm of our social life in which something approaching public opinion can be formed. Access is guaranteed to all citizens. A portion of the public sphere comes into being in every conversation in which private individuals assemble to form a public body . . . Citizens behave as a public body when they confer in an unrestricted fashion – that is, with the guarantee of freedom of assembly and association and the freedom to express and publish their opinions – about matters of general interest.
>
> (Habermas 1989: 136)

This definition and Habermas's related analysis of the historical transformation of the structural conditions of the public sphere have attracted a substantial amount of critical appraisal and scrutiny (Held 1990; Holub 1992; Calhoun 1993; Garnham 1993; Thompson 1993). Before giving this background I will briefly highlight here the key aspects of Habermas's model and the particular relevance of its critique to the political dimension of football.

The theoretical framework through which Habermas (1974) develops his notion of the public sphere is problematic. Departing from the inclusive notion of the public sphere cited above, he identifies an ideal type of the public sphere in the political discourse of the eighteenth- and early nineteenth-century English bourgeoisie, and its attempt to emancipate itself from the feudal system. According to Habermas, the public sphere of the time was based on open-ended political discourse within a civil society, often taking place in coffee houses and saloons, and the circulation of non profit orientated media operated by members of the public. Mirroring the massification angst of the Frankfurt School, Habermas argues that this ideal type of the public sphere is under threat in the age of the (mass) welfare state:

> With the interweaving of public and private realms, not only do the political authorities assume certain functions in the sphere of commodity exchange and social labour, but, conversely, social powers now assume political functions. This leads to a kind of 'refeudalization' of the public sphere. Large organizations strive for political compromises with the state and with one another, excluding the public sphere whenever possible.
>
> (Habermas 1989: 141)

Both assumptions – the existence of an ideal type of a public sphere in the eighteenth century and its refeudalization in mass consumption societies – are, I believe, incorrect. Habermas reaches these conclusions as his concept suffers from a too narrow, too specific interpretation of the public, politics and participation.

The reasons for this failure are manifold. Firstly, some of Habermas's assumptions are historically incorrect. These historical inaccuracies have been well documented elsewhere (Curran 1991) and do not need to be repeated here. Although Habermas acknowledges (1974) the link between the rise of the public sphere in eighteenth-century Europe and the development of capitalism, he does not interpret the public sphere as an inherent part of the mediascape developing in industrial society and instead believes it to be refeudalized by the mass media. Secondly, Habermas's notion of the public sphere is not only historically incorrect, it is a normative ideological evaluation and idealization. Yet the public sphere is constituted by its technological and social foundations including cultural realities such as football, not by ideal types of political participation or communication. Incidentally the ideal types of political participation have often proved to be anything but ideal: for example during the eighteenth century large proportions of the population including women and members of the lower classes were excluded from the public sphere. This normative misinterpretation is heightened by the English term 'public sphere' (Habermas 1989, 1992) as opposed to the German *Öffentlichkeit* originally used in Habermas's work. *Öffentlichkeit* as opposed to 'public sphere' describes a state, not a space, as the term 'sphere' suggests. *Öffentlichkeit* has no place, no plural. It is an intrinsic feature of modern, (mass) media-based society. *Öffentlichkeit* in its literal sense refers to a state of being open (*offen*) in opposition to the enclosed, the private. Thus, as in Habermas's original definition, *Öffentlichkeit* exists when knowledge or texts are open and accessible, though not necessarily universal, information.[2] Subsequently, however, Habermas confines the public sphere to defined socio-demographic groups. Therefore he implies that there is a space to *Öffentlichkeit* and, thus, that there may be other, alternative public spheres. This is, I think, incorrect. The interrelation between consumption and production, giving rise to a dynamic interaction between football and politics, points to the need for a different typology of the public sphere and political participation.

Much of the criticism directed at Habermas's work, such as the feminist critique by Fraser (1990, 1992; see also McLaughlin 1993), follows precisely these misleading implications by pleading for a model taking account of different public spheres. While I agree with their objections against Habermas's exclusive notion of the public sphere, the conclusions they draw, speaking of public *spheres*, inherit the misconceptualization of Habermas's work. Habermas himself, further departing from his originally correct definition of *Öffentlichkeit*, is at ease with this critique and adopts a position that speaks of different spheres:

> It is wrong to speak of one single public . . . a different picture emerges if *from the beginning* one admits the coexistence of competing public spheres and takes account of the dynamics of those processes of communication that are excluded from the dominant public sphere.
>
> (Habermas 1992: 424–5)

While the historical premises of Habermas's revised position are correct, the theoretical abstraction is not. While one cannot dispute the existence of many conflicting social groups and communities reflecting social, cultural and economic distinctions within the public sphere, it is only through Habermas's normative rather than empirical definition of the public sphere that we come to see these groups as public spheres in their own right. By disputing that the public sphere constitutes a condition of modern societies rather than a space (or spaces) within them, and by ignoring the inclusive plurality of the public sphere, the actual focus shifts away from investigating *Öffentlichkeit*. Those scholars liable to such approaches in fact speak about social groups or subcultures when they intend to talk about public sphere(s). When, for example, Dayan speaks (1998) about 'publics', what he really pays attention to are communities or audiences. If football and its fans constituted their separate public sphere, none of the political themes discussed above would bear any relevance in the discourse of this public. If we accept the notion of multiple publics we eliminate the analytical value of the category 'public', as it is precisely in the interaction of different groups and through dialogue that the public sphere is formed. What Habermas's historical framing of the public sphere as well as much of its critique have in common is that both hinder the analysis of the complex interconnectivity of modern culture and the public sphere. It is only through a conceptualization of the public sphere as a unified yet fragmented condition in which the accelerating interchange of information takes place that we can meaningfully analyse how football and politics inform each other, how citizens become fans, and fans citizens. It is precisely because football and its fans are part of a single – though not coherent   public that themes such as religion, sexuality, party politics and ethnicity inform and reflect their discourse.

Two aspects of the public sphere are of particular significance to my argument, then. Firstly, the public sphere is not a normative ideal type confined to bourgeois, liberal political interaction, but a condition of modernity arising – much like Association football – out of the cultural, social and technological premises of industrial capitalism. Secondly, with the expanding role of electronic mass media, the public sphere has been undergoing far-reaching structural transformations, in that it has become more complex, fragmented and, as I will argue, inclusive. In this context it is worth remembering our previous observation concerning the degree to which football is embedded into the fabric of the everyday life of football fans through set patterns of consumption many fans report:

> I follow football on a daily basis. I watch *täglich ran* [daily football news], ten minutes or how long it takes. As far as football is concerned, there is also always Eurosport, the Under-21s played yesterday. Yes, I always watch football if it is on, actually.
>
> (Mr Schmidt, Bayer Leverkusen fan)

Football, well, it is part of my life. During the week I always check teletext, watch all sorts of things on television, and then we talk about it in school. Especially on Fridays, when school is over and you know tonight or tomorrow there is an important game. You go home, listen to the Bayer CD, lie down on the bed and you look forward to the weekend.

(Thorsten, Bayer Leverkusen fan)

The degree to which media use is integrated into the structure of everyday life is the premise of the increasingly inclusive, yet fragmented, condition of the public sphere. In the Habermasian conceptualization of the public sphere with its rigid distinction between the public and the private, between the state and the domestic, between politics and entertainment, such everyday consumption, often taking place within the home, is per se excluded as an aspect of the public sphere. What is needed instead is a broader understanding of the public sphere that takes account of its collapsing boundaries. Such an approach informs John Hartley's critique:

My argument is that, like the imperial archive of knowledge, the public sphere is more real as a fantasy, an ideal type, than as a historical achievement. The critical pessimism of twentieth-century social theorists who lament the passing of an informed, rational public sphere and the rise of popular entertainment has simultaneously overplayed the achievement and social extent of the Enlightenment public sphere, and also proved to be an impediment to understanding the role that the popular media do play in producing and distributing knowledge, visualizing and teaching public issues in the midst of private consumption, writing the truths of time on the bodies of those image-saturated 'telebrities' whose cultural function is to embody, circulate, dramatize and teach certain public virtues within a suburban cultural context.

(Hartley 1997: 181)

Hartley develops an alternative paradigm that takes account of the role of popular media, and of the subtle and complex ways political meanings and beliefs are negotiated in today's public sphere. This model provides us with a useful starting point to examine the political dimension of football fandom. Hartley in contrast to many recent discussions of the public sphere maintains the unity of the public sphere as a multiple and complex yet intrinsically cross-communicating semiotic system:

The postmodern (media) public sphere, which like suburbia is not a place at all, is the locus for the development of new political agendas based on comfort, privacy and self-building. I would argue that the major contemporary political issues, including environmental, ethnic, sexual and youth movements, were all generated *outside* the classic public sphere, but they

were (and are) informed shaped, developed and contested within the priva-
tized public sphere of suburban media consumerism.

(Hartley 1997: 182)

It should be noted that Hartley does not argue (1996) that liberal political discourses have ceased to exist, but rather that the classical public sphere still
remains part of the larger postmodern public sphere, which – drawing on the
work of the Russian cultural literary theorist Yuri Lotman – he terms 'semiosphere'. In between both, 'the mediasphere has developed . . . connecting the
public (political) sphere and the much larger (cultural) sphere, within the period
of modernity' (Hartley 1996: 78).

Like Habermas's work, Hartley's approach has its limitations and shortcom-
ings which spring from a questionable research basis. The main problem in
Hartley's work lies in the fact that he, as Couldry points out (2000), excludes
the possibility of audience research (Hartley 1987) but develops a theoretical
model largely based on assumptions about audiences and their interaction with
media texts. Thus Hartley does not prove conclusively that the 'major contemporary political issues' are indeed generated through media consumption, as well
as by the media themselves. However, it is such qualitative audience research
that I draw on in this discussion of the contemporary public spheres and model
of political and cultural participation, further confirming Hartley's position.

Assessing the cultural space in which fans project their own values and beliefs
in their fandom highlights the implications of fandom as an extension of self.
The semiosphere, according to Hartley (1997: 182), is the space 'where personal, family, political and cultural meanings are reproduced – a place where
people make themselves out of the semiotic and other resources to hand'. Football fandom in turn connects the self with the semiosphere or public sphere, as it
becomes the space in which semiotic meanings are negotiated and formed into
an extension of self. It is the fan's agent to the outside world. It is here that
popular discourses and self-projection are juxtaposed. It is here that the politics
of everyday life manifest themselves. The following extract demonstrates how
fans choose and draw upon selected discourses and negotiate them on the
grounds of their own fandom:

> Bayern München is an international, cosmopolitan club. Because, when they
> tell Carsten Jancker [Bayern München forward], 'look, all the skinheads
> think you are cool, you have to let your hair grow', then this shows that
> political correctness matters to the club.

(Pascal, football fan)

This statement demonstrates both how the political discourse is generated and
how it is subsequently negotiated in fandom. The haircut of a player is considered a signifier of a political discourse (the problem of racism and neo-Nazism).
Pascal evaluates the club's action according to his political stance. In fact, he
expresses his own position on racism rather than the club's. Indeed, there is no

evidence that Bayern München ever sought to influence the player's appearance. Pascal thus performs a political role and participates in a public political discourse. In this sense, fans not only fulfil a political role, but they actively exercise citizenship. In contrast to the narrower definition of citizenship in political theory, they are citizens projecting themselves onto and communicating through the clubs they support. They are, to return to Hartley's work, DIY citizens. Hartley's concept (1999) of DIY citizenship is based on his assumption that television is a medium of convergence and as such transmodern:

> The convergence in question marks a return to a decidedly 'pre-modern' concept of citizenship, derived from the political theory of the ancient Hellenic city state, where (at least for free, male, adult natives – in other words citizens) democracy, drama and didactics were one and the same thing, practised in the same place by and for the same people, whose assembly in sight of each other *constituted* the polity and whose collective actions of hearing orators, actors and leaders *constituted* the audience . . . Television . . . is thus a '*transmodern*' *medium* – pre-modern and postmodern all at once.
>
> (Hartley 1999: 7)

In this sense, television offers a medium of difference through which identity and citizenship are formed. Yet such citizenship – and this is where Hartley's concept is informative to the study of football fandom – is self-determined. Similarly, Fiske (1989a) – who himself has compared television to a form of DIY kit[3] (Fiske 1987) – interprets consumption as an act of semiotic self-determination and thus as 'the empowerment to the disempowered' (Fiske 1989b: 25). While football fans indeed engage in acts of semiotic determination, I have also sought to emphasize that the generating of meaning in the reading of fan texts constitutes an act of self-reflection, which for reasons highlighted in the discussion of Bourdieu (1984) must not be mistaken as a simple matter of choice or empowerment. The DIY analogy is nevertheless useful in exploring the consequences of political communication within popular culture:

> In Britain, 'DIY' is familiar as the amateur end of home-improvement – installing the material basis for the ideology of domesticity in the form of particle-board, paint and a patio. I borrow the term to describe the Do-It-Yourself citizen; the practice of putting together an identity from the available choices, patterns and opportunities on offer in the semiosphere and mediasphere . . . Citizenship is no longer simply a matter of a social contract between state and the subject, no longer even a matter of acculturation to the heritage of a given community; DIY citizenship is a choice people can make for themselves . . . The places where you can find DIY citizens exercising their semiotic self-determination are on television and among its audience.
>
> (Hartley 1999: 178–9)

And, we may add, inside the stadium, in the local pub and in all other places where football is consumed. While television, as the backbone of both the contemporary mediasphere and semiosphere, is crucial in the constitution of citizenship, the example of football fans reading fanzines, listening to the radio and attending football matches at the ground illustrates that other media add to television's capacity to form citizenship. Hartley's concept thus captures important themes I have discussed in relation to football fandom. It emphasizes the home as the crucial place of identity construction and thus reflects the rise of football fandom as a form of modern, domestic leisure. It corresponds to the conceptualization of fandom as a form of consumption and communication. It highlights the transformations of the public sphere that manifest themselves, among others, in the cultural proliferation of football. It helps us to understand fandom as a form of identity and political participation. Most importantly, it helps us to analyse to what effect football fandom functions as an extension of self.

A case study: DIY citizenship and the negotiation of the Le Saux–Fowler incident

Fandom as a form of interaction between the self and the public offers a space in which citizenship is generated and politics are shaped. I will further analyse this relationship between football fandom and politics in the discussion of a final example: the row between Chelsea and England winger Graeme Le Saux and fellow England international Robbie Fowler and the subsequent discourse on the incident among fans.

During Chelsea's home game with Liverpool on 27 February 1999, Liverpool striker Robbie Fowler engaged in (alleged) verbal and (clearly visible) extra-verbal references to homosexuality and sodomy directed at Le Saux. Fowler's actions were accompanied by the chants of a substantial number of Liverpool supporters voicing their belief that, in their words, Le Saux 'takes it up the arse'. The situation escalated after Fowler, following a foul on Le Saux, for which he was cautioned, used the break in play to bend over and present his backside to Le Saux in a suggestive fashion. Later Le Saux elbowed Fowler in an incident that was caught by the television cameras inside the ground but missed by the match officials. It was later discussed in the BBC's highlights programme *Match of the Day*, prompting calls for the FA to take disciplinary action against Le Saux.

Several aspects of this incident are significant in the exploration of how identity and political discourse are formed and cultivated among football fans. Firstly, the incident highlights the complex interconnectivity of the public sphere. Aside from the obvious dimension of sexuality, the incident raised seemingly unrelated themes. Fowler and Le Saux, as public figures, embodying and dramatizing cultural meaning, provided the wider context for the reading of the incident. Fowler was already a familiar figure in the wider political and cultural discourse surrounding British football. The semiotic themes he cultivated range from raising awareness for workers threatened by job losses (he wore a shirt in support of striking Liverpool dockers) to drug addiction, as rumours had linked him with cocaine abuse.[4] Le Saux, on the other hand, has been usually portrayed by the mainstream sports media as an outsider, hot-tempered,[5] and distanced from his team-mates, with emphasis being laid on his middle-class roots and his upbringing on the Channel Island of Jersey. This perception was highlighted in the media discourse following his clash with Fowler. Some commentators therefore pointed to deeper roots of the incident than straightforward homophobia. The nationwide fanzine *When Saturday Comes* felt that sexual orientation was not the real issue:

> Fowler's point was simple. Football is for men who conform to a certain ideal of what a man is: aggressive, inarticulate, misogynic and definitely one of the lads. Players who don't conform, like the notoriously antique-collecting, *Guardian*-reading Le Saux, are favoured with the worst insult the lads can think of. It's the fact that he's a bit different that bothers them, not his actual sexuality which, as coincidentally made plain in the programme for the Liverpool game, is conventionally hetero.
>
> (*When Saturday Comes*, no. 149, 1999: 4)

In this interpretation the conflict between Le Saux and Fowler is not a conflict concerning sexuality; rather it expresses the tension between 'lads' and intellectuals and hints at a conflict between classes. This approach, not surprisingly, was taken further by the paper that itself came to occupy the role of an exhibit in the Fowler–Le Saux discourse, *The Guardian*:

> In this country of conformists, footballers read the *Sun* or the *Daily Sport*, and are expected to be working-class, badly-spoken, ignorant, right-wing. Piers Morgan, editor of the *Mirror*, summed it up nicely: 'Nobody cares if Le Saux is gay or not. It is the fact that he openly admits to reading the *Guardian* that makes him the most reviled man in football.' Le Saux, by the general reckoning, is a victim of his own urbanity; after 11 years in the game he is still a stranger to its culture. With all his arcane interests, no wonder the rest of his profession dismiss him as a poof.
>
> (*The Guardian*, 'Weekend' section, 15 May 1999: 10)

While the extract echoes the general approach of the *When Saturday Comes* editorial, that Le Saux does not conform with the laddish culture within professional English football teams, it also introduces further oppositions: educated versus badly spoken, urbane versus ignorant, liberal versus right-wing and, underlying all those distinctions, middle class versus working class. Such dichotomies went well beyond the scale of interpretation of other mass circulation and subcultural media, ranging from the tabloid press to fanzines.[6] All these media, by interpreting the incident in accordance with the socio-cultural positioning of their readership, actively constructed oppositions within a political discourse. Fans thus encountered a multiplicity of discourses in the public sphere in and through football.

On a side note the Le Saux–Fowler incident also demonstrates the cultivation of discourses within the public sphere through different mass media. In a painful attempt to avoid the word 'gay' that makes for a worthy case study of televisual representation, the BBC misrepresented the incident by focusing on Le Saux's elbow check and ignored the previous taunting. In the BBC's Saturday-night highlights programme *Match of the Day* panellist Trevor Brooking merely concluded that 'both players come out with very little credit', while match commentator John Motson, when Fowler was seen to bend over spreading his buttocks, guessed 'I suppose he was insisting on the ten yards', leaving the fanzine *When Saturday Comes* wondering whether Motson 'is in a world of his own or just terminally dim' (*When Saturday Comes*, no. 146, 1999: 4). Similarly, broadsheet papers did not refer to Fowler's homophobic abuse until the *Daily Mail* eventually broke the story by identifying Fowler's part in the incident and its sexual connotations. Subsequently, other papers and television took up the story.

In the following I will illustrate how fandom invites political action and the formation of (DIY) citizenship on the basis of such media texts. As much as the media coverage of the incident was diverse and emphasized different aspects of the case, respondents took varying positions and came to different types of reading of the incident. Their accounts can be subdivided into three broad categories:

Hegemonic reading

The majority of Chelsea fans sought to justify Le Saux's behaviour, as he was considered to be part of the club and, hence, an object of fandom acting as symbolic or semiotic extension of the fan. These participants felt offended by Fowler's suggestion that Le Saux might be gay, which they – as does Fowler – understand as an insult. They considered, to a varying degree, Le Saux's physical retaliation as justified ('he had to do something to defend himself', 'it wasn't right, but he can't take that kind of insult') and emphasized his and thereby their own heterosexuality. Such readings were informed by papers such as the *Daily Mail* and *The Mirror*.[7] While these texts do not necessarily share the homophobic sentiments of some of their readers, they can still be negotiated within a hegemonic heterosexual reading that regards the suggestion of homosexuality as an insult, and hence the incident as an attack on Le Saux's 'appropriate' heterosexuality.

Liberal reading

The same texts, however, allowed for a different reading, one in which Fowler was singled out for criticism as his actions were read as an act of homophobia,

I.M. MARSH LIBRARY LIVERPOOL L17 6BD
TEL 0151 231 5216/5299

insulting gay people as much as Le Saux. As one reader of a Chelsea fanzine writes, Fowler 'is such a raving homophobe that he makes Bernard Manning seem like Julian Clary' (*Chelsea Independent*, no. 101, 1999). Such liberal readings were particularly prominent among higher-educated, middle-class fans, drawing on the wider context of the incident as suggested in *When Saturday Comes* or *The Guardian*. For these fans Le Saux became the symbolic representative of their own left-wing or liberal urbanism and cosmopolitanism. A further important dimension that, although largely absent in the media coverage, was prominent in the above quotes as well as other hegemonic and liberal readings of the case is a regional divide that follows, broadly, north/south divisions, which in turn expressed class relations (northern working class versus southern middle class).[8] Thus Le Saux also became a signifier of the supposedly 'cultured' and 'liberal' south, thus representing the geographical position of many Chelsea fans.

Radical reading

The interpretation of the incident by a small number of Chelsea fans ran counter to the dominant reading of the case. Their different reading resulted from their unwillingness to accept the polarization of the hegemonic and liberal model. These fans criticized Le Saux's obvious outrage at the suggestion he might be homosexual and the less than humorous way he dealt with this incident:

> It is also like the Le Saux thing. He has got to be straight, because he has got a wife, what a wonderful idea! They were talking about Robbie Fowler is a homophobic, but to me, he is a lot less homophobic than Graeme Le Saux, who will always say, 'no, no, no, I am not'. And that means, there are Chelsea fans that are, how does that make them feel, how, how does it make *them* feel? . . . If Graeme Le Saux would be half the man he thinks he is, when Fowler showed him his arse, he should have gone up to him and pretended to have sex with him. That would have been the end of the story.
>
> (Jarrett, Chelsea fan)

In this account the dominant dichotomies of the case are radically reworked and appropriated to the fans' own *Weltanschauung*. Interestingly, such readings were found among particularly committed fans, following the team home and away. The reason for this lies in the different focus of their fandom. The actual object of their fandom consists of their fellow fans and their own fan activity, in which a critical examination of the mainstream reading of events surrounding the club is in itself constitutive of their fandom. Their criticism of Le Saux illustrates their struggle for spaces of self-reflection through the club that suit their radical and alternative readings.

If we were to include Liverpool fans and 'neutral' viewers of the incident, further distinct patterns of reading would emerge. Yet even the small sample focusing on

Chelsea fans illustrates the relationship between football fandom and the public sphere. Differences and self-positioning are manifested through the multiplicity of readings of cultural icons and texts. The relative textual openness of these discourses allows fans a form of semiotic self-determination. The multiple readings of, for instance, the Le Saux–Fowler incident express difference and socio-cultural positioning and thus confirm and communicate identity. Because of the interconnectedness of the public sphere, they also give rise to citizenship as fans actively participate in a discourse of a political nature. This participation, like most other aspects of everyday life, is not directly translated into parliamentary politics, but nevertheless constitutes a form of political action in which the codes of communal coexistence are scrutinized, negotiated and transformed. To take Hartley's analogy of the DIY citizenship further, such citizenship, based on political participation in the public sphere, seeks to 'redecorate' the lifeworld of individuals – its ultimate aim is 'home improvement'.

Yet it is also important to bear in mind the limitations of this semiotic self-determination. The notion of DIY citizenship reflects the structure of fandom as a dialectic form of consumption. Fandom provides spaces for the projection of values and (political) beliefs and as such implies forms of political participation. Yet neither citizenship nor identity is made 'from scratch' as the DIY analogy might suggest. They are, as I have argued drawing on Bourdieu's work (1984), structured by the social, cultural and economic position of individuals and confirmed and communicated through acts of consumption. On the other hand, both my argument concerning fandom as extension of self and the above examples of the cultural universalization of football indicate that fans negotiate values, beliefs and political participation, neither independent of nor fully determined by the social, cultural and economic position of fans, partly because – through the narcissistic foundation of fandom – fans are subject to the influence arising out of the external transformations of the semiotic spaces of self-reflection in fandom. Nevertheless, football fans communicate their values and beliefs, in other words their image of self, and do so in relation to others and their own fandom (as well as its object) in and through a public space. Football fans are indeed DIY citizens in that they 'select' their own stances and readings from the multiplicity of meanings of the public sphere (in which television occupies a central role) according to their self-image. Given the socio-demographic inclusiveness of the contemporary public discourses and the cross-cultural spread of football, football fandom bears democratizing potential. No doubt, more and wider political participation is within the grasp of more sections of the population than during the nineteenth century, upon which Habermas's romanticized vision of the bourgeois public sphere is based. However, we need to pay attention to the cultural and economic basis of both fandom and the place in which it is lived. The principles of rationalization and standardization which are inherent within them – most notably through their dependence upon television – serve as a reminder that notions of football fandom as a sphere of semiotic self-determination and political democratization might be overly optimistic. Without necessarily subscribing to their historically grounded pessimism, it is worth recalling Horkheimer and Adorno's assessment of the seeming choices of industrial capitalism:

> In the culture industry the individual is an illusion not merely because of the standardization of the means of production. He [*sic*] is tolerated only so long as his complete identification with the generality is unquestioned. Pseudo-individuality is rife: from the standardized jazz improvisation to the exceptional film star whose hair curls over her eyes to demonstrate her originality. What is individual is no more than the generality's power to stamp the accidental detail so firmly that it is accepted as such . . . Mass culture discloses the fictitious character of the 'individual' in the bourgeois era.[9]
>
> (Horkheimer and Adorno 1972: 154–5)

Similarly, the DIY analogy might be an accurate, yet not entirely optimistic, terminology describing media-based forms of political participation. After all, DIY does not always result in outstanding creativity, but its uniform effects often underline the standardized nature of modern (suburban) living. Its most popular manifestation is found in the assembly of pre-designed furniture purchased from large DIY chains and transnational furniture stores. While it is important to demonstrate how football fans assemble their own meaning through the consumption of football, we must not ignore the context of this consumption. The structures framing football, television and other media are all reflected in its content. Television, structurally dependent upon attracting large cross-demographic audiences, had to be, in Hartley's words (1999: 172), a good neighbour that 'avoided political partisanship, tried hard not to insult anyone . . . It was a truly caring neighbour'. Yet there seems to be a problem with television's caring neighbourliness. Television's role in the Le Saux–Fowler incident illustrates how television in its attempt to be a good neighbour to everyone might not be a good neighbour to anyone. Television, as much as other objects of mass consumption, is 'pre-digested, pasteurised' (Silverstone 1994: 174).[10] If fans, however, 'build' their citizenship out of pasteurized and standardized assembly kits, if they inevitably all end up with similar products, then DIY citizenship might be more accurately described as IKEA citizenship, with all its frustrations, missing parts and uniform products. While the usefulness of the notion of DIY citizenship in exploring the interrelation between the universalization of football and football fandom is accepted, there is also a need for further analysis of the wider structural context of football fandom in modern society. Before I examine themes of rationalization and simulation in the final chapter, I thus turn to another, related phenomenon of the cultural expansion of football. Football has become more universal not only culturally and socially within societies, but also physically and geographically between societies. Thus the condition of professional football is becoming increasingly global.

Chapter 5

Football and cultural globalization

Spectator football has evolved into a truly global phenomenon. At the time of writing, the world football organization FIFA counts 204 member states. The top events such as World Cup finals, the European Champions League and large domestic leagues are transmitted by television across the world. On British terrestrial television alone viewers can now choose between English, Scottish, Italian, Dutch and North and South American football. Alongside these distribution patterns, football clubs have themselves become increasingly international. During the research for this book Chelsea FC employed four Italians, three Frenchmen and two Danes as well as players from Nigeria, Uruguay, Spain, Finland, Norway and Russia in addition to their ten English players. In Germany 205 out of the 495 players in the Bundesliga were carrying a non-German passport at the beginning of the 1999/2000 season.

These figures indicate the growing 'complex connectivity' (Tomlinson 1999) between societies and the increasing erosion of boundaries between nation states. The structural transformations of the public sphere discussed in the previous chapter already reflect such interconnectivity. In addition to integrating personal and public life, the impact of television and other electronic media on the public has fundamentally altered notions of 'here' and 'there'. In this sense the proliferation of football across different social and cultural spheres within one national state is already part of a wider globalization process. While the increasingly supranational state of the game is largely uncontroversial, the academic debates surrounding globalization are not. In the following, I will focus primarily on the cultural aspects of globalization and identify its premises and consequences, which in turn are also to be found outside the cultural realm. In doing so I will follow the core themes John Tomlinson identifies (1998: 236) as being at the heart of the globalization debate: 'time–space distanciation, disembedding, hybridity, deterritorialization, glocalization, virtually mediated quasi-interaction' and 'the network society'.

These themes have, with varying theoretical emphasis, been explored by a range of theorists, including Giddens (1990, 1991, 1997), Beck (1992, 2000), Featherstone (1990, 1995) Hannerz (1990, 1997), Robertson (1990) and Tomlinson (1991, 1999). In contrast, despite a growing body of work in this field these themes have only been dealt with in a partial fashion in the analysis of contemporary sport. Many contributions to the field describe the internationalization rather than the globalization of sport (Williams 1994a, 1994b; Giulianotti and Williams 1994). Other work on sport and globalization has focused on national identity and cultural hegemony (Jarvie and Maguire 1993; Maguire 1993, 1994; Houlihan 1994) or examined the local transformation of sport or football in particular national settings (Boyle and Haynes 1996; Horne 1996). In contrast to such accounts I seek to move beyond the nation state in identifying the structural and economic foundations of the globalization of football and thus to juxtapose the global production of professional football and its local consumption.

For club and company: the economic globalization of football

In a similar vein to the historical interdependency of modern football and industrialism, the cultural globalization of football must be analysed before the background of its social, institutional and economic framing. Over the past hundred years various international footballing organizations have been formed. These include continental associations such as CONCACAF or UEFA as well as the world governing body FIFA. As multilateral representatives of the nation state system Giddens (1990, 1997) identifies international bodies as key agents of globalization. Organizations such as FIFA are indeed global in both scale and scope. In their recent investigation of FIFA John Sugden and Alan Tomlinson (1998: 214) argue that FIFA has become part of the global political economy of the sport, merging its interests with those of multinational corporations and regional elites. Global institutions such as FIFA, in the words of Martin Shaw (1997: 33), 'affirm global society'. Alongside institutional globalization, the international division of labour, which Giddens (1990) identifies as a further cornerstone of globalization, has resulted in the spiralling labour migration of professional athletes across the globe reflected in the figures above (see also Arabena 1993; Bale and Maguire 1994). The link between a capitalist (world) economy, industrialism and the globalization of football becomes even more evident in the analysis of football clubs as central units of production in international football.

Whereas club football has traditionally been considered the counterpart to international football competitions such as European Championships or World Cups, domestic or 'national' leagues are becoming transnational in terms of both production (teams and players) and distribution (broadcasting). Particularly the football leagues in populous, economically powerful western European countries such as England, Germany, Italy and Spain are increasingly represented on television screens around the world. Jürgen von Einem, at the time of the interview head of sport and sponsorship at Bayer AG, assesses the international distribution of domestic league competitions in Europe:

It is absolutely global, not only the Champions League but also the Bundesliga by now. In the future we might sell the international television rights separately from the domestic television rights, because that is something which we will have to pay more attention to. In any case, the Bundesliga . . . has got contracts with 160 television stations around the globe. And they show many, many live games, those games broadcast as pay-TV by Premiere here, as well as highlights programmes. In other words, the Bundesliga is marketed around the world. There are two leagues that dominate in this sector, the Premier League in England and the Bundesliga.

(Jürgen von Einem, interview 15 December 1998)

This clear statement of the distinctly global strategy of contemporary players in the football and sponsorship market in turn reflects the increasingly global state system of consumer markets and distribution patterns. Bayer 04 Leverkusen, owned by Bayer AG, is an example of this tendency of the globalizing football industry. Football clubs have formed so-called 'strategic partnerships' with transnational corporations (TNCs) who pursue their global advertising and promotional interests through such cooperation. Examples of TNCs controlling major European football clubs include Philips (PSV Eindhoven), Peugeot (FC Souchaux) and Volvo/Ford (IFK Gothenburg) (Hoehn and Symanski 1999). Wealthy industrialists such as the Agnelli family (Fiat) and Silvio Berlusconi control the two most successful Italian clubs of the last decade, Juventus Turin and AC Milan. In the Japanese J-League, founded in 1993, all 15 teams at the time of writing are owned by large Japanese corporations including well-known global enterprises such as Nissan (Antler Kashima), Mazda (Sanfrece Hiroshima), Matushita (Gamba Osaka) and Toyota (Grampus Eight, Nagoya) (Horne 1996). In Mexico 17 out of the 18 first division clubs are owned by media companies (Taylor 1998). A similar picture emerges in the United States where most investors in the 12 newly formed Major League Soccer clubs come from the media sector. Alongside such direct ownership many professional clubs have developed far-reaching ties with major capitalist enterprises through sponsorship and promotional deals.[1] The aim of media companies in seeking to control football clubs is vertical integration.[2] Canal+ ownership of Paris St Germain or BSkyB's failed takeover bid for Manchester United, as well as the subsequent purchase of minority stakes in, among others, Leeds United and Chelsea FC by the Murdoch-controlled satellite television provider, illustrates broadcasters' desire, especially in the pay-TV market, to secure future distribution rights through the ownership of clubs. In contrast, the interests of other industry sectors in football are more subtle. Ultimately such companies seek to enhance their brand image through sport sponsorship:

The point, apart from brand recognition, is that when major corporations [Großkonzerne] conduct their market research every two years . . . and look at what the actual conclusions are, they must recognize two components.

They are basically the same from industry sector to industry sector. Firstly, people have a high technical respect for major corporations, yet simultaneously the sympathy rankings of large corporations are rather low, because they are removed from the consumer and not transparent to him or her. There is nothing with higher sympathy rankings than sport . . . thus sport promises actually the plus in sympathy rankings that is the weakness of major enterprises . . . If you ask people what BASF or Hoechst do, they say 'I don't know', but about Bayer they say 'Aspirin and football' . . . That's the company image, that's something much closer to the consumer than the pharmaceutical and chemical industry in general.

(Jürgen von Einem, interview 15 December 1998)

Enterprises thus seek to forge a link between fandom and brand image. The indications are that continuous football sponsorship by Bayer AG has succeeded in merging brand image and football fandom. As one Bayer fan remembers,

I did some market research for the Bayer company, it was about its sympathy rankings five years ago and today. You wouldn't believe how many sympathies Bayer has won through football. Out of curiosity I asked some people why they liked Bayer. 'They play good football', they said, no one actually saw the company any more.

(Dominik, Bayer Leverkusen fan)

Such successful examples of sponsorship illustrate how sponsors aim to become integrated into the reflection of self through the club in football fandom. As Lash and Urry have argued (1994: 15), the branding of goods takes place in the process of consumption rather than production. Yet while consumption is described by Bourdieu (1984) as an unconscious articulation of the social, cultural and economic position of the consumer, brands aim to initiate an explicitly conscious habitus in which commodities are bought and consumed in an attempt to articulate a particular image. Previously, I have identified such self-projection on the grounds of a more conscious habitus as modus operandi of football fandom. Hence sponsors aim for the advertised brand to become part of football fans' fandom. In the ideal case, the sponsor is included in the categorized 'we'; sponsor and brand are recognized as part of the projected self-image of the fan:

It's an automatism. If the club's badge occurs next to a brand, you develop completely different sympathies for the brand than otherwise . . . Last time we went to Cologne, when we were standing on the terraces – their main sponsor is Ford – a Ford car was driven around the ground. And suddenly all the Bayern fans shouted 'Opel, Opel' [Bayern München's shirt sponsor] It was just a means to an end, but there is certainly some form of identification with Opel.

(Lukas, Bayern München fan)

In this case the symbol of the car manufacturer Opel is employed by fans in communicating their fandom. Such symbolic identification also manifests itself in consumption decisions of fans:

> When Coors sponsored Chelsea a couple of years ago, I started drinking it. And it is not a very nice beer, so I was glad when they stopped the sponsorship, then I stopped pretending to drink it.
>
> (Samuel, Chelsea fan)

> When Coors used to sponsor Chelsea, my dad always used to buy Coors instead of Foster's or something, because he thought that helped Chelsea out.
>
> (Catherine, Chelsea fan)

> *Question*: Can you recall any sponsors of Major League Soccer?
> *Larry*: Mastercard, Pepsi. I do pick Pepsi over Coke for this reason with what soda I buy.
>
> (Larry, DC United fan)

Thus the sign value of the brand intertwined with football fandom converts into actual monetary profit for the sponsoring party. Football clubs have recognized their marketing potential and diversified into the production of further commodities and services ranging from hotels or fitness clubs to all sorts of merchandizing goods:

> *Tina*: She buys almost everything.
> *Anna*: Yes, I have got three Leverkusen shirts, scarves.
> *Tanya*: And a lot of little things.
> *Tina*: Usually I get some presents from my sister: lighter, toothbrush, cups, bed linen, socks, shoes, earrings . . .
> *Chris*: . . . unfortunately they don't sell underwear yet, but apart from that we buy everything.
>
> (Anna, Chris, Tina and Tanya, all Bayer Leverkusen fans)

Following the commercial success of football clubs' merchandizing activities the link between fandom and capitalist consumerism constitutes a crucial premise in the globalization of football. Capitalist enterprises such as sponsors and football clubs, in light of their own diversification attempts and following the inner logic of capitalist exchange, constantly seek to enlarge their potential market and hence enter transnational competition. As professional football is economically dependent upon sponsoring and merchandizing, it is integrated into a globalizing marketplace organized by transnational commercial interests. Hence professional football is transformed according to the economic globalization imperative of late twentieth-century capitalism. It is within this process, driven by the fundamental mechanisms of capitalism and industrialism, that the forces of economic and cultural globalization inform each other. Parallel to the extension of capitalist trade from narrowly defined regions to a global marketplace, the focus of professional football has shifted from local and national to continental and global competitions. Many relatively new competitions, including the European Champions League and the Latin American Copa Libertadores, represent tendencies of europeanization or hispanicization, which Maguire describes (1993: 311) as competing sub-processes of contemporary global flows. These competitions articulate the interests and the economic needs of TNCs:

> *von Einem*: The German market used to be of comparably higher significance than today. Today it is about 20 per cent of the total turnover of the company, and what we are doing in football today we wouldn't do under national considerations alone . . . As much as Europe has become our new home market, the weight now shifts towards European competitions.
> *Question*: Such as the Champions League?
> *von Einem*: Yes, without that it doesn't make any sense any more.
> (Jürgen von Einem, interview 15 December 1999)

On a first level, then, capitalist exchange and profit accumulation are driving forces in the globalization of football. However, in order to understand how culture and economic order shape and transform each other, we also need to take a closer look at football's global and local cultures.

Football, globalization and localization

In the following I rely on a broad definition of culture and, consequently, of cultural globalization. The universal nature of culture as the ground on which everyday life is exercised is well captured in Tomlinson's definition:

> [C]ulture can be understood as the order of life in which human beings construct meaning through practices of symbolic representation . . . if we are talking culture we mean the ways in which people make their lives, individually and collectively, meaningful by communicating with each other.
> (Tomlinson 1999: 18)

This definition is useful in two respects. Firstly, it helps us to recognize fandom as an act of communication through consumption, as a way in which fans make their lives meaningful in relation to others, as a cultural phenomenon. Secondly, Tomlinson's inclusive definition points to the interconnectivity between the cultural, social and economic processes of globalization. I will verify this link further by examining international and national club competitions, which structurally mirror the interests of capitalist enterprises while equally contributing to the processes of cultural globalization such as virtualization, deterritorialization, homogenization, fragmentation and localization.

The number of club games on an international level has increased continuously since the introduction of the European Cup in 1955/56. With the arrival of the Champions League in 1991 and its expansion to now 32 clubs, European cup competitions have been transformed into a league format. The Champions League as well as the international distribution of domestic competitions has created new transnational audiences. In response to the increasing number of international games, new – if relatively small – transnational audiences have emerged:

> I watch a lot of football . . . especially the World Cup, European championships and UEFA Cup. They are really important to me, because I have also lived abroad. I have watched *ran* [German Bundesliga highlights programme] just twice over the last one and a half years. It doesn't really offer me that much. Wolfsburg and so on, that just doesn't give me anything. But UEFA Cup, Champions League, those are the games I am just looking forward to as a football fan. And I am happy that I have got the opportunity to watch the really good games with skilled players and big clubs.
>
> (Pascal, football fan)

> I get slaughtered by my friends for being for Italy now . . . I have strong opinions against the English football, the way they play and the way the English fans are. That's all . . . that [European league] would be good, because I would get to see more of the foreign clubs. So that would be great.
>
> (Brendon, Chelsea fan)

Two aspects are worth noting here. Firstly, the above extracts reflect the multiple layers of the globalization process. Pascal – as does Brendon earlier in the interview – explains his preference for international competitions in terms of recent migrational movements and family ties ('they are really important to me, because I have also lived abroad'). While transnational football alone does not construct transnational social relations, football fandom offers the space to project and communicate the transnational identities of fans. Secondly, these accounts illustrate how for some viewers transnational club competitions are the focal point of their fandom. The fandom for transnational competitions bypasses the nation state as the cultural ground for the manifestations of their interests and preferences. In conversations about European and global football they are quick to refer to selected club teams from around the world they follow:

> There are many clubs abroad that are my favourites. Especially in France . . . I particularly like Marseille. Paris, I quite like them too, because my mother is from Paris . . . I like Manchester, Manchester United.
>
> (Pascal, football fan)

> I have always been interested in European football anyway. Even before it was shown on satellite I used to go to Italian bars and watch the Italian football on Wednesday night in the pub. So, I have been to about 30 major European cup finals . . . in 22 years; I have always been interested in European football. I love the way, I just love the way they think about the game, technique and it wasn't all about this smashing the ball down the field and running after it, kicking some guy.
>
> (Will, Chelsea fan)

The foundation of the fandom of such football fans is one that goes beyond national frontiers of culture and communication. In this sense transnational football competitions contribute to what Mike Featherstone (1990, 1995) labels 'third cultures':

> We can point to the existence of a global culture in the restricted sense of 'third cultures': sets of practice, bodies of knowledge, conventions and life-styles that have developed in ways which have become increasingly independent of nation states. In effect there are a number of trans-societal institutions, cultures and cultural producers who cannot be understood as merely agents and representatives of their nation states.
>
> (Featherstone 1995: 114)

The academic attention that has been dedicated to the question of sport and nationalism (see Blain *et al.* 1993; Blain and O'Donnell 1994; O'Donnell 1994) in general and football in particular (Goksøyr 1994; Carrington 1998; Crolley *et al.* 1998) indicates that such global 'third cultures' continue to exist alongside national and local cultures. Similarly, a number of fans in my study emphasized the significance of national competitions and national teams, while fewer fans centred their fandom on such 'third cultures' of transnational football. The latter was most common among younger viewers. However, most fans felt that the transnational dimensions of football corresponded with the changing structure of their everyday life consumption:

> All the brands, everything comes from all over the world. You can read newspapers from all over the world on the Internet. Football is almost lagging behind a bit.
>
> (Axel, Bayer Leverkusen fan)

> It all becomes increasingly international . . . the world becomes smaller and foreign football comes over here.
>
> (Wilfried, male football fan)

Many interviewees welcomed such globalizing tendencies in professional football:

> The days are gone by when there was a huge difference between the style of the football that was played in England, Italy, Germany, France, but now

everything is just blending. Every team is now full of players from every country . . . I hope in a funny way that football could actually help to make the English more international-minded.

(Will, Chelsea fan)

In light of these transnational dimensions of contemporary football, the continuing emphasis on the nation in academic investigations of football fandom, I think, is misleading in that these studies ignore the crucial transformations football fandom is currently undergoing. What they fail to account for is the changing dynamic between local, national and global (transnational) cultures in the globalization process.

Even globalization theorists remain surprisingly cautious concerning the implications of the interrelation of local and global for national cultures. Featherstone, for instance, reduces the analytical value of his conceptualization of 'third cultures' by arguing that it is:

> misleading to conceive a global culture as necessarily entailing a weakening of the sovereignty of nation states which, under the impetus of some form of teleological evolutionism or other master-logic, will necessarily become absorbed into larger units and eventually a world state which produces cultural homogeneity and integration.

(Featherstone 1990: 1)

Naturally, a global culture will not automatically cause the dissolution of the nation state as a result of teleological evolutionism. Yet, by combining all possible implications into a single scenario, Featherstone limits the value of the notion of 'third cultures', as they emerge as a static, separate category. He forgoes their actual relevance by excluding them as an influence weakening the nation state. While I agree with Featherstone that this may not follow out of the teleological logic, the case of football fandom (and a similar case might be made for other forms of popular culture) demonstrates that 'third cultures' have the capacity to alter the structure and position of national cultures. In football fandom global cultures fundamentally re-shift the relation between local and national cultures. While football fans participate in all three sets of cultures (local, global and national), these different cultural dimensions are not negotiated independently but inform and reshape each other. Exploring fans' negotiation of the national, global and local layers of professional football, an intrinsic connection between the global and the local emerges. Most interviewees in my study read the transnational and potentially global dimension of football through a heightened emphasis on the local, their own team:

> Talking about highlights I definitely have to name the matches against Barcelona and then Bayern winning the UEFA Cup, that was good. Er, Schalke was quite all right, too. Actually, I could name almost every year of

LIVERPOOL JOHN MOORES UNIVERSITY
LEARNING SERVICES

the Champions League, because since it exists, there have always been really good games, really interesting highlights. From my Bayern perspective anyway.

(Moritz, Bayern München fan)

Question: Do domestic competitions, such as winning the Premier League, matter to you most?
Jeff: We haven't done it yet, we haven't done it yet, so it is a difficult one to answer. Previously I'd have said yes. But with the changing attitude of Chelsea, there may be teams like Barcelona coming over, the crowd might get together more as a unit, but against Barcelona as being the opposition rather than against Tottenham. I mean I have noticed the atmosphere against the continental teams we were playing in the European Cup-Winners' Cup has sometimes been a lot better, towards the later stages, in a lot of the home games.

(Jeff, Chelsea fan)

In these cases the transnational competition constitutes the space in which fandom is positioned and acted out, yet it is negotiated by the fan through the prism of the local. Yet the notion of the 'local' itself requires further exploration.[3] The local, signified by the club which functions as a representative of the self, is integrated and interpreted before the transnational background of an increasingly encompassing public. Moreover, the local stipulates the global and vice versa. On the one hand, the global is constructed and made sense of through the local. On the other, the local itself is constituted through the local appropriation of the global. As Daniel Miller argues (1992: 181) in his investigation of the Trinidadian audience for the American soap *The Young and the Restless*, 'authenticity has increasingly to be judged *a posteriori* not a priori, according to local consequences not local origins'. Drawing on Miller, Morley has underlined the intrinsic interdependence of global and local cultures:

> The 'local' is not to be considered as an indigenous source of cultural identity, which remains 'authentic' only in so far as it is unsullied by contact with the global. Rather, the 'local' is itself often produced by means of the 'indigenization' of global resources and inputs.
>
> (Morley 1991: 9–10)

Morley's and Miller's conclusions are crucial in the investigation of the local and global dimensions of fandom. In the face of a globalizing football industry, the local in contemporary football fandom is created through the indigenization of global resources. The locally based object of football fandom (a club or team) draws extensively on the international labour market of professional footballers. Consequently, fans of Chelsea FC, for instance, based their fandom upon the local appropriation of their increasingly international squad. The influx of international football players (and cultures) formed the basis for what fans considered their local team:

> I always supported Chelsea and you have to live with the hard times and the good times at the moment . . . I think it's changed a bit recently. Before, I would have just said, it is like a good team, a good stable team. But now it's sort of more exciting and there is lots of foreign players and it has become quite trendy.
>
> (Catherine, Chelsea fan)

> I appreciate the majority of the players because they have all got certain attributes, Zola, who is just world class and he is such a nice guy. Flo, what a fantastic person, always takes time to talk to you and then you have got the likes of Dan Petrescu and Frank Leboeuf . . . so normally if I just see one on the street and occasionally I do meet them, I always ask them, 'do you mind, have you got five minutes to talk?'. If not, I leave them alone. So you have to appreciate their response. Rather than rush out, they come and talk to you. Yeah, it's just good manners.
>
> (Jack, Chelsea fan)

In these accounts the global and the local meet to form the spaces of self-projection which football fandom is based upon. The transnational squad becomes not only a signifier of local pride but actively constitutes the semiotic context of the club ('there is lots of foreign players and it has become quite trendy'). Similarly, players from all quarters of the world become part of local everyday life through fandom and face-to-face contact, illustrating how the local is formed through 'indigenization'. In turn, fans in countries on the economic periphery or semi-periphery of world football – including, in marked contrast to common power relations in the geopolitical or economic realm, the USA – are subject to a reverse globalization–localization process, in which they relate to distant locales through the exodus of local players:

> I follow with interest European clubs that have American players, such as Claudio Reyna of Rangers, John O'Brien with Ajax, Frankie Hejduk, John Thorrington and Landon Donovan of Bayer Leverkusen, Tony Sanneh, a former DC United player, with Hertha Berlin, and of course Kasey Keller with Rayo Vallecano, and Brad Friedel in Liverpool.
>
> (Ben, DC United fan)

> I follow and support international teams for which Americans play: Rangers, Rayo Vallecano, Hertha Berlin, Bayer Leverkusen, Liverpool.
>
> (Peter, DC United fan)

Similarly, Glasgow-born Greenock Morton fan Logan, now living in London, is particularly keen for Scottish players and managers to succeed in the English

Premier League and fellow Glaswegian and Manchester United manager Alex Ferguson in particular:

> I . . . support the Scottish team, and indeed support teams that are managed by Scottish ex-players or managers. So at the moment I am following Manchester United with a tremendous amount of ambivalence, because I don't think it would be a good thing for football in this country, indeed football anywhere, for Rupert Murdoch to gain control of Manchester United. But on the other hand, I would like to see Alex Ferguson succeed, although there are sadly no Scottish players in the Manchester United team.
>
> (Logan, Greenock Morton fan)

The local, however phantasmagoric, thus presents the space where the global is manifested, appropriated and reworked. Lash and Urry argue (1994) that spatial proximity and the trust-based systems of locality counteract globalization anxieties. Similarly, the consumption of global resources locally appropriated provides the ground on which fans seek to position themselves – even, as Logan's example demonstrates, in opposition to the core forces behind globalization processes. In the interaction between local and global culture, football fandom thus nevertheless becomes an act of lived globalization in its capacity to appropriate parts of the sign system of global football into local contexts and thus to provide spaces of self-reflection. In turn such self-reflection functions as an agent and external representation of the football fan in transnational cultures:

> When I was with my brother in New York, we were able to relate to a group of people from Brazil, and other South American countries via Chelsea and football.
>
> (Jerry, Chelsea fan)

> It is much more international now, I didn't notice it that much before, but now I do, because of all the Champions League games. I think, it is always an experience like recently against Glasgow Rangers, when they were here. We were walking to the stadium and next to us were three or four people from Glasgow, and we talked to them all along the way. But not only about football, about all sorts of general things, what to do in Leverkusen, etc.
>
> (Manfred, Bayer Leverkusen fan)

> It does become more international . . . for clubs like us. And there are people who are fans of us who wouldn't have known anything about us just a few short years ago. So I have been on holiday and talked to people about the club and they didn't know anything about us. That is not the case now.
>
> (Dean, Chelsea fan)

Fans position themselves through their football fandom in a transnational system, in which they are represented through their object of fandom. As clubs

grow increasingly transnational, fandom becomes a universal agent of representation and communication:

> I have not missed a Chelsea European game. And the great thing about
> European games is to meet the fans, is to be able to speak to them, in a bar
> with fans from different countries, talk about football in their country, in
> our country . . . There is just something very special about being able to do
> that.
>
> (Karen, Chelsea fan)

Football fandom is thus itself globalizing: through her football fandom Karen
the fan is integrated into a transnational culture, activities and travel while following Chelsea abroad. These transnational dimensions of football fandom form
– to return to Featherstone's terminology – 'third cultures', which do not exist
in separation but in constant interaction with the local and national dimensions
of the game. This dynamic between local and global cultures has a profound
effect on national cultural spheres. Again, this is not to say that nation states will
disappear as a central form of political organization in the near future. However,
'national cultures' and nation-state-based societies are all subject to deep-
running transformations. As the local is increasingly positioned within a
transnational framework, global and local interconnectivities form a nexus that
calls into question the role of the nation state as socio-cultural ground of everyday experience. The transnational nature of the European Cup competition has
served to undermine partisan identification on the basis of the nation state in
such competitions. Even for fans that had previously underlined their patriotic
stands in general, national categories did not determine their patterns of identification in inter-local European and global competitions:

> If it is Man United, I definitely support the other club. No way, even if
> Manchester United is the only English club left in the competition, I would
> not want them to win. I would rather England to go out . . . I hate Leices-
> ter, there are certain clubs you wouldn't want to win . . . I think Manchester
> United, I am certain we don't want them to win. We cheer for Dynamo
> Kiev or whoever Man United are playing.
>
> (Karen, Chelsea fan)

To the overwhelming majority of interviewees the national origin of club teams
in transnational competitions seemed of no importance but for the heightened
rivalry with domestic competitors:

> I was cheering when Juventus went two up against Manchester United . . . I
> know a lot of Man United fans who thought it was brilliant that we lost.
> There was no, 'oh, it is an English club', it was 'ha ha'!
>
> (Ken, Chelsea fan)

It is only usually when Inter or Barcelona are playing that I have a personal stake. I normally just watch the game for itself, I don't worry. I don't have any nationalistic [feelings].

(Ally, Chelsea fan)

Samuel: I'd rather see Juventus play Marseilles than United play Inter, for instance. Obviously two teams other than an English team.
Question: But if you do watch Manchester United?
Samuel: I would rather see them lose, oh, definitely.

(Samuel, Chelsea fan)

In these accounts it becomes clear how national partisanship is superseded by internal rivalry in the face of transnational competition. Some fans even express clear preferences for teams from other countries in transnational competitions:

If, for example, Arsenal would play against Hamburg SV, I don't know, because I think Arsenal are really great.

(Richard, Bayer Leverkusen fan)

I really want Arsenal to win the Champions League.

(Tina, Bayer Leverkusen fan)

The local, as signified by the club team, also emerges as more significant than national categories in the construction of fandom and identity to the majority of fans:

I have been to England matches at Wembley . . . but it is not the same. Going to Wembley with Chelsea, my personal experience in '94, was, I was watching a game of England walking down Wembley Way, but I would rather walk down Wembley Way with Chelsea in a Cup Final.

(Jack, Chelsea fan)

I still put club before country.

(Ken, Chelsea fan)

I watch the national team, it is a bit of an *Ersatz*, but I think club football is more interesting. I can identify with it much more.

(Thilo, Preußen Köln fan)

The focus on local objects of fandom which are positioned in an increasingly global context, then, reduces the significance of the notion of the national in everyday football fandom. As the nation is bypassed as the organizational level of club football, nationality becomes a more marginal category in the identity and identification of football fans. The following accounts mirror the decreasing significance of the nation state in the formation of football fandom:

Question: Do you follow the German national team, too?

Mr Schmidt: Well, somehow, after the war it was more like that. It has all faded today. Back then I had a much stronger sense of national identity. I usually don't think a lot about such things any more. All that 'it is an honour to play for your country', that should stay out of football.

(Mr Schmidt, Bayer Leverkusen fan)

Total disinterest. I am not a Germany fan. Even football aside, I don't care whether I am German, Belgian, Turkish or whatever, and that's why the national team doesn't interest me whatsoever.

(Dominik, Bayer Leverkusen fan)

I don't care whether they win or lose. For instance, when England played Italy at Wembley in a World Cup match last year and Zola scored, I was happy, because it was a Chelsea player scoring. So, it doesn't matter to me at all.

(Samuel, Chelsea fan)

Such accounts do not prove that the national dimension will eventually be rendered irrelevant or meaningless. Equally, they reflect two particular cases of national identity in large-scale, industrialized nations and do not allow for conclusions across different countries and continents. Yet, as the processes of globalization and localization progress, nations and national identities will not remain untouched by these forces. Some players in the football industry themselves seem in no doubt about the future role of national dimensions in a transnational market for professional football:

[Club football] becomes more international, and it is the logical outcome of an international integration process . . . If we have, for instance, a unified Europe one day, then a game between England and Italy might be as interesting as a game between Prussia and Bavaria . . . European competition on a national level in a unified Europe will become redundant, that's no question.

(Jürgen von Einem, interview 15 December 1999)

It goes without saying that such processes are far from their conclusion. While the national dimensions of football and its consumption have been reshaped, there seems to be no end to processes of globalization and localization. Whether the nation and nationality will cease to play a prominent role in local and global tensions remains to be seen. What is important, however, is the ways in which local, national and global cultures inform and, crucially, reshape each other. Moreover, if we accept the profound impact of globalization and localization on the everyday life of fans that has been evident in the above accounts, then understanding the global and local dimensions of football as driving forces behind such changes to the lifeworld of fans constitutes the first step of a meaningful exploration of fandom and globalization. This confirms my earlier claim that capitalistic principles of profit maximization account for the economic premises of the globalization of the football industry, but do not illuminate how and by what means such global markets are constructed.

Television football and globalization

The key to the examination of the premises and implications of the global markets of football, then, lies in the technological as much as economic role of the modern electronic mass media, most notably television. Television provides the cultural and social basis of the globalization of football fandom. In the following I will therefore verify and analyse the link between both economic and cultural globalization and television. The close link between TNCs and the football industry has resulted in increasingly transnational and global marketplaces. Television, alongside other mass media, provides the technological and cultural ground which has enabled capitalist enterprises to reach potential buyers freed from territorial constraints. It should be noted that such 'reach' has, of course, been symbolic rather than physical. Television and other mass media have not brought consumers in touch with the actual, physical commodities produced by capitalist enterprises, but with a system of semiotic codes and images which signify actual commodities. Advertising, sponsoring and product placement, underlying the everyday discourse of consumer products cultivated by the mass media, have provided the very foundations of consumerism. In this sense, global capitalism, reflecting 'the culture-ideology of consumerism' (Sklair 1995: 87–91), has become an 'economy of sign and space', as Lash and Urry (1994) have summarized the symbolic, deterritorialized nature of brand-based capitalism. It is thus through television – more than any other medium – in its capacity to convey images and signs, that capitalist enterprises seek to employ the sign value of football clubs. Through television, consumerism articulates its messages on a global scale and thus globalizes its semiotic vehicle, football. The case of the sponsoring activities of Bayer AG again draws attention to the economic mechanisms behind the globalization of football:

> When Bayer Leverkusen plays Schalke 04 and this is broadcast live in Brazil, it is a wonderful thing for us. We have a big company there, Bayer do Brasil, we sell aspirin there, hence this has a great value to us. To Schalke 04 it has no value at all. What would they want with a live transmission in Brazil? And Veltins [German beer brand and shirt sponsor of Schalke 04] is not drunk a great deal at the Copacabaña either.
> (Jürgen von Einem, interview 15 December 1999)

Football's economic value is aggregated through its televisual representation. The expanding, deregulated television market was considered by Bayer the crucial premise for its heightened sponsorship activities in order to shape the semiotic code of its products, in other words its brands:

> Brands are crucial as you will know, so there are various measures we take . . . Sport and economy developed a closer relationship with the beginning of commercial television in the early '80s . . . If the media resonance hadn't been increased in the mid-'80s because of commercial television, then we would have still been involved in sport, but on a drastically smaller scale.
>
> (Jürgen von Einem, interview 15 December 1999)

In this account, von Einem therefore identifies television as the technological premise behind the proliferation of football sponsorship and, consequently, its increasing globalization. In turn, television provides the modus operandi, as much as forms an expression, of contemporary consumerism. Given our earlier observation of the historical link between the rise of television- and home-centred, suburban consumerism in the United States and to a lesser degree in Europe in the post-war era, television articulates consumerism in its form and in its content. This further confirms the link between economic and cultural globalization processes, as well as the interrelation between production and consumption. Harvey rightfully warns,

> It is conventional these days . . . to dismiss out of hand any suggestion that the 'economy' . . . might be determinant of cultural life even in (as Engels and later Althusser suggested) 'the last instance'. The odd thing about postmodern cultural production is how much sheer profit-seeking is determinant in the first instance.
>
> (Harvey 1990: 336)

Yet Harvey pays little attention to the interrelation between production and consumption. The degree to which a global capitalist system is promoted through the mass media is partly dependent upon the readings of media texts by diverse audiences. The further structural link between economy and culture, however, lies in the modes of information and communication they share. As global economies of sign and space are based on global mass media and most prominently television, the everyday cultural spheres of consumers are shaped and structured through the consumption of precisely these media. As television is employed by the football industry to market products beyond geographical frontiers, it is the central medium through which football fans become integrated into a global semiotic system:

> I think [football] is more international. It is because of the media, because you see more and more of the Italian league, the English league, they show more and more games. And the Champions League is also very popular . . .

> I think it is part of some globalization process, more players are being exchanged. We are increasingly integrated into a network, and maybe that's why we are more interested in what happens abroad.
>
> (Sabine, Borussia Mönchengladbach fan)

Sabine thus identifies a global 'network' as the basis of the increasingly trans-national character of everyday life. Broadcasting games from around the world, television prepares the ground for the proliferation of transnational practices, which in turn are the basis of the global system (Sklair 1995). Many interviewees identified the consumption of non-domestic league football on television as part of their football fandom:

> When I turn on the television and there are any games from Spain, Italy, England on DSF or Eurosport or so, I always enjoy watching them.
>
> (Hilmar, Bayer Leverkusen fan)

> I was watching some Asian football the other night. At three o'clock in the morning . . . I was awake, put the TV on, it's Asian football on, so I will watch a bit of that. If it is on, the telly would be on, there is football on, I will end up watching it.
>
> (Matt, Chelsea fan)

Multi-channel and digital television, in particular, bypass the established patterns of nation-centred public broadcasting, reflecting regimes of flexible accumulation and its principles of outsourcing, subcontracting and flexibilization (Harvey 1990):

> *Chris*: We watch Celtic, sometimes Real Madrid, we check the teletext about what is going on in the Italian league . . .
>
> *Tina*: Because of digital television we have a lot of football from England now, I am totally looking forward to that, because they always sing, they have proper lyrics.
>
> *Tanya*: I don't know, I don't have Premiere German pay-TV, I can only watch Eurosport or so.
>
> (Chris and Tanya, Bayer Leverkusen fans)

This short discussion among a group of fans demonstrates the intrinsic interrela-tion between the ownership of multi-channel television (such as satellite and digital) and the consumption of transnational football. It is through the televisual consumption of football that global, 'third' cultures are increasingly integrated into the everyday lifeworld of fans:

> Now, there is so much football to watch, and European football. You could never see any European football in this country until ten years ago, it was of

no interest. But now you have got *Football Italia* on Channel 4, you have got Spanish football on Sky, the European Cup spread over Tuesday to Wednesdays and Thursdays. I'd probably be watching football every single day of my life, but I have to sort of draw a line somewhere.

(Will, Chelsea fan)

On Wednesday nights and Tuesday nights it is UEFA Cup, and then you have many more opportunities now because of DSF or Eurosport. For instance, I really like to watch *Eurogoals*, because it just interests me . . . I always like to watch Madrid, Barcelona or Nice, France or something like that, because I just think it is great and all the different players the teams have.

(Christoph, Bayer Leverkusen fan)

Global football is experienced through the means of mass communication that television and to a lesser extent other media such as the Internet provide. Similarly, as transnational media texts are appropriated by fans, global cultures become subject to localized everyday discourse:

I like European football, it is different . . . It definitely has become easier to watch, especially since I have got cable as well, you can watch *Eurogoals*, Eurocups, the Cup-Winners' Cup live, the UEFA Cup live. You see many different teams, many interesting players . . . I mean, at the end of the day, if you like football, you are a bit of a nerd in some ways. Because you store all this information, you want more and more and more, and you get more and more and more obscure, like people can name Man United's first team. [I have] my friend from Belgium, so I have someone to talk with about it.

(Constantine, Queens Park Rangers fan)

On telly we get Italian games and the world is becoming a smaller place. So the fact that we can see what is going on in the French league or what is going on in the Italian league or German league and you can keep track of the players, because of the movement of the players, where they are coming from, you can relate more, so-and-so used to play for this or that club in Europe. And you get an attachment, interest in how they are going on now. And the same about players you come up against, Tottenham, West Ham or Arsenal, when they are playing another team in Europe . . . that makes Europe a smaller place. Before most of these names, they meant nothing, just teams, but because of the coverage they get, it's now associated with fine players.

(Gary, Chelsea fan)

In these accounts television emerges as the crucial link between the global and local dimension of contemporary football fandom, due to its unique capacity to consume and bridge space as well as place. Similarly, television not only reflects global structures but acts as an agent of cultural and economic globalization.

On a basic level the above accounts of football fans all share one theme: their fandom is (partly) constructed through the consumption of mediated, distant events. The degree to which spatial distance has been rendered insignificant is verified by the rising number of fans following their favourite team from afar. In the following extracts, for instance, fans of Chelsea FC living in South Africa describe how their fandom is based on events transmitted through a range of electronic media:

> With the very good TV coverage we get, we seem to see a large majority of games plus we see all the goals on a British soccer programme we see. Also the Internet helps with the link to the CFC [Chelsea FC] site plus the Internet papers. Also I speak regularly with my brother in the UK who is a season-ticket holder.
>
> (Stan, Chelsea fan)

> If you subscribe to our pay-TV channel then you are able to watch *Match of the Day*, etc. . . . . If there are other things to do or the chance to go somewhere and Chelsea are playing, then watching the team play takes preference.
>
> (Jerrell, Chelsea fan)

These examples underline how fandom is constructed by drawing on semiotic resources and information generated outside the locale, in other words a global public. Interestingly, Jerrell had no other social or cultural bonds with England and London than football. Similarly, during my research on Chelsea FC, I found a number of supporters from Scandinavian and Benelux countries whose fandom for Chelsea was initially based on media consumption:

> *Espen*: We have a long tradition of English football in Norway, it started in '68 I think . . .
>
> *Roar*: . . . '69 . . .
>
> *Espen*: . . . '69, Wolverhampton–Sunderland I think . . .
>
> *Roar*: . . . yeah, I think so . . .
>
> *Espen*: The first match broadcast from England. And ever since, since '69 it has been on all Saturdays. English match of the day, 4 o'clock on Saturdays, live games.
>
> *Roar*: Today, they show Chelsea–Liverpool in Norway.
>
> *Espen*: On Channel Plus, this French pay-TV.
>
> *Roar*: They broadcast live games from the matches over here.
>
> *Question*: Is it as prominent as Norwegian football, then?
>
> *Espen*: Yes, it is more in Norway, you see on the whole range of Norwegian TV channels, it is more English football than Norwegian football. As

you said on Saturday, Sunday, Monday it is now football from England. And also the FA Cup, Saturday, Sunday and also Wednesday the re-matches, so it is a lot of English football on Norwegian television.

(Espen and Roar, Chelsea fans)

Such forms of spatially distant fandom emerge both transnationally and within national boundaries. The popular cliché of Manchester United fans living every-where but in Manchester highlighted in the introduction to this part coincides with data collected concerning the location of Chelsea season-ticket holders, suggesting a growing separation of the everyday locale and the geographical positioning of the object of fandom (see Table 5.1 overleaf). The same holds true for fans whose fandom is mainly based on spatially unbound media con-sumption. The following accounts of Bayern München fans verify such claims:

Moritz: I was in Berlin until I was six, then in Bonn up to sixth grade, in Prague until ninth grade and since then I have been back here.
Question: So you have never lived in south Germany?
Moritz: No . . . I have been to Munich, but never to see a football match.

(Moritz, Bayern München fan)

Bengt: The contact to football and being a fan came through television . . . Around this time when you are six or seven, you start watching tele-vision and it was also through my father . . .
Question: So you have always lived in Bonn?
Bengt: Yes.
Lukas: I moved to Bonn pretty early too, when I was seven. My parents lived in Bochum when I was born . . . There is still some link to Bochum, but it is not a very nice town . . . Bonn is a great city, I love it.

(Bengt and Lukas, Bayern Munchen fans)

Further quantitative data substantiates claims of a growing geographical separa-tion between fans and their clubs. In the previously mentioned UFA study (1998), Bayer Leverkusen, for instance, was three times more popular in the eastern states of Berlin, Mecklenburg, Brandenburg and Sachsen-Anhalt than in its own western region. While some clubs such as Hamburger SV or VfB Stuttgart enjoyed significantly higher popularity in their own region, larger recently successful clubs such as Schalke 04, Borussia Dortmund and the at the time runaway leader of the Bundesliga, 1.FC Kaiserslautern, were popular throughout all German regions. Similarly, while Germany's biggest, though not most popular, club Bayern München enjoyed its highest popularity in Bavaria (34 per cent), it had a larger following in the western state of Northrhine-Westphalia (18 per cent) than the regionally based teams 1.FC Köln (14 per cent), MSV Duisburg (10 per cent) and Bayer Leverkusen (10 per cent) (UFA 1998).

Table 5.1 Geographical distribution of Chelsea season-ticket holders (1998/9)

Postcode area	no.	%
Fulham and Chelsea	674	4.35
South-west London, other	1,611	10.40
London, other	2,821	18.21
UK, outside London	10,335	66.73
Overseas	34	0.21
Total*	15,488	99.9

Note
* No postcode information available for 13 season-ticket holders.

Based upon televisual consumption, the lifeworld of fans is thus intertwined with distant points of relation and influences. Television therefore emerges as a crucial force behind the growing spatial interconnectivity of different locales, which Giddens describes as increasingly phantasmagoric:

> In conditions of modernity, place becomes increasingly *phantasmagoric*: that is to say, locales are thoroughly penetrated by and shaped in terms of social influences quite distant from them. What structures the locale is not simply that which is present on scene; the 'visible form' of the locale conceals the distanciated relations which determine its nature.
>
> (Giddens 1990: 18–19)

The increasingly phantasmagoric nature of place reflects the forces of modern industrialism and globalization which are intrinsically linked with television. The televisual mediation of football accelerates the dramatically shifting relation between time and space in the age of modernity. Television has furthered processes that have been described as time–space distanciation as well as time–space compression. Both terms describe different aspects of the same phenomenon. Giddens's idea of time–space distanciation pays little attention to the impact of modern media in the changing relation of time and space. Instead, he emphasizes the importance of the introduction of mechanically measured clock time. While this holds true for the transitional period from premodernity to the rise of industrialism, the accounts of fans discussed above suggest that electronic mass media play an increasingly important role. As a driving force of time–space separation they have made distant places virtually accessible at every time of day. The consumption of football has neither its time nor its place any more. Football can be consumed far away from its actual place, the stadium, through television. The event exists in a sphere globally and simultaneously accessible, unbound by physical settings. Consequently, as football is separated from a singular territorial context, it loses its place in time. Matt, for example, watches football from Asia at night when he can't sleep. Other interviewees watched Italian football on Sunday afternoon, a time not traditionally associated with football in Britain. Similarly, Harvey (1990) emphasizes the impact of modern media on the shifting relation between time and space. He argues that in modernity, time and space have been compressed, as a result of the availability of modern means of travel and electronic media. The accounts of fans drawing on a wide range of fan texts transmitted through television from around the world, often simultaneously with other audiences around the globe, support Harvey's argument. While time and space have become distanciated from each other, they become variable and compressed. Harvey emphasizes television's contribution to the process of time–space compression: referring to events like the 'World Cup, the fall of a dictator [or] a political summit', Harvey observes how 'television . . . makes it possible to experience a rush of images from different spaces almost simultaneously, collapsing the world's space into a series of images on a television screen' (Harvey 1990: 293). Harvey also warns (1990: 305) that the radical transformations of shifting experience of time and space trigger 'an omnipresent danger that our mental maps will not match current realities'.[4] However, Harvey's warning suffers from a romanticized notion of premodernity: he notably fails to investigate his implicit claim that in premodernity mental maps did in fact match an objectifiable, universal reality. What is needed, then, is a closer examination of how globalization and localization change our everyday life, our sense of identity, our social organization and belonging.

Deterritorialization, fandom and community

Many of the transformations described above can be summed up in the term 'deterritorialization' (cf. Appadurai 1990; Morley and Robins 1995; Tomlinson 1999), meaning a process in which social, cultural and economic life is detached from specific locales. This, however, is to argue neither that such separate, untouched locales ever existed, nor that they allowed the construction of mental maps matching contemporary realities. There are two issues that are of importance in relation to my overall argument on football and fandom in the age of globalization. Firstly, there is the question of to what extent we can speak of *de*territorialization, which in turn is dependent upon the question of whether it is accurate to speak of 'authentic' local places and cultures in the first place. Morley and Robins (1995) dispute the existence of untouched, homogeneous and authentic local cultures, independent of cultural flows and interaction. Yet, while raising an important aspect by countering romanticized notions of local cultures, their critique must not be misunderstood as an argument against the existence of deterritorialization and the need for further academic exploration of this phenomenon. As John Tomlinson argues in reply to Morley and Robins:

> The deterritorialization that we have instanced certainly implies a movement
> away from a prior state in which cultural experience was linked more closely

to place, but this need not involve the sort of myths of indigenousness that are rightly criticized.

(Tomlinson 1999: 129)

The changing horizon and boundaries of football consumption support Tomlinson's argument. The significance of televisual texts in the framing of fandom, and in turn the significance of fandom in the projection of self and construction of identity in contemporary societies, demonstrate how the position of physical place in constructing social and cultural realities has changed. My point is therefore the following: on the one hand, deterritorialization constitutes a fundamental shift in the cultural and social construction of place. On the other, we must bear in mind Morley and Robins's warning of an over-simplified notion in which the territory is synonymous with authenticity, insularity and an expression of organic communities or culture. Or, in light of Harvey's argument, we must not assume that there ever was some universal reality that was understood through the congruence and coherence of social experience and place.

The logical conclusion of Harvey's argument is to claim that everyday life unbound of place becomes inauthentic, that the increasing fragmentation of local place *ipso facto* results in the dissolution of organic communities or, as in Meyrowitz's argument (1985), that the primacy of locality has given way to a televisually transmitted sense of a 'generalized elsewhere'. None of this, I believe, can be assumed so easily. First we need to define a key term in the discussion of place and deterritorialization: community. On a basic level, *community* describes a group of people who have something in *common*, based upon *communication*. Significantly, communities are experienced subjectively. They are realized through the subjective feeling of membership. As Silverstone observes,

> Community always involves a claim. It is not just a matter of structure: of the institutions that enable participation and the organization of membership. It is also a matter of belief, of a set of claims to be part of something shareable and particular, a set of claims whose effectiveness is realized precisely and only in our acceptance of them. Communities are lived.
>
> (Silverstone 1999: 97)

The question I want to investigate is how such communities are lived by football fans, and how they are transformed through deterritorialization. So far I have focused on the relation between football and individuals rather than social groups. This emphasis mirrors the central position the self and identity occupy in a deterritorialized lifeworld bound by mass media. On the other hand, all dimensions of fandom I have investigated – communication, extension and distinction, identity and citizenship – are preconditions of the formation of communities.[5] Weeks (1990: 89) summarizes identity in simple terms as 'what you have in common with some people and differentiates you from others'. In this sense identity and community become an expression of the process of self-positioning in the modern world. It is, on a rudimentary level, with those people with whom we have something in common that we form communities. This is equally true for communities in a globalizing, deterritorialized world and for communities in premodern times. However, the fundamental difference, I think, between premodern and contemporary communities lies in the fact that the latter have become increasingly voluntary. In premodern times what people had in common with each other was largely defined by the shared place they inhabited. Communities were a fixed given, rarely to be overcome by an individual. This is increasingly less the case in contemporary societies. Fandom, as I have argued, can now be forged by drawing on an endless variety of texts originating in modern mass media and first of all television. This is not to argue that identification with local clubs has ceased, but that it has become optional, as both the previously discussed qualitative and quantitative data demonstrate. As football fandom is a space of self-reflection, communities become voluntary social groups who function as a mirror to their members. This must not be misread as a lack of desire of individual fans to be part of communities. On the contrary, the search for membership of communities and the construction of a sense of belonging are an integral part of football fandom. I have already discussed the use of a categorized 'we' by fans. In some cases the use of 'we' expressed both the bond between themselves and fellow fans and the bond between the fan and the club:

> *Question*: Do you identify with the club?
> *Ken*: It is with the fellow supporters. I can't relate to the executive area at Chelsea. Even though, I go to Tottenham and go to the executive area, but I just know, if you go there, there is no passion, no feeling about the club . . . The players I have met, I can actually relate to . . . I don't hold the view that they are all mercenaries, because I don't believe Chelsea are paying them more than they could get elsewhere. They pay them well but that's their market value. So I identify with the supporters, I identify with some of the players I have met, I don't identify with the East Stand middle tier, I don't identify with the executive area, but I do identify with Ken Bates [the chairman]. I understand exactly what he is trying to do. It is a shame he couldn't do it ten years ago, because we would be a superpower now, he is doing the right thing.
> (Ken, Chelsea fan)

This account illustrates the complex and hybrid construction and articulation of communities in football fandom. Belonging to a community is part of the wider process of selective projection in fandom. Ken carefully constructs his object of fandom in accordance with his own values and beliefs. Hence the community of which he sees himself a part functions as self-reflection in that it excludes those who are assumed not to share the common ground of fandom ('I don't identify with the East Stand middle tier') while including others who are a suitable back-ground for self-reflection (loyal fellow fans, players who still treasure comradeship, a smart club chairman). In other words, the common element in such communi-ties is essentially imagined. Communities constructed through football fandom are imagined in a double sense. Firstly, they are *imagined in content* as individual fans claim membership of such a community drawing on their individual reading of the values and attributes that the members of the community are imagined to have in common. Secondly, such communities are *imagined in structure* in the sense in which Benedict Anderson describes nations as imagined communities. Anderson argues (1991: 6) that the nation 'is *imagined* because the members of even the smallest nation will never know most of their fellow members, meet them, or even hear of them, yet in the minds of each lives the image of their com-munion'. Football fans are part of an imagined community, whose borders as much as content are imagined by every individual member. Therefore audiences for football (whether *in situ* or on television) do not constitute a community a priori. Rather, segments of the audience are transformed into imagined communi-ties through common patterns of reading and appropriation. To describe, for example, the entire television audience for a Premier League match between Chelsea FC and Manchester United as a community would be of limited analyti-cal benefit. Rather, several communities manifest themselves within the audience through a shared and common reading of the text, such as Chelsea fans or Man-chester United fans. As it is dependent upon the reading of almost universally available texts, membership of such communities is not only imagined but volun-tary. Consequently, fan communities reflect the conscious habitus of fans. As the self-reflection in football fandom prestructures membership of fan communities, these communities are themselves increasingly unbound of physical space and therefore deterritorialized.

My argument concerning deterritorialization can thus be summarized as follows. Firstly, deterritorialized communities are as authentic or inauthentic as other large-scale communities in modernity. Secondly, in the discussion of deter-ritorialization we must take account of the inevitable local remanifestation of all cultural and social exchange, again mirroring the wider dialectic between global and local dimensions. As far as the latter point is concerned, Tomlinson argues,

> there is the simple but important fact that we are all, as human beings, *embodied and physically located*. In this fundamental material sense the ties of culture to location can never be completely severed and the locality contin-ues to exercise its claims upon us as the physical situation of our lifeworld. So deterritorialization cannot ultimately mean the end of locality, but its transformation into a more complex cultural space.
>
> (Tomlinson 1999: 149, original emphasis)

In this sense, I now turn to the transformation of locales into 'complex cultural spaces' as well as the interrelation between deterritorialized information flow and face-to-face interaction as they emerge in the investigation of the interaction between contemporary fan communities. Communities are as much defined by their spaces of inclusion as by their spaces of exclusion and the construction of the imagined 'other'. This is epitomized in football fandom by particular rivalry between particular teams. Such rivalry often emerges between clubs that share a narrowly defined geographical space such as cities or regions.[6] Bayer Leverkusen fans, for instance, univocally identified 1.FC Köln, the largest football club in the neighbouring town of Cologne, as their main rival:

> *Question*: Do you have any rivalry with any other clubs?
> *Hilmar*: Köln.
> *Axel*: Not as rival, because they aren't any competition for us any more, they can't be any more, but as unpleasant and disliked neighbours . . . They are full of shit.
> *Hilmar*: Köln really accumulates all negative attributes a club can have.
> *Axel*: That's not because you have had any bad experiences with the FC [1.FC Köln], it just simply is like that. You can't be a Bayer fan and say, Köln is actually a quite nice club, that just isn't a possibility.
> (Hilmar and Axel, Bayer fans from Leverkusen)

Similar sentiments to those above were echoed in the accounts of a large number of Bayer fans. The long-standing rivalry between the fan communities of Bayer Leverkusen and of 1.FC Köln was also evident in a survey conducted among fans, in which they ranked all Bundesliga clubs as well as the recently relegated 1.FC Köln according to their sympathies, and has been observed in earlier writing on football cultures in Germany (Bode 1990). With an average ranking of –4.19[7] the Cologne club emerged as the least-liked opposition among participants in my study (see Table 5.2 overleaf).[8]

However, the contrasting example of Chelsea FC demonstrates that even such rivalry, which has been crucial in the local construction of football fandom, is being transformed under the impact of deterritorialization. This development mirrors Joshua Meyrowitz's argument that communities become increasingly liberated from spatial locality:

> Because of the relationship between places and situations, group identities have usually been closely linked to shared but special access to physical locations . . . Access to a group's territory was once the primary means of incorporation into a group . . . By severing the traditional link between physical location and social situation, for example, electronic media may begin to blur previously distinct group identities by allowing people to 'escape' informationally from place-defined groups and by permitting outsiders to 'invade' many groups' territories without ever entering them.
> (Meyrowitz 1985: 57)

Table 5.2 Popularity of Bundesliga clubs among Bayer Leverkusen fans

Club	Value
Bayer 04 Leverkusen	5.00
Borussia Mönchengladbach	0.00
VfB Stuttgart	−0.26
TSV 1860 München	−0.48
1.FC Nürnberg	−0.59
VfL Bochum	−0.70
Schalke 04	−0.70
SC Freiburg	−0.81
Eintracht Frankfurt	−1.11
Hamburger SV	−1.11
1.FC Kaiserslautern	−1.19
Hertha BSC Berlin	−1.22
MSV Duisburg	−1.63
Hansa Rostock	−1.78
VfL Wolfsburg	−2.22
Werder Bremen	−2.48
Borussia Dortmund	−2.59
FC Bayern München	−2.93
1.FC Köln	−4.19

Note
Participants: 27; scale −5 (dislike a lot) to +5 (like a lot), survey period: August to December 1998.

Yet rather than being externally eroded, as Meyrowitz implies, these 'group territories' themselves undergo a transformation from territory to semiotic space. This transformation fuels the increasing deterritorialization of football communities evident in the case of Chelsea FC fans. Asked about their main local rival, Chelsea fans seemed unsure whether there was an actual local rival:

> I don't think we have a local rivalry.
>
> (Ally, Chelsea fan from east London)

> I don't know, we always liked Fulham, but Fulham hates us. Because they are jealous of us. Everyone hates Tottenham and Arsenal, I don't think Chelsea actually have a particular rival, they detest Man United, like really. I know most people do, but they do like because of history . . . there is not really a local rival. I don't think there is a particular one.
>
> (Catherine, Chelsea fan from south-west London, living in Brighton)

Instead, all but one Chelsea fan referred also to rivalries with clubs outside London and the south-east of England:

I don't mind Arsenal. It is just Spurs, I have always been, Chelsea have always hated Spurs, the same way we always hated Leeds, we always hated Man United.

(Samuel, Chelsea fan from Wimbledon)

In both qualitative and quantitative data, Manchester United frequently emerges as the main rival. When asked to rank the Premier League clubs according to their sympathy, Chelsea fans ranked a number of smaller London teams (Charlton Athletic and Wimbledon) highest, while the northern clubs Leeds and particularly Manchester United were among the least popular (see Table 5.3).

Manchester United also emerged as the main rival in the verbal accounts of Chelsea fans:

I am not sure what all the thing about Tottenham is. It seems a bit, on the surface it seems racial, because it is an anti-Jewish feeling. I am not sure that they actually mean that, it is just going along. I doubt they know how it all

Table 5.3 Popularity of Premier League clubs among Chelsea fans

Club	Value
Chelsea FC	5.00
Charlton Athletic	1.90
Wimbledon FC	0.73
Sheffield Wednesday	0.23
Southampton FC	0.17
Derby County	0.13
Newcastle United	0.07
Nottingham Forest	−0.07
Aston Villa	−0.17
Coventry City	−0.17
Everton FC	−0.77
Blackburn Rovers	−0.87
Middlesbrough FC	−0.87
Leicester City	−0.97
Liverpool FC	−1.07
West Ham United	−1.57
Arsenal FC	−1.83
Leeds United	−2.77
Tottenham Hotspur	−2.93
Manchester United	−4.20

Note
Participants: 30; scale −5 (dislike a lot) to +5 (like a lot), survey period: January to June 1999.

started, so I don't really mind. Our main rivalry now is with Manchester United, it is just pure jealousy, we haven't won a league game since, but again, that is the only rivalry.

(Will, Chelsea fan from north London)

In Will's account, the shared space of competition is identified as the main reason for the rivalry with Manchester United ('it is just pure jealousy, we haven't won a league game since'). Similarly, many fans of Major League Soccer, which has a comparatively small number of teams spread across the vast territory of the United States, based their rivalry not on geographical but on competitive parameters:

I am especially pleased with beating other top teams, Columbus is our closest rival, in 1996 New York/New Jersey was a rival and I love beating LA.

(Jamie, DC United fan)

I really dislike LA and Miami. I don't like LA because I consider them our main rival.

(Bob, DC United fan)

I like beating Chicago, who took our third crown from us.

(Donald, DC United fan)

Alongside shared spaces of competition in large-scale national leagues, a further element fuelled intense rivalries with clubs outside a given locality:

Manchester United, I know I should get [*pauses*], I suppose, it is because I don't come from London, so I don't get too worked up about West Ham, about Tottenham, about Arsenal. I actually think it is quite, my need to beat them is completely dependent on the opposing fans. It is probably because West Ham fans, Tottenham fans, Arsenal fans, aren't in the same bracket as Manchester United fans. I find certain fans particularly irritating, because they have never been to Old Trafford. I can relate to Tottenham fans and Arsenal fans, people I know they go and watch it, so all credit to them. If they beat us, they give us stick, fine, I do the same thing. But I can't take stick from any Man United fans and they never go to the games, and ten years ago they probably supported Liverpool or Nottingham Forest.

(Gary, Chelsea fan from Colchester, Essex)

Gary's account points to new forms of 'local' rivalry. Here local rivalry is to be understood in terms not of a shared territory but of a shared symbolic space such as league competition. In the second account, the relation between the local reterritorialization and appropriation of deterritorialized semiotic spaces and discourses is highlighted. Firstly, Gary refers to the fact that his own fandom is not situated in London but situated in his own local lifeworld ('because I don't come from London, so I don't get too worked up about West Ham, about Tottenham, about Arsenal'). Secondly, his account underlines that while communities are deterritorialized and imagined, they still continue to be manifested locally. This includes face-to-face interaction, as he explicitly refers to Manchester United fans he encounters in his own locality ('but I can't take stick from any Man United fans'). Communities, whether deterritorialized or not (and this is, I think, what Tomlinson argues when he speaks of the transformation of localities into complex cultural spaces), manifest themselves in local, day-to-day social encounters:

Question: So do you know any Manchester United supporters?
Jack: Oh, I do, yeah, a lot of them come from London. Yeah, I can't stand it when I see kids walking around the street in a Man United shirt, unfortunately children as children, they don't want to be seen to support anyone other than the top one. My son was like that.

(Jack, Chelsea fan from Sutton)

I was at a school in north London, a third of the school supported Man United and for no other reason than there is an air crash and they all support them. Now, I live a hundred miles away, the whole town supports them. And they never go. I go to Manchester more than they do . . . A lot of friends, not friends, work colleagues, they all support them.

(Michael, Chelsea fan from Cheltenham)

Comparing the interlocal, deterritorialized group of Chelsea fans to traditional high-modern imagined communities such as nations, face-to-face interaction notably emerges as more significant in the former, globally and locally constituted community. Thereby football fandom reflects another aspect of the dialectic between global and local forces: fragmentation and homogenization. Appadurai identifies homogenization and fragmentation as processes at the heart of globalization.

The central problem of today's global interactions is the tension between cultural homogenization and cultural heterogenization. A vast array of empirical facts could be brought to bear on the side of the 'homogenization' argument . . . What these accounts fail to consider is that at least as rapidly as forces from various metropolises are brought into new societies they tend to be indigenized in one or other way.

(Appadurai 1990: 295)

Fragmentation and homogenization reflect localization and globalization processes that in turn express the dialectic between global production (and distribution) and local consumption. Contemporary football fandom simultaneously fragments and homogenizes. It homogenizes in that a few 'super-clubs' (Bale

1993: 179) recruit large groups of fans from countries around the world. The ongoing demise of lower leagues in the face of bigger turnovers and profits in the top football leagues of the core national and continental federations substantiates such homogenization claims. In contemporary football, fewer clubs recruit larger fan groups. During my fieldwork in London, I interviewed a student from Malaysia who supported Liverpool FC:

> *Question*: Do you consider yourself as a fan, then?
> *Dinh*: Yeah, definitely, because from when I was seven, at that time I was in primary school, and the teacher asked us to look at and pick some cartoons and I flicked through the papers. And I saw Liverpool and it just started there.
>
> (Dinh, Liverpool fan)

As football clubs attract fans from different and distant localities around the world, their fan communities both are fragmented in space and fragment space. They are fragmented in space as fans are dispersed around the globe. They fragment space as the traditional link between territory and communities identified by Meyrowitz (1985: 56) has been progressively undermined. As Morley argues,

> locality is not simply subsumed in a national or global sphere; rather it is increasingly bypassed in both directions: experience is both unified beyond localities and fragmented within them. Such fragmentation, however, is rarely random, nor is it a matter of merely individual differences or 'choices'. Rather it is a question of the socially – and culturally – determined lines of division along which 'fragmentation' occurs.
>
> (Morley 1991: 8)

The way in which fans project their beliefs and their image of self onto the club powerfully underlines Morley's assessment that such fragmentation is not a mere matter of individual choice. Yet what makes membership of such communities voluntary in comparison to earlier epochs is that 'the socially – and culturally – determined lines of division' have been dramatically transformed in the light of globalization processes: the territorial location of individuals is no longer the overshadowing determinant of their membership of communities. I will substantiate this further with a number of examples. The homogenization and fragmentation of communities is illustrated by the numerous Chelsea fans living outside the UK. Chelsea FC currently has 31 fan clubs in 17 countries outside the UK.[9] These fans are part of a deterritorialized community, which is manifested in everyday interaction with members of the same or other communities within a (distant) locale. In the following example, two Norwegian Chelsea fans describe contact with other deterritorialized communities within their lifeworld:

Espen: Everybody in Norway has their favourite teams in England, if you ask someone what is your favourite team in England, they normally have an answer.
Roar: My brothers, I have two brothers, one is a United fan and the other one is a Tottenham fan. But it is fun, we always have something to talk about.
Espen: Some stick. [*laughs*]
Roar: We get together every weekend.

(Espen and Roar, Chelsea fans)

The local appropriation of larger homogenized communities, such as Chelsea, Tottenham or Manchester United fans, fragments social groups and cohesion within the locale of the two interviewees. Simultaneously, while communities are both unified beyond and fragmented within localities, membership of these communities reshapes the structure of everyday life. Hence, despite the deterritorialization of communities, their significance to local life must not be underestimated. As Espen later explains,

We are on the board of our supporters' club, so we use a lot of time, also for these activities, to organize travels, tickets for home games and we myself, try to make some activities in Norway, people getting together. We have our football cup in Oslo every year. We are playing in Chelsea shirts against other teams from Norway, play Manchester United and Arsenal and Liverpool and everybody. So I would say, football is one of the top priorities in life. And Chelsea is one of the top priorities.

(Espen, Chelsea fan)

Thus deterritorialized communities are integrated into the local everyday life of fans. This local remanifestation of deterritorialized communities also answers questions raised concerning their authenticity. As Silverstone argues (1999: 97), 'if people believe something to be real, then as the American sociologist W. I. Thomas famously noted, it is real in its consequences'. This is verified by the ease with which fans identify these communities as part of their local social environment, as illustrated in the question about local rivalry:

Question: Do you feel something as local rivalry living so far away? Maybe with any teams in Norway?
Roar: The best teams, of course. I hate Liverpool.
Espen: Not for me. My main enemy is United. It was Tottenham . . . Tottenham I always disliked. So for me it is United, Arsenal and Tottenham.
Roar: For me it is United, Arsenal and Liverpool. Almost all of my friends are Liverpool fans.
Espen: For me it is Manchester United, you see that on the Norwegian telly, it is always about Manchester United, always about Solskjaer, his

scoring goals and hurrah, a lot of minutes on the news, anything happens in Manchester. It is also about the newspapers and TV.

(Espen and Roar, Chelsea fans)

In all but one account of the Chelsea fans living outside the UK, they named other English teams such as Manchester United, Liverpool or other London clubs as their local rivals.[10] The symbolic space of shared competition emerges as more important in the construction of self-identity and group membership than the actual geographical place inhabited by fans. The reasons Espen gives for his dislike of Manchester United, however, point to a further dimension in the interrelation of deterritorialization and fan communities that is also evident in the other accounts discussed above, in which fans of clubs such as Manchester United are criticized for their fandom's dependence on mass media. What Espen uncovers is the tension among different degrees of media usage, among different fan groups, reflecting varying degrees of deterritorialization and the forces behind it – most notably the media-driven rationalization of the consumption of football. As much as this rational technological capacity has occupied a key role in the globalization of television, it is equally significant for a parallel phenomenon: the proliferation of postmodern (football) culture.

Summary to Part II

Football fandom, as it is firmly integrated into an increasingly global sphere of semiotic exchange, functions as a vehicle for the articulation of values and beliefs. As fans actively participate in the discourses of the public sphere through the patterns of their consumption, their fandom manifests a form of 'DIY citizenship'. The nature of such participation in public discourse is in turn structured by the economic, social and cultural macro transformations of rationalized, consumerist capitalism. Similarly, I have documented how capitalist consumerism has been instrumental in the rise of global 'third cultures', which have translated into a growing transnational system of signs and texts. Through the growing interrelation between local and global dimensions of everyday life in a process of distanciation of space and time, fans are able to choose from an endless variety of semiotic resources. This, in turn, provides the ground on which social, cultural and political discourses and citizenship are formed and membership of communities becomes voluntary. Communities have thus lost their singular link to territorial place, which is replaced by a complex interrelation between global, deterritorialized communities and local face-to-face interaction. These processes form the spaces in which fandom is exercised as an extension of self. In the global semiotic system every act of consumption becomes a matter of choice (even though such choices are predetermined) and thus of articulation and communication. All accounts in this study illustrate these choices, which at the same time reflect the values and beliefs of fans. These are choices made in a global mediasphere and lived locally. Whether fans choose to support a club on the other side of the world in order to express their identity (for example white fans of Chelsea FC in South Africa) or choose to support a club on the other side of town (for example fans in Leverkusen), such choices reflect fans' *Weltanschauung* and ultimately function as an extension of fans into the world. Thus fans cannot escape from globalization, yet the way in which they participate in global cultures constitutes a form of self-expression. The implications of this dialogue between global production and local indigenization and consumption are manifold. The nation, formerly marking the boundaries of the public sphere and providing borderlines of semiotic exchange, appears to occupy an increasingly marginal position in the dynamic interaction between local and global dimensions in the everyday life of fans. Consequently, the condition of modern football fandom is not formed by the cultural or economic hegemony of nation states. In contrast to general claims of the americanization of sport (Houlihan 1994), fandom has been shaped by contemporary global consumerism. What is at stake in football fandom is not the hegemonic struggle for power by nation states but the interrelation of diverging cultural and economic forces.

All the implications of the globalization (and universalization) of football I have identified – localization, time–space distanciation and deterritorialization – reflect the forces of the rationalization momentum of global consumerism. They are the ground for the semiotic diversity of contemporary football, which provides fans with a variety of clubs and fan texts. This textual polysemy forms the background against which fans themselves reflect a sense of self through their consumption choices. At the same time, however, the rationalization imperative that underlies the consumerist system undermines precisely such choice. The forced deterritorialization of the fandom of many Chelsea fans who have become unable to afford the *in situ* consumption of matches indicates how rationalized consumerism eradicates the choices it creates. It is this dialectic that I will examine further in the final part of this book.

Part III

Football and postmodernity

The monks of Tibet devoted themselves to the fastidious work of transcribing the 99 billion names of God, after which the world will be accomplished, and it will end. Exhausted by this everlasting spelling of the names of God, they call IBM computer experts who complete the work in a few months . . . For with this virtual countdown of the names of God, the great promise of the end was realized; and the technicians of IBM, who left the site after work (and didn't believe of course in the prophecy), saw the stars in the sky fading and vanishing one by one.

(Baudrillard 1997: 23)

Former England manager Graham Taylor was once believed to have found the key to success in modern football. Having analysed hundreds of goals in domestic and international competition, Taylor noted that 80 per cent of goals were scored from three passes or less (Ward and Taylor 1995). He then sought to rationalize the play of the teams he coached accordingly, relying on standardized tactical patterns such as long passes. This Taylorization of football, however, was short lived. England never made any impression under Taylor's reign and failed to qualify for the 1994 World Cup. As former England striker Gary Lineker has pointed out, Taylor's formal rationality had ignored too many variables, such as the share of ball possession (Ward and Taylor 1995: 330). While Taylor soon fell victim to the irrationalities of the rigid rationalism of his scientific game plan, it is off rather than on the pitch that regimes of formal rationality have had their most lasting impact on the game and its fans.

Turning to questions of rationalization, simulation and postmodernity moves my argument into a third and final stage. I began the analysis of football fandom by emphasizing the historical link between football, modernity and industrialism as well as television and consumerism. I also defined football fandom as a series of set patterns of consumption, which in turn communicate the self through self-reflection. In a second step, I examined the implications of fandom as an extension of self in relation to the cultural and territorial expansion of football with particular reference to processes such as the structural transformation of the public sphere and globalization. These macro processes are juxtaposed with acts of consumption and hence appropriation, resulting in localization and citizenship. Yet the limits of appropriation are ultimately dependent on the mechanisms behind the transformation of processes of production. To explore these mechanisms and their implications is the aim of the remainder of this book and I will begin, once more, with the economic realm and the inherent rationalization of processes in the production of modern football.

Chapter 6

Football, formal rationality and standardization

The forces of rationalization and standardization have long been identified as important principles and articulations of industrial modernity. Max Weber famously pointed to the role of rationalization, and related tendencies such as bureaucratization, as the central transformational force behind industrialism. His investigations also warn us of the irrational consequences of the *Zweckrationalität* (formal rationality) arising out of the micro orientation of production and organization in industrial societies (Weber 1921). Weber's substantial analysis of the nature of industrial capitalism still offers particular insights to the understanding of present-day practices of production and consumption in professional football. Using Weber's distinction between formal and substantive rationality, I now want to turn to the analysis of the fundamental transformations of the production of football and its consequences for the construction of fandom. Firstly I examine the application of formal rationality in the production of contemporary football drawing on Ritzer's (1996; 1998) notion of McDonaldization, before turning to an exploration of the consequences of the rationalization and standardization of production and distribution regimes. As part of this endeavour I will particularly focus on the far-reaching changes to place as territorial context of football consumption arising out of the rationalization of professional football.

Football and McDonaldization

George Ritzer's investigation (1996; 1998) into the production principles of the fast food industry – and American burger giant McDonald's in particular – constitutes one of the most notable efforts to apply Weber's concerns regarding the nature of rationality to consumer capitalism. His notion of McDonaldization has thus attracted much recent critical attention. Aside from some largely polemical critique (Wynyard 1998; O'Neill 1999), more substantial approaches scrutinize the fact that Ritzer focuses on rational production regimes and pays little attention to consumers and their own appropriation of McDonaldized products (Parker 1998; Jary 1999). Some critics, such as Miles (1998) and Alfino (1998), have even suggested that Ritzer fundamentally misreads the mechanisms of consumerism: 'Ritzer cannot be forgiven for presenting a theory which misunderstands a consumer society in which the complexities of structure and agency are played out and negotiated by consumers throughout the course of their everyday lives' (Miles 1998: 65).

Miles's argument is based on his participant observations in a sports store, where he investigates the way mass produced sports articles are being appropriated by consumers to their own social and cultural needs. However, while attacking Ritzer for his lack of attention to the 'semiotic power of consumers' (Fiske 1989b), Miles loses sight of how the global patterns of rational production prestructure such semiotic power. In applying the McDonaldization framework to professional football, I examine both the production and consumption of contemporary football.[1] In this sense, I will begin my discussion of the rationalization of football by juxtaposing the recent transformations of football and football fandom with the rationalization of fast food production and consumption in an attempt to illustrate parallels and discrepancies between these areas.

McDonald's as well as other fast food chains have become firmly integrated into the contemporary landscapes of sports.[2] As one Bayer Leverkusen fan observed:

> There is nothing to object against the McDonald's. I only mind commercialization that affects the fans, like the hotel. They just took away two rows of seating. But I don't mind the McDonald's.
>
> (Simon, Bayer Leverkusen fan)

McDonald's, as the epitome of rationalization, is thus happily accepted by a fan who is otherwise critical of the modernization and commercialization of both sport and society. Yet the McDonaldization of modern sports and in particular football goes well beyond the growing presence and interest of fast food chains in sports. The sports industry has adopted the formal rational principles of McDonaldization in producing and packaging spectator sport. I will outline those rationalization tendencies of sports' production by following the four dimensions of the McDonaldization process Ritzer identifies (1996): efficiency, calculability, control and predictability.

Efficiency

McDonaldized means of production are marked by their search for greatest efficiency. In economic terms enterprises seek to achieve maximal profit with a minimal use of material and human resources. Again, the rationale behind such systems is mathematically quantifiable *Zweckrationalität* (formal rationality) reflected in monetary profit. For fast food restaurants this means selling as many burgers, fries and drinks as possible using the fewest possible (financial, rather than environmental) resources. Ritzer describes (1996) the efforts made by fast food restaurants to heighten the efficiency of their business by streamlining, standardizing and automating the production process[3] as well as speeding up the consumption process. The search for formal efficiency of fast food restaurants is mirrored in areas of cultural production. Football clubs seek to heighten their profits by making maximal use of their assets. Much as McDonaldized fast food services seek to produce and sell as many burgers as possible, generally with little regard for their actual quality, football clubs have steadily increased the number of games played per season, which has led to widespread concern among the sport's medical consultants. New or enlarged competitions such as domestic league cups, the UEFA Intertoto Cup, designed to fill the gaps in the football calendar and to keep the football-based lotteries and pools games afloat during the summer months, or the Champions League, originate in clubs' attempts to make maximal usage of their means of production, in other words stadia and coaching and playing staff. Additional and extended competitions inflating the number of games played each season have prioritized quantity over quality, hinting at one of the many irrational consequences of formal rationality which has been a core concern of both Weber's original work (1921) as well as Ritzer's McDonaldization thesis (1996; 1998).

Ritzer highlights (1996) the degree to which fast food restaurants put their customers to work by delegating to them various tasks such as the preparation of soft drinks or adding toppings to their burgers, serving their own food and disposing of the leftovers once their meal is finished. The role of customers as 'unpaid workers' is even more noteworthy in professional football. Through their singing, chanting, clapping and other forms of acoustic and visual support fans fulfil a crucial role in the production of professional football as widely consumed events. In an age in which the overwhelming majority of football consumption takes place through television, the comparatively small number of direct customers of football cubs – fans at the ground – are put to work performing the atmospheric packaging of a football game, which is an indispensable part of the end product. This is Jürgen von Einem, head of Bayer's sports sponsoring:

> The role of the spectator [at the ground] has changed. It has a different significance today than it did 10 or 20 years ago. The budget of football clubs depended to 80 per cent on gate takings. Today it is 25 per cent, even less in our case . . . Something else is important . . . The crucial factor is the atmospheric quality of an event. This is not only about sport, it is about the atmospheric quality and a common and communal experience. And that is what people are looking for and what is immensely important for the popularity of an event. It must not be the case that a ground is half empty, deconstructing the event. If television technology continues to develop as it has done . . . the competition between stadium and home will become even harder . . . You will only win this competition where a positive communal experience is guaranteed at every game. Clubs with stadia that offer the according level of comfort, the according communal experiences, the

according facilities, etc., will survive this competition from television, because television is not able to generate this communal experience.

(Jürgen von Einem, interview 15 December 1998)

Thus *in situ* spectators are an indispensable part of the production of football as televisual event. Ground spectators, despite being paying customers confronted with rising admission prices (though less in Leverkusen than elsewhere, further demonstrating the club's awareness to this extent), perform indispensable tasks in the production of spectator football. Like other consumers in contemporary capitalism they are utilized as sources of capital accumulation:

We perform a variety of work-like tasks as consumers in fast food restaurants. Similarly we work during our treks to shopping malls, supermarkets, and even Las Vegas casinos . . . Capitalism *wants* to keep us at it because instead of paying workers, people are willing, even eager, to pay for the privilege of working as consumers . . . As a result of the necessity for ever-increasing consumption, the focus of capitalism has shifted from exploiting workers to exploiting consumers.

(Ritzer 1998: 120–1)

Ritzer's observations hold equally true for the realm of professional football. With amateurism and maximum wages only distant memories, football players enjoy one of the highest-paid occupations of their age group. While players' wages have multiplied, fans face steadily rising admission prices:

The pricing is outrageous, it is my biggest [expense], for football . . . I just paid for the season ticket, for me and my two boys, £780. My first ever season ticket I bought was £25. Obviously prices go up, but especially Chelsea, we are overpriced in everything.

(Benny, Chelsea fan)

Ground spectators thus both finance the clubs they support and prepare the ground for the further profitability as their 'labour contribution' forms the *conditio sine qua non* in the production of professional football's main and most profitable product: the televisual event. As the stadium becomes a site of production, the efficiency imperative of rationalized industrial production constitutes the parameters of planning modern sports arenas. Having emphasized the need for spectators in the construction of football as a televisual event, von Einem further explains the considerations behind the planning of modern stadia, such as Bayer Leverkusen's BayArena which has one of the smallest capacities in contemporary top flight football with 22,500 seats:

All this is only possible if you build a stadium – which after all is a production site for Bundesliga and European Cup games – that is not larger than just above its average capacity. If you walk into the Bayer executive planning commission 'Investment and Technology' and tell them what a great project you have, then the first question they ask is what kind of average use of the capacity you plan. And if you answer 60 per cent or 50 per cent you might just as well take your stuff and leave right away . . . That's like a company saying there is a need for maximum capacity three times a year and during the rest of the time we just let it run with 50 per cent. This costs an enormous amount of money, investments, running costs, maintenance, personnel, and one day, when it starts to crumble, further investments become necessary. Such planning is completely idiotic and unprofessional.

(Jürgen von Einem, interview 15 December 1998)

Efficiency thus emerges as a central theme in the planning of football stadia.[4] It is worth pointing out that such maximal efficiency for producers does not translate into similar advantages for consumers. Whereas recent accounts of the transformations of contemporary capitalism have observed an increasing flexibilization of production (Harvey 1990; Lash and Urry 1994), the consumers in McDonaldized systems ranging from professional sports to fast food restaurants are often left with less choice than in the heyday of Fordism. Similarly, the decentring pressure on such consumption has increased. While the number of football games available on television has multiplied in recent years, the consumption of live games has grown increasingly difficult. Stadia's maximum capacities being unequal to the demand for tickets, the heightened efficiency of football clubs results in increasingly rigid consumption patterns for fans. Given high demand for a limited number of seats, many football clubs have tripled admission prices within the last decade. Moreover, with fewer seats available, the pressure on fans to purchase season tickets or join (expensive) membership schemes increases. Non-season-ticket holders are rarely able to attend more than a few selected games – if they want to do so, it requires careful and time-consuming planning. This Queens Park Rangers fan from London describes how the rationalization efforts of football clubs have made it more difficult to attend games:

It is hard to go to games nowadays. I can't remember having any problems back then, I was a little kid . . . it is definitely different though. I remember going to White Hart Lane, because I watched anything really. Apart from QPR I would go and watch Spurs, Chelsea, Arsenal, whoever, and I would go to White Hart Lane and you can't see a thing, but in a way it was more enjoyable. It is really organized now. Really, really regulated, come in from exit so and so, go to toilet so and so.

(Constantine, Queens Park Rangers fan)

Similarly, many Chelsea fans found it difficult to watch the away games they wanted and used to, as tickets for these games are sold to season-ticket holders first:

I don't get to go to many away games, because I am not a season-ticket holder and it is now virtually impossible to get tickets. I mean the days when you used to just turn up on the day and pay are gone and that's when we used to go to away matches really. So I haven't seen an away Chelsea match for a couple of seasons. The last one I saw was at Wimbledon and that was because it was easy to get a ticket. But, now, the away tickets go to season-ticket holders and never come on sale.

(Dan, Chelsea fan)

The amount of planning that the consumption of *in situ* football requires is also highlighted in the following account of a Chelsea fan. The quote indicates the wider effects such rigid consumption patterns have on the structure of everyday life:

The basic joy of going to a game disappeared. When we can meet up at two o'clock in a pub, have a drink and then leave the pub at five to three and go around to the ground and stand on the terrace and, you know, huge amount of bonding about it. I really liked that, I really miss that. Now, we have to get match tickets seven, eight months in advance when we go to a game, that just takes it to a different plane. You can't just decide in Sunday lunch time, let's go to a game, because you can't get a ticket. So that has taken away . . . now it is much more kind of planned activity, so we buy a ticket months in advance, we arrange to go for a meal beforehand, and because it is much more of a set thing. It is a bit more stilted really, not as unique as it was.

(Samuel, Chelsea fan)

Hence the search for more efficiency by football clubs who regard the stadium as a site of production has resulted in rigid regimes of inflexible consumption. Fans are only able to attend games if they are prepared to organize their everyday life in accordance with the demands of the rationalized production of such events by football clubs. Seeking to heighten their revenue from television, English and German clubs have abolished the traditional Saturday afternoon scheduling of all games. Spreading single match days over two, three or even four days multiplies the number of matches that can be transmitted live on television, hence maximizing both audiences and broadcast hours for one match day.[5] As broadcasters, in their own search for maximal efficiency and revenue, are eager to broadcast live those games that have a particular relevance to the current fight for the championship and, to a lesser degree, the relegation struggle, decisions about which games are rescheduled are often made at short notice and well after fans have purchased their season tickets or match tickets.[6] A Chelsea season-ticket holder describes the impact the constant rescheduling of games has on the structure of his private life:

I mean the problem is Sky TV. It probably causes more arguments between the wife and I than anything. Because she is happy for me to go off for football with the kid, but recently I haven't known which day I am going to football, because it keeps changing. I can't arrange this, I can't do that. We tried to arrange my daughter's birthday party and we couldn't, we actually had to book it a month away, because it was difficult to find out what Saturday or Sunday were free, because they were all up for being changed. I mean, I object to the Tottenham game being changed to a Monday night, I think that is obscene. I bought my kid a ticket, I can't take him on a Monday night, he has got school.

(Ken, Chelsea fan)

This account highlights the flexibility that is expected of spectators at the ground as well as the often severe impact on their families. Moreover, television, as the rationale behind professional football, is singled out as the decisive factor in the dilution of match days and the flexibilization of scheduling ('I mean the problem is Sky TV'). As with the strict formal rationality and efficiency imperative of the fast food system, which prioritizes quantity over quality, many fans express their concern that the extensive televisual broadcasting of games throughout the week threatens and undermines the value of the experience and the emotional quality of watching football matches:

They play at different times Sunday. Sunday evening and then they play for European cups Tuesday, Wednesday, Thursday, so there is the team that want to play on Saturday[7] because it plays on Tuesday, etc. So this kind of thing I don't like at all. Okay, television is more money and people enjoy more football watching it on television. But still, it is not necessary, because the emotion, the enjoyment, would be the same. Only those like this, who want to watch football by itself, without any big feelings behind it . . . The important thing is not to destroy the emotions behind it.

(Roberto, SSC Napoli fan)

Similarly, fans observed that the social context of their fan consumption was altered through the scheduling of matches throughout the week:

It is easy to get to all games, but it is harder to meet because kick-off is at 7:45, people can't get away from work early enough to meet up.

(Samuel, Chelsea fan)

Saturdays and Wednesday nights is when football should be played and no other day. I hate Sunday matches, when we played in the FA Cup semi-final '97 we played Wimbledon on a Sunday morning at 11 o'clock . . . it is horrible, it is a ritual, going in, having a drink, meeting your friends, having a chat.

(Jarrett, Chelsea fan)

Because of television's dominance of football schedules, the consumption context of *in situ* football has thus been transformed in parallel with the decentred and individualized consumption of football on television. While fans are still able to arrange to attend games at the ground, the flexibilization of schedules leaves little or no space for the communal context ('having a drink, meeting your friends, having a chat') of ground visits. Despite attending the game *in situ*, such fans consume football matches in an increasingly similar fashion to their televisual counterparts. This transformation of the consumption patterns of modern leisure practices such as football also sheds a different light on the arguments concerning the proliferation of the post-Fordist stage of flexible accumulation. Even if processes of production have become more flexible and niche-orientated – although the concentration of markets for football teams and the increasing link between large-scale TNCs and football clubs points in the opposite direction – then this has not led to a flexibilization of consumption choices for most fans and spectators.

Calculability

The notion of calculability describes principles by which enterprises seek to create impressions of added value for consumers. The emphasis on quantity is the most apparent strategy employed in this context. Ritzer defines (1996: 59) calculability as 'an emphasis on things that can be calculated, counted, quantified. In fact, quantity (especially a large quantity) tends to become a surrogate for quality.' In pursuit of this strategy McDonald's and its competitors seek to emphasize the measured, rational dimensions of their products, labelling them 'Big Mac' or 'Quarter Pounder' (Ritzer 1996: 61). Little or no attention is paid to what lies beyond the mathematically quantifiable dimensions, how the product tastes, what effects it has on the human organism or whether it is produced in an ecologically sustainable way. Modern sports share with McDonaldized systems this focus on formally quantifiable systems. According to the laws of Association football, the quality of a goal scored is irrelevant: the match-up between two teams is summarized in the ultimate standardized form of two single numbers.[8] Goals and points, RBIs and home runs, records and league tables determine success or failure in the world of modern sports.[9] Given this common emphasis on calculability and quantifiable information such as 'the record or the size of a burger', sport becomes the ideal vehicle to articulate McDonaldized enterprises' message of quantifiable high performance. In turn the sports industry has sought to emulate this formal rational emphasis on calculability. Ritzer refers (1996: 73–4) to the measures taken in professional basketball as well as baseball in order to secure high-scoring games, thus prioritizing (formally measured) quantity.[10] Likewise football clubs and associations have sought to maximize the number of goals scored and the time played.[11]

Off the pitch, the way in which football matches and tournaments have been marketed also places the emphasis firmly on calculability. Whether in relation to

World Cups, European Championships, the Champions League or even domestic competitions, the event is described as the 'biggest match of the year' or
'the biggest tournament ever'. As many games in the past have demonstrated,
the 'biggest' matches are often a long way from being the most enjoyable. A
further attempt to sustain a certain quantity of play can be seen in the sport's
governing bodies' endeavour to minimize loss of time through injuries by order-
ing that injured players must be immediately carried off the pitch and treated
elsewhere. As the automated drink dispensers in fast food restaurants guarantee
an exact 0.4 litre of every soft drink, the reduction of injury breaks aims to guarantee fans a more or less precise 90 minutes of play. Thus the search for
calculability in itself furthers the standardization of the game.

Control

The increased control over production and consumption processes by producers
constitutes a further dimension of McDonaldization. In McDonaldized systems
control is achieved through the replacement of human with non-human technologies. 'The great source of uncertainty, unpredictability and inefficiency in
any rationalizing system is people – either those who work within it or those
served by it. Hence, the efforts to increase control are usually aimed at people'
(Ritzer 1996: 101). At first sight, these observations do not translate easily to
the football industry as they do not accurately reflect the power relations
between workers (professional footballers and managers) and employers
(clubs).[12] It is, however, the degree to which McDonaldized businesses seek to
control their customers that bears a striking resemblance to professional football.
Ritzer refers (1996) to the efforts by fast food franchises to regulate customer
conduct on their premises as well as to minimize the time they spend in the
restaurant. The plain, anonymous, fluorescent-lit interior of fast food restaurants
is a case in point. Football clubs are known for even more rigid measures of
control. Until the Hillsborough disaster in which 97 Liverpool supporters were
crushed to death in April 1989, spectators were routinely fenced in and directly
supervised by the police. Today the control mechanisms inside football stadia
have become more subtle, but are no less rigid. Fences disappeared in the wake
of Hillsborough, and stadia in Britain now operate on the basis of designated
seats for each spectator. This guarantees an even distribution of fans to the dif
ferent entrances of a stand and a higher degree of efficiency in the employment
of stewards and gate security as it allows the crowd to be monitored more easily.
In the following extract a Chelsea fan summarizes the implications of such strict
control for the conduct of spectators:

> It's worse at Old Trafford than anywhere. 55,000 people have to sit down
> all the time. You are allowed to stand up when they score a goal, but you
> are not allowed to stand up any other time. It is a bit like that at Chelsea.
>
> (John, Chelsea fan)

Violence, abusive singing and chanting, the use of fireworks and critical banners have thus been driven out of football stadia. While in the case of violence and racist and sexist abuse this may be morally desirable, such increased control over customers has also rewarded football clubs with increased revenues, as violence and abuse used to prevent clubs from making the most efficient use of stadia by attracting high-spending customers. The above extract also shows that such heightened control goes beyond the mere prevention of violence or abuse by determining precise ways in which a game has to be consumed. Therefore clubs have not only intensified their control over customers but also sought to select their customers from particular socio-demographic groups while marginalizing others:

> It has been the aim of clubs to make football socially acceptable. In the '80s you only had social dropouts here, now it is all about business interests. All the rich people are coming now. Many fans were banned from the stadia in the 1980s, because clubs wanted to make money.
>
> (Achim, Bayer Leverkusen fan)

This exercise of control by football clubs is a clear intervention in favour of what has been labelled somewhat mistakenly 'new consumers' (King 1998). During my fieldwork in Leverkusen a manifest conflict between new fans and organized, often adolescent fans was evident in the accounts of many spectators:

> *Jens*: If you look at our stadium, there is more comfort and more money, but the atmosphere has suffered . . . Now they build a hotel behind the fan section of the stadium, that's complete rubbish. It's like the bigwigs are looking down at the anti-social riff-raff.
> *Achim*: Yes, we won't be allowed to stand any more if the hotel is behind us.
> *Sabrina*: All the old people are already complaining if someone stands up in front of them. They should just sit somewhere on the grandstand.
>
> (Achim, Jens and Sabrina, Bayer Leverkusen fans)

The interests of these organized fan club members run counter to the more regulated and predictable, in other words McDonaldized, consumption contexts that many newer fans and spectators prefer. In the following a father of three who first developed an interest in the sport and Bayer Leverkusen about three years ago explains his preference for all-seater stadia:

> I like all-seater stadia . . . I know from a case when a fan club were standing during the entire game. Behind them was a man with a leg put in plaster and a small child and they couldn't see anything. They call themselves the true fans but to me they are just riot gangs. They don't have any class or style whatsoever. If you have got a stadium with seats, you should sit down

and enjoy it. You can stand up if something dramatic happens but apart from that you should sit down. Those who want to stand, they should put them all in one section, take the roof away and put metal barriers up and then they can stand there, yell and knock back their beer. I couldn't care. I believe, because of all the seats more cultured people have been coming, because people didn't want to stand there in the rain for one and a half hours. But they say, 'okay, I enjoy football, I have got a roof and a seat and take pleasure from the game'.

(Manfred, Bayer Leverkusen fan)

These opposing points of view are representative of the open confrontation between fan groups I noticed throughout my participant observations in Leverkusen.[13] Although the club did not directly intervene on behalf of those fans preferring to sit, it clearly furthered the transformation of its spectator profile by the introduction of what was at the time Germany's only all-seater stadium. The desire to attract certain social and, for that matter, economic groups to the stadium, while excluding others, is even more evident in the case of Chelsea FC. In the 1970s and early 1980s Chelsea, like many other professional clubs in England, Germany and other European countries, was presented with a dwindling socio-demographic bracket of fans containing almost exclusively male adolescents often prone to violence:

There was a reputation that at Chelsea were a lot of hooligans, definitely. And in the bad old days there was a lot of right-wing activity, the National Front people, a lot of racism. It was really awful at some stage.

(Will, Chelsea fan)

I have been involved in the violence of the '80s and I suppose as a teenager, although I was never a perpetrator of violence, but I certainly ran with the crowd, like a lot of us did . . . It was complete lawlessness . . . It wasn't like it is now. There weren't women. There weren't old men. There weren't families. It was a very adolescent type, aggressive crowd that followed the club and had notorious trouble.

(Dan, Chelsea fan)

Through a number of measures to control the socio-demographic profile of spectators – such as all-seater stadia, new facilities and rising admission prices – the club succeeded in driving out many of the fans who had earned the club an infamous reputation for violence and hooliganism in the mid-1980s.[14]

When I said I am a Chelsea supporter, I was seen as a hooligan . . . It is changing now, it is really. It is a different class, not the British lad class, more sort of middle class at Chelsea now.

(Will, Chelsea fan)

> I remember an away game at Fulham, a local derby, when they were turning over cars and things. It is hard to believe, I am very glad that all this has gone from football. I sometimes take my nine-year-old daughter, I have four children . . . she loves to come, but there is no way in the past you could have taken a nine-year-old child to a football match.
>
> (Dan, Chelsea fan)

The recruitment of new, economically sound spectators to the ground leads to a second level of control. Football clubs seek to select spectators according to their economic capital and to exercise control over their spending and consumption patterns through diversification.

Although diversification is not traditionally understood as a component of McDonaldization,[15] it aids us in illuminating the motivations behind the application of principles of McDonaldization. Diversifying their products from mere football to the production and retailing of consumer goods such as clothing, music and a wide range of services, football clubs aim to gain control over the consumption patterns of their fans well beyond football. Diversification efforts have physically manifested themselves in the reconstruction of stadia to accommodate new services. Both Chelsea and Leverkusen were at the forefront of such developments.[16] The idea behind the diversification of football clubs is that the fixed patterns of consumption, which fandom rests upon, can be employed in consumption areas other than football within the semiotic framing of the club. The attempts of clubs to explore the loyalty of fans appears almost shameless. In a match day programme during my fieldwork Chelsea chairman Ken Bates writes,

> Last summer Man U spent £30m on players, we spent £14m . . . This is why I am urging you to buy your insurance through us, book your holiday and travel arrangements with us, buy a CPO [Chelsea Pitch Owner] share, have a Chelsea Credit Card and book your Christmas, Birthday and business function here at Chelsea Village, stay in the Hotel and eat in the restaurants and drink in the bars . . . If you spend your money here, all the profits go towards buying the next world class player – and it costs you nothing because you spend the money anyway.
>
> (Ken Bates in *Chelsea*, 1 May 1999)

It goes without saying that fans are actually asked to spend money well in excess of their usual spending.[17] However, as few Chelsea fans I interviewed considered the diversified business interests of Chelsea Village plc related to the club as their object of fandom, its commercial success has been limited:[18]

> I am not someone who goes into the Megastore very much. Sometimes I have a drink in the Shed Bar, but normally, when I have a drink after a game, I would go to a pub . . . they are too expensive. They were advertising a special offer for lager in a bar in the new Matthew Harding Stand, for

£2.20 a pint. That was the special offer up to Christmas, no way I am gonna do that.

(Will, Chelsea fan)

I won't use it. They overcharge for poor quality, and I love Chelsea and I don't want them to be poor, but I refuse to believe, if I buy fish and chips for £13.99 at Fishnets, it will make me a better fan. It won't. I drink away from the ground.

(Jarrett, Chelsea fan)

I use the ticket office. I do not go in bars or restaurants, and I avoid using the facilities in the family section . . . because it is overpriced and rubbish. They could do a little bit more for it.

(Ken, Chelsea fan)

However, whether fans choose to use or to avoid the new rationalized and diversified service football clubs offer in and around modern stadia, the context of their fandom is ultimately affected by it. The McDonaldized structure of such services leads to new requirements on the overall policy clubs pursue. The large investments in hotels, restaurants and other diversified facilities trigger the necessity for clubs such as Chelsea FC to attract spectators from places well outside the London area, preferably abroad, who will be inclined to spend more on their 'special day' than regular visitors.[19] Through diversification, which in turn follows the principles of rationalization inherent in McDonaldization, football clubs have thus come to increasingly resemble other sections of the leisure industry such as theme parks, which have frequently been identified as an expression of postmodern and hyperreal dimensions of contemporary leisure (Eco 1986; Ritzer 1998; Bryman 1999).

Predictability

The application of the final category of McDonaldization to spectator sports seems most paradoxical at first sight. The enjoyment of sport is generally understood to be dependent on the unpredictability of its outcome. Yet Ritzer observes (1996) how professional teams in, for instance, baseball have furthered the predictability of sport itself through dome stadia and artificial surfaces. Rather than focus on the actual game, I will concentrate here on the increasing predictability of the consumption context of sport. Ritzer describes the role of predictability in rationalized systems as follows:

In a [rationalized] society, people prefer to know what to expect in most settings and at most times. They neither desire nor expect surprises . . . From the consumer's point of view, predictability makes for much peace of mind in day-to-day dealings . . . To managers and owners, predictability makes it easier to manage both workers and customers. It also makes other things easier such as anticipating needs for supplies and materials, personnel requirements, income, and profits.

(Ritzer 1996: 79)

In this sense, the transformations in the production and therefore the consumption of modern football have made football as an event – rather than the game itself – more predictable. Attending football games was previously associated with various unpredictable factors. Fans had to stand wherever they found a place. Old stadia with open architecture offered no protection against the elements. With hugely varying attendance figures, the atmospheric quality of the game varied significantly. Today clubs have sought to largely eliminate such variables. Leverkusen's BayArena as well as Chelsea's Stamford Bridge are prime examples of such efforts. Both grounds are all-seater stadia in which each spectator is assigned a fixed seat. Roofing protects fans from rain and extensive sun exposure. At Leverkusen's BayArena the club has even installed radiators in the roof construction which heat the stands during the winter months. The comparatively small capacity of both grounds guarantees near sell-out crowds and accordingly the appropriate atmosphere at every match. Modern plastic seats with integrated back support promise maximum comfort, almost comparable to sitting arrangements at home. It is indeed in juxtaposition with the unrivalled degree of predictability the home offers that football clubs are seeking to maximize the predictability of the *in situ* consumption of football. Television as a home consumed medium sets the pace for the demand for predictability in contemporary football. No form of football consumption is more predictable and surprise-free than the consumption of the televisually transmitted images of the game in one's own living room. The efforts of football clubs to increase the predictability of football consumption thus are a direct response to practices of consumption fostered through television.

The heightened predictability of sports events is in turn based upon principles of standardization. As Ritzer argues (1996: 79), 'rationalization involves the increasing effort to ensure predictability from one time or place to another'. For time and place to become predictable they must be standardized and become therefore interchangeable. McDonald's restaurants all over the world offer, with minor variations, the same menu around the clock. In a similar fashion football has developed supranational competitions that are based on standardized formats and are accessible from most quarters of the world. Interestingly, the consumption of standardized, supralocal competitions such as the Champions League or national leagues is often directly interrelated with the usage of other McDonaldized services, particularly fast food:

McDonald's has a particular meaning – it just stands for football. When we are going to away games, you just go and eat something quickly at McDonald's.

(Dominik, Bayer Leverkusen fan)

In this extract the predictability of fast food systems fits well into the require-ments of fans who despite travelling seek the highest possible degree of predictability. While fans can expect similar conditions and levels of comfort around the country, McDonald's offers them an equally unsurprising range of food. A prime example of standardization and predictability in the football industry is the – coincidentally McDonald's-sponsored – UEFA Champions League. All games are played at 19:45 GMT or BST, as appropriate.[20] Participat-ing clubs are required to display identical billboard advertisements; the size and layout of match programmes are regulated, as are the size, colour and design of the tickets to Champions League matches. Bayer Leverkusen fan Dominik recalls his experiences during Bayer's first Champions League season, 1997/98:

> The Champions League was just horrible. Everything was regulated, what the programme has to look like, what interviews you are allowed to do, how long they are, just everything.
>
> (Dominik, Bayer Leverkusen)

As Dominik notes, the televisual representation of the Champions League was even more regulated than the event at the ground.[21] The Champions League thus offers a highly predictable consumption experience. Like the patrons of fast food restaurants, spectators face little if any surprises when attending a Champi-ons League match. They can follow the Champions League regardless of their actual location in Europe, or – given the Champions League's global redistribu-tion – around the world. A number of fans welcome the standardization and predictability of contemporary football and of the Champions League in particu-lar. The fixed times and dates of the competition, the universal availability and the broadly coherent level of play were seen by these fans as advantages of the competition. Pascal explains his preference for Champions League football as follows:

> You don't meet up when some unimportant, small team plays anyone else. But it is just, Wednesdays, you just know, it is Champions League. You just know it is going to be a good game. And even if it is like [Bayern München v. Bröndby Copenhagen], you can see another attractive game like Inter v. Real and Barcelona v. Manchester.
>
> (Pascal, football fan)

Fans whose fandom is largely based on televisual consumption often explain their preference for the Champions League with what they consider the similar quality of the games. Rather than taking the risk of watching matches involving smaller domestic competitors, they believe the match-up of European top teams guarantees a certain degree of entertainment. Another fan, following football exclusively through television, explains why he prefers the Champions League to domestic competitions:

> The teams in the Champions League are the only teams that are good enough to watch really. Kiev, for example, they play really good football . . . The Champions League games are full of highlights, they are really good games, every single year.
>
> (Moritz, Bayern München fan)

Due to its standardized global distribution the Champions League has attracted viewers outside Europe as well:

> I am more attracted to the Champions League than for example the Premier League . . . There are some good games that you don't see very often, so that is really attractive to see that.
>
> (Pablo, Boca Juniors fan from Argentina)

To other fans the predictability of the availability rather than the quality of Champions League football is the main advantage of the standardized format of the competition. Chelsea fans living in Belgium, Norway and outside Europe displayed a particular interest in European cup competitions and the Champions League:

> *Espen*: If you are going to enter the Champions League, that will be our number one priority.
> *Roar*: Yeah.
> *Espen*: For me I would rather lose the league [English Premier League] and win the Cup-Winners' Cup again.
>
> (Espen and Roar, Chelsea fans from Norway)

> To me the Champions League is particularly important.
>
> (Jerrell, Chelsea fan from South Africa)

This leads us back to the earlier discussion of globalization and deterritorialization. As the Champions League offers a standardized product of universal availability, dimensions of time and place are eroded. The rationalization of football, which is itself rooted in the conditions of industrial formal rationality, forms the precondition of the increasing independence of consumption from physical or structural referents such as time, place, class or other socio-demographic factors.

Thus there are two important conclusions from my analysis so far. Firstly, I have demonstrated the profound and lasting effects the application of formal rationality in the production of football has on the construction of fandom. Changing schedules and McDonaldized services affect the individual consumption context as much as the wider patterns of the everyday life of fans. Secondly, the object of consumption is reshaped through rationalization and McDonaldization. Visits to the ground and the viewing of games on television emerge as increasingly uniform and standardized, reflecting the formal rational principles of efficiency, calculability, control and predictability.

In this sense the rationalization and McDonaldization of football constitute the economic ground upon which its current cultural order rests. It is important to remember that processes such as McDonaldization result from a continuity of industrial production rather than from a sharp departure from Fordist regimes of capitalist production. This becomes particularly visible by identifying the historical context out of which post-war processes such as McDonaldization arose:

> McDonaldization did not occur in a historical vacuum; it had important precursors that remain important to this day. These precursors provided the principles – of the assembly line, scientific management, and bureaucracy – on which fast food restaurant chains were built. Furthermore, they provided the ground these chains needed to thrive – large numbers of factory workers and bureaucrats who worked great distances from their suburban dwellings, who possessed automobiles to transport them not only to and from work but also to and from the fast food restaurants they increasingly needed and desired, and who visited the shopping mall that would house many fast food restaurants and their rationalized derivatives.
>
> (Ritzer 1996: 32–3)

The origin of McDonaldization not only in particular production regimes but also in a particular cultural landscape, the American suburb, points to a third, crucial dimension in the analysis of the McDonaldization and rationalization of football: its profound impact on human landscapes and the relation between place, space and consumption.

Place, space and standardization

The landscapes of professional football such as stadia have been dramatically transformed by processes of rationalization. Simultaneously, the consumption of football has increasingly shifted away from stadia and grounds to the spaces of consumption created by the mass media, most notably television. In both cases the very features constituting 'place' have come under threat. Before turning to the further investigation of these transformations, the notion of 'place' requires further clarification. Both 'space' and 'place' have been used with different, sometimes diametrically opposed, meanings. While Michel de Certeau (1984) defines space as practised and frequented place, the sense in which I intend to use both terms runs contrary to such a definition. Seeking to express the opposition between place and rationalized placelessness, I draw on a different definition of place:

> Place, as defined here . . . is place in the established and symbolized sense, anthropological place . . . We include in the notion of anthropological place

the possibility of the journeys made in it, and the language characterizing it. And the notion of space, in the way it is used at present . . . seems to apply usefully, through the very fact of its lack of characterization, to the non-symbolized surfaces of the planet . . . The term 'space' is more abstract in itself than the term 'place', whose usage at least refers to an event (which has taken place), a myth (said to have taken place) or a history (high places). It is applied much the same way to an area, a distance between two things or points . . . or to a temporal expanse . . . It is thus eminently abstract.

(Augé 1995: 81–2)

Augé's distinction between place and space points to the need to understand places as intrinsically human territories that bear reference to their human construction. Places in this sense are, as Silverstone argues (1994: 27), 'human spaces, the focus of experience and intentions, memories and desires.' Yet, such places have come under threat from the regime of formal rationality. The geographer Edward Relph has summarized (1976: 118) such rationalized places as a placeless geography 'in which different localities both look and feel alike, and in which distinctive places are experienced only through superficial and stereotyped images, and as "indistinct and unstable" backgrounds to our social and economic roles'; the consumption of football through television constitutes a process in which 'distinctive places are experienced only through superficial and stereotyped images'. Taking this superficiality to its extreme – the reduction of all levels of experience to vision and sound – television represents a placeless space. Before pursuing this line of thought further, the shift within football towards placeless environments in terms of physical rather than televisual space is worth exploring. For Relph (1976) placelessness manifests itself in five dominant features: firstly, Relph notes (1976: 18) an 'other-directedness' in places that can be detected in landscapes created for tourism and consumption, such as entertainment districts and theme parks. He singles out 'Disneyfied' and 'museumfied places' as 'synthetic or pseudo places'. I have illustrated such other-directedness in places in the case of diversified football stadia, which now offer a theme-parkesque range of services. The conversion of football grounds into increasingly regulated all-seater stadia reflects a second feature of placelessness: the 'uniformity and standardization in places' (Relph 1976: 118). In the extracts below, football fans acknowledge and deplore the increasing interchangeability of football stadia:

I think some top teams are very much alike in most countries.

(Remi, Bayern München fan)

All stadia will more or less look alike. Maybe not in terms of every architectural detail, but there is a tendency towards multi-functional stadia.

(Marco, MSV Duisburg and AC Milan fan)

People take more holidays, get broader minded, but in a way everything becomes the same, really. Sometimes you forget where you are. I think that's a shame . . . Because it is so much composed of other places, clubs lose that local element.

(Vanessa, Manchester United fan)

Everyone builds a nice, new stadium, it all looks pretty much the same.

(Thilo, Preußen Köln fan)

Alongside football stadia, 'new towns and suburbs, industrial commercial developments, roads and airports' as well as 'international styles in design and architecture' are further examples of such uniformity (Relph 1976: 118). Thirdly, placelessness is marked by the 'formlessness and lack of human scale or order in places' (Relph 1976: 119). Sports stadia, ranging from the Nazi-built Olympic stadium in Berlin to the towers of the old Wembley, have often suffered from such gigantism in which 'individual features are unrelated to cultural and physical setting'. Football stadia often share the architectural style and the lack of human scale apparent in other venues of mass production such as factory halls. The outside of Nottingham Forest's City Ground (see Figure 6.1 overleaf), for instance, bears a remarkable resemblance to the industrial appearance of factory halls, airport terminals, multiplex cinemas or shopping centres.

The tendency towards formlessness and lack of human scale has been enhanced by the rationalization and partial suburbanization of football landscapes. While inner city stadia, such as Arsenal's (soon to be abandoned) Highbury stadium, are embedded in local housing and neighbourhoods, new rationalized stadia, built in the metropolitan suburbs, such as the Stade de France in Saint-Denis, or along motorways, such as the Giants Stadium in New Jersey, are characterized by an increasing absence of human scale and order. Finally, Relph identifies (1976: 119) 'place destruction' and the 'impermanence and instability of places' as further features of placelessness. While these two aspects are not as prominent within the landscapes of modern football as those discussed above, cases such as the abandonment of grounds like Sunderland's Roker Park and the above-mentioned Highbury stadium (in 2005), or the ongoing redevelopment of stadia like Stamford Bridge or Leverkusen's BayArena, further verify the largely placeless nature of modern football stadia.

The growing placelessness of the landscapes of professional football reflects the search by football clubs for maximum efficiency, control, predictability and calculability. As a result football's landscapes have become standardized and interchangeable, lacking historical and human referents. Fans critical of the standardization of football often identify consumerism and the speeding up of consumption in McDonaldized systems as the causes of such developments:

Apart from the size, most stadia will look like Leverkusen in a few years' time. That all starts with everything that is taking place around the game,

Figure 6.1 The outside of Nottingham Forest's City Ground

like American football in the USA. All the party and everything, restaurants, hotels and everything that is now coming to the foreground.

(Thomas, Bayer Leverkusen fan)

Everything is becoming short lived and fast moving, American chains: fast food, döner, pizza, whatever. And the same is happening in football.

(Axel, Bayer Leverkusen fan)

The critique of the standardization of football is first and foremost directed at football's McDonaldized structures and competitions. While Perry describes (1998: 153) McDonaldization as a form of global standardization, the semiotic emptying of places represents the physical equivalent to the standardization of everyday products such as food, adding to the long list of irrational consequences of formal rationality.

This tendency towards placelessness stands in sharp contrast to the 'topophilic' nature (Bale 1993) of football fandom and its heightened emphasis on place and territory expressed through various fan practices. Yet placelessness is nevertheless intrinsic to modern sports and football. Bale argues (1998: 267) that historically 'the football landscape ought to be one of placelessness'. Bale's claim coincides with my assessment of football as rooted in the rationalization framework of industrialism and its active employment of formal rational regimes leading to its integration into a global capitalist system. Consequently, the rationalization of football landscapes resulting in increasing placelessness is inherent in the historical context and the economic structure of football. Bale develops this argument by claiming that the tendency towards placelessness in football is reflective of the very nature of the sport:

In most areas of life where placelessness exists it seems to result from factors *extrinsic* to the activity upon which it is imposed. For example, McDonald's restaurants do not *have* to be the same in order for hamburgers to be produced. Likewise, suburban homes do not *have* to be the same for purposes of residential occupation. High rise buildings do not *have* to be standardised for office work to take place. It may be more efficient and more rational but it is not absolutely necessary. Placelessness in such contexts . . . is not intrinsic to the activities carried out at the places. In sport, on the other hand . . . placelessness *is* intrinsic to the activity involved. It is a part of the norms of sport, a part – often hidden – in its underlying (and sometimes conflicting) ideologies of fair play and achievement orientation.

(Bale 1998: 268)

In other words, the ideology of football strives for placeless environments: 'football seeks to eliminate place (a unique area or peopled space) and replace it with space – or non-place or placelessness' (Bale 1998: 268), as the fair play and achievement orientation of football express the rational requirements of modern capitalism. Both Bale's argument and mine rest upon the assumption that standardization serves as a crucial premise of placelessness (Bale 1998). In turn the standardization of place creates the semiotically emptied environments contributing to football clubs' growing lack of referentiality and thus 'contentlessness'.

The contentlessness of football clubs is highlighted in the emergence of, in Bale's words (1993: 179), 'super-clubs'. While an increasing number of transnational 'super-clubs' are followed by a growing number of fans around the world, many smaller, locally rooted and less rationalized clubs are threatened with extinction. Smaller clubs are under increasing commercial pressure from large, televisually omnipresent super-clubs.

> The small clubs are being pushed to the margins. HJK Helsinki has to play eight times to qualify for the Champions League. Why can't just one national champion play against another national champion?
>
> (Richard, Bayer Leverkusen fan)

Again, the McDonaldization framework helps us to analyse this concentration process. While small local restaurants offering authentic cuisine have to compete with global, rationalized fast food corporations, small football clubs playing in lower divisions with a local following are confronted by diversified super-clubs who draw their income mainly from their global televisual redistribution. These super-clubs, then, in turn express the larger rationalization framework of contemporary societies:

> In the future the mega-clubs will stage dramatic spectacles on a continental sporting stage . . . The achievement space of sports mirrors that of society with its motorways, supersonic airline networks, concrete tower blocks, and shopping malls – straight-lined and efficient but often bland and boring. Such landscapes of achievement will be a response to the didactics of sport as a business and, at the same time, its associated concerns with the *citius, altius, fortius* ethos and the safety and comfort of spectators. But as in other modern landscapes they will make people feel less like persons and more like things (Gregory 1989: 370) . . . The super-clubs will provide spectacles which may symbolize community but it will only *symbolize* it. At this level at least, and in David Harvey's words, 'place and community' will have given way to 'space and capital'.
>
> (Bale 1993: 179)

Bale correctly underlines the mirror function of sport in relation to modern industrial capitalism and the degree to which place has been transformed into space in the consumption of contemporary football. Moreover, he identifies the implications of the application of formal rationality as 'bland and boring'. Blandness notably emerges as the modus operandi of the diversified standardization of rationalized production regimes, as a form of semiotic emptiness. In McDonald's restaurants we do not find exceptionally spicy or adventurous food. There is no room for traditional dishes or for specific tastes. Instead McDonald's caters for its patrons with what it perceives to be the lowest common denominator. The Big Mac has become a global and universal food item thanks to its lack of any specificity in taste. Football's super-clubs are of course not predominantly in the business of producing burgers – although most of them do sell their own burgers now – but of producing fan texts. Through the employment of formal rational production processes clubs have aimed to produce texts that represent their version of the smallest common denominator. Because of global televisual redistribution, such clubs are accessible in most quarters of the world and derive their popularity, just like McDonald's, from the plain and uniform products they offer around the world. Hence, the attractiveness of professional football clubs in the age of mass consumption is largely based upon their textual openness bordering a semiotic zero level. As we have seen in the various accounts of fans, there is no common reading of clubs such as Chelsea or Bayer Leverkusen. For their increasingly standardized nature and structure such clubs have no generally recognized a priori meaning. Similarly, as Bale argues, clubs have largely eliminated their links to actual places or communities. They are, in other words, the Big Macs of modern sports.

In that they represent no pre-given meaning, clubs are inoffensive to any potential consumer and, moreover, provide ideal spaces of self-reflection. I have identified self-reflection and the construction of a categorized 'we' between the club and the fan as the modus operandi of football fandom. As football clubs such as Manchester United, Juventus Turin and Bayern München produce increasingly polysemic, open texts, they attract fans from diverse geographical, social, cultural and economic backgrounds. In the same way as football's landscapes are becoming placeless, football clubs grow increasingly contentless. This contentlessness forms the premise of their universal accessibility. The textual openness of clubs based upon rationalization and standardization is in turn embedded in the exchange logic of capitalism, which in itself is standardizing. Whereas football clubs historically represented certain cultural, social or geographical groups, the focus on monetary profits – with money as the ultimate standardized exchange value – has made the privileging of particular social and cultural groups – those economically most potent aside – undesirable. Similarly, the interest in global markets reflects the universal interchangeability of money.

I will further illustrate this with a number of examples. As Bradley in his study of Scottish football (1995) observes, the two Old Firm clubs Glasgow Rangers and Glasgow Celtic – as well as many other Scottish clubs – have traditionally been associated with certain religious groups, which in turn express cultural, political[22] and social differences. Similar cases are evident in many other European countries including Spain, Belgium and Turkey[23] (Duke and Crolley 1996) as well as around the world (Kuper 1994; Taylor 1998). In the course of the increasing commercialization and globalization of football, these clubs have actively sought to overcome the particular socio-political and cultural concepts they have traditionally signified. Glasgow Rangers, for example, a club that has repeatedly stressed its eagerness to join a large-scale European league, has sought to dissociate itself from its traditional semiotic meaning. In 1989 Rangers broke their tradition of employing only Protestant players and signed a former Celtic player and Scottish Catholic Maurice Johnston. In his account of the transformations of Scottish football, Moorhouse (1991) linked this ground-breaking move with the internationalization and professionalization – and, we might add, rationalization – of the game. Today, the question of the religious affiliation of Rangers players has ceased to bear widely perceived relevance.[24] Although Rangers, at least within Scotland, continues to be perceived as a Protestant and Unionist club, it has sought to establish itself as a 'normal' European club, aiming at the textual openness of its competitors throughout the continent. Thus Rangers have partly successfully abandoned their historical referents. Interestingly, football clubs located in the core regions of global consumerism are generally those that have reached the highest degree of semiotic emptiness and referentlessness, while clubs on the semi-periphery and periphery of global consumerism continue to be of direct political, cultural or social signification value.[25] My investigations of Bayer Leverkusen and Chelsea FC verify this point. Located in the consumerist heartland of Europe, both clubs have attempted to overcome their historical referents as a TNC-controlled club in the case of Bayer and as a club with a violence-prone hooligan following in the case of Chelsea FC. The largely divergent readings of their object of fandom by Chelsea and Bayer Leverkusen fans indicate the degree to which both clubs have succeeded in constructing polysemic fan texts that allow ever wider possibilities of reading.

Within the standardized and diversified landscapes of football, super-clubs are turned into the plain spaces that fans employ as spaces of projection and reflection. Nowhere in football are non-place and contentlessness realized as much as in the spaces of vision offered by television. The rationalization potential of television lies in its unparalleled capacity to multiply, represent and simulate games endlessly. However, television does not reproduce the game *event* itself but merely a *vision* of the event. Meyrowitz has argued (1985: 117) that in the realm of electronic mediation the definitions of situations and behaviours are no longer determined by physical location. In the case of television football the game, which forms the key fan text, is separated from its territorial environment. Hence the game event, which *in situ* spectators experience with all senses, is reduced to the dimensions of vision and sound. The consumption of such environments matches Relph's (1976) description of placeless environments. Despite the increasing placelessness of football landscapes, even the most rationalized and placeless stadia fall short of the far reaching elimination of the difference between places that occurs when they are represented on television. The previous example of Glasgow Rangers illustrates this point. Although Rangers' Ibrox Park is a modern and rationalized stadium, its traditional signification value has not been fully eliminated. It is still located in a distinct territorial place and frequented by a large number of supporters to whom Rangers represent principles such as Unionism and Protestantism. Catholic supporters are still unlikely to want to watch, let alone support, Rangers under such circumstances. Yet in the televisual broadcasts from Ibrox most of these geographical, social and political referents are eliminated. Televisual representation, by predominantly focusing on the playing field, reduces the signification capacity of clubs to the colours of their shirts and their style of play. The broadcast of Rangers' matches in, for example, the Champions League is equally accessible to fans from all social, cultural and religious backgrounds across Europe. In their televisual representation Rangers become freed from their traditional signification value. On television the club becomes placeless and contentless.

Place and geographical territory, alongside a wide range of cultural, social and historical referents, have thus disappeared in the televisual representation of football. The fandom of those following football predominantly on television is independent of the actual geographical location of their club. I have already referred to the number of Bayern München fans I interviewed in the Rhine region. Despite the fact that their fandom often forms a central pattern of their everyday life, the experience of place is absent from their fandom:

> *Lukas*: I shouldn't be telling this to anyone, but I have actually never been to the Olympiastadion [Munich's home ground]. I have never been to Munich. I have never been to Munich at all, not the city, not the stadium, nothing.
> *Bengt*: I have been there once, when I was ten or eleven, but there was no game or anything.
>
> (Lukas and Bengt, Bayern München fans)

> *Question*: Have you ever been to Munich, then?
> *Wojtek*: No, never . . . I have heard though it is supposed to be a very nice place and worth seeing.
>
> (Wojtek, Bayern München fan)

Moreover, the Bayern München fan quoted below explains that despite having been to Munich, he has no particular relationship to the place:

> I have been to Munich but not to watch any football there . . . It is a nice city, but I wouldn't want to live there. It is too expensive. Maybe football, but really it is not my idea of a place to live, I would rather live in Hamburg.
>
> (Moritz, Bayern München fan)

Similarly, many fans I interviewed in the London area supported clubs from afar through television without any other connection to the location of these clubs. This is a Liverpool fan from Malaysia, now living in London:

The truth is, I have never been there . . . but, basically, it is a beautiful city.
(Dinh, Liverpool fan)

These fans experience their object of fandom isolated from its original place and the meanings it communicates. What they experience on television is a vision of standardized playing fields, more or less identical from stadium to stadium. Place on television becomes its own simulated shadow. To television viewers, for instance, there is virtually no difference between the most fundamental distinction in terms of place in football – home and away games. For television audiences the image of the pitch and its surroundings constitutes the featureless, always similar space within which football is played and consumed. Here the above-quoted Bengt and Lukas explain their relationship to Bayern München's stadium:

> *Lukas*: No, I don't have any attachment to it.
> *Bengt*: No, me neither. It would be more upsetting for me if they would knock down the Müngerdorfer Stadion.[26] I have more a sense of home there – as sad as it is – than in the Olympiastadion.
> (Bengt and Lukas, Bayern München fans)

The central role of the mass media in furthering the tendency towards placelessness in modern landscapes is also captured in Relph's original account of placelessness:

> An inauthentic attitude towards places is transmitted through a number of processes, or perhaps more accurately 'media', which directly or indirectly encourage 'placelessness', that is, a weakening of the identity of places to the point where they not only look alike but feel alike and offer the same bland possibilities of experience. These media include mass communication, mass culture, big business, powerful central authorities, and the economic system which embraces all these . . . In short, mass communication appears to result in growing uniformity of landscapes and a lessening diversity of places by encouraging and transmitting general and standardised tastes and fashions.
> (Relph 1976: 90–2)

In addition to the standardized content Relph refers to ('tastes and fashions'), the standardized vision of television has been instrumental in creating spaces of placeless consumption. Relph emphasizes the interrelation between mass communication and placelessness. It is important to note that television, beyond constructing a placeless world in its representation of place, also contributes to the increasing placelessness of contemporary landscapes. Television, crucially, not only constitutes another manifestation of placelessness – reflecting the rationalization and standardization regime of capitalism – but occupies a key role in setting the pace of this development. Because of its central position in the lifeworld of fans, television has fundamentally changed the way place is experienced. The experience of unmediated place has itself become increasingly superficial. This superficiality is grounded in the increasingly function-orientated nature of spaces and places of consumption. On television the represented place and the physical space football are consumed in do not endorse any meaning but merely provide the context for the consumption of the actual object of fandom. In other words, the predominant function of the landscapes of football is to provide the stage for the production of the television representation of football. This is Dominik, a 22-year-old Bayer Leverkusen fan:

> In the past I went to the ground with my father and then we went home and watched football. And it was something completely different. I stood on the terraces and watched everything and on television it all seemed completely different. Today when you are in the stadium, at least that is my impression in Leverkusen by now, it is the same, whether I watch the game on television or in the stadium. Because the Haberlandstadion has just become a big box, where television takes up the largest part and the fans are just the decoration. And I feel home games are just the big packaging for it all.
>
> (Dominik, Bayer Leverkusen fan)

This account illustrates how the experience of football landscapes by *in situ* spectators has shifted profoundly and increasingly resembles the (non-)relation between place and consumption of television football. Similarly, many Chelsea fans living outside the club's west London neighbourhood yet regularly attending home games had no initial relation but football to the club's stadium and its immediate environment on and around Fulham Road:

> If it wasn't for the football, I don't think I would have ever been to Fulham Broadway. It is out of the way, and there really isn't anything else there. The nearest I would have got to it, if Chelsea weren't there, would be walking down King's Road.
>
> (John, Chelsea fan from Watford, now living in south London)

> I don't mind [the location of the ground]. Because I wasn't born and bred in Chelsea – I was in the other end of town.
>
> (Ally, Chelsea fan from east London)

> No, I don't have any attachment to the area. No, because we are in sort of a transient area.
>
> (Dean, Chelsea fan from Twickenham)

> My connection to Chelsea is purely football.
>
> (Nick, Chelsea fan from Southampton)

In these accounts the experience of the physical landscape of football resembles the experience of football on television, since fans have no relation to place except as a stage for the consumption of football. The object of fandom (the club) and its environment are semiotically divorced. As fans' experiences of place are contextual and superficial, the landscapes of modern football are increasingly placeless. Therefore clubs sustain textual polysemy and neutrality in televisual as well as *in situ* consumption. At the same time, being increasingly circumstantial, the landscapes of football grow more and more interchangeable.

However, in the discussion of the growing placelessness of spaces of consumption, it is not the actual state of landscapes but their appropriation that ultimately constitutes their meaning and significance to the lifeworlds of fans. Despite the fact that many Chelsea fans have no connection to west London or Fulham, the area surrounding the stadium on Fulham Road bears significance to their fandom, taking on a sense of home and belonging. This is John, whom I cited above explaining that he had no previous connection to Chelsea but football:

> *Question*: Do you have an emotional attachment to the ground, though?
> *John*: Yeah, I suppose I do have, I have started to get more and more. Especially since the '80s I would go, five or six times a year . . . And now, it is really just being on Fulham Road at a match day, that I have an emotional attachment to. Because that is being home – the first time at the beginning of the season, we got back, [asking each other] 'did you have a good summer?'.
>
> (John, Chelsea fan)

This extract illustrates how seemingly placeless spaces such as football stadia and their landscapes are negotiated and appropriated by fans. Over time even standardized spaces of consumption are appropriated to the lifeworld of individuals. Tomlinson (1999: 117) has made similar observations for other spaces of consumption such as supermarkets, and concludes that such non-places are not automatically culturally sterile. As they are frequented by people, non-places are filled with cultural and social significance, with human history. While non-places might be standardized and widely lacking any actual referents, they nevertheless become spaces of human interaction (Tomlinson 1999) and therefore culture. John identifies such interaction between fans as the crucial element in constructing a sense of belonging and home ('Because that is being home'). Thus even the most featureless and placeless landscapes of consumption are transformed into places of referentiality and meaning for fans.

This reminds us that conceptualizations of place and placelessness are theoretical abstractions for analytical purposes. Neither place nor non-places exist in the absolute:

> We should add that the same things apply to the non-place as to the place. It never exists in pure form; places reconstitute themselves in it; relations are

restored and resumed in it; the 'millennial ruses' of 'the invention of every-day' and 'the arts of doing', so subtly analysed by Michel de Certeau, can clear a path there and deploy their strategies. Place and non-place are rather like opposed polarities: the first is never completely erased, the second never totally completed.

(Augé 1995: 78–9)

This interaction between the opposed polarities of place and non-place is evident in the accounts of fans above. While stadia have for themselves become a place-less landscape, they are experienced as places of interaction and culture by the fans populating them. Similarly, Bale, having argued that placelessness is intrinsic to Association football, acknowledges the opposing polarities between production and consumption, between human convention and human action:

Spectators/consumers at sports events create a problem for my theory of sport as a model of placelessness because, as noted above, in even the most sterile stadium the crowd acts as a form of 'noise', creating a place out of nothing . . . We may have a synthetic isotropic plane, we may have a deterritorialized space, but because of the place-making quality of people as sports spectators it might seem that my emphasis on placelessness has been misplaced. What seems to exist instead is a constant tension between place and space in an activity where placelessness would seem to be logically paramount.

(Bale 1998: 271–2)

The divide Bale acknowledges between the structural heritage and foundations of Association football – and, we should add, its economic rational regimes – and the way it is consumed and appropriated by fans is also verified by my study. Most fans and supporters I interviewed regularly frequented rationalized, placeless stadia, yet expressed, nevertheless, a strong sense of belonging to such environments. These accounts echo the appropriation of placeless landscape to the lifeworld of fans and the resulting signification value of such spaces of consumption:

If they moved, I wouldn't like it . . . you sort of get attached to it . . . It's nice walking down there . . . especially coming back from Brighton, 'cause when I am walking down there with my dad and I am going to chat with him, and more people come to the ground. It is really nice.

(Catherine, Chelsea fan)

One Chelsea fan even accredited Stamford Bridge with transcendent importance:

I have an emotional attachment to the ground, yes. Because if I die, my ashes will be scattered there. I told the wife and kids, when I die, don't be

[sad], just my ashes on the ground, just sprinkle it, that will do . . . They couldn't move it, no, it's got to stay there, it is our home.

(Jack, Chelsea fan)

Despite the standardized and placeless landscapes of their home club, many fans experienced them as unique:

I would claim our stadium is something really special . . . It is our domain, you can see it from afar when you are on the motorway. And when the floodlights are on during dusk, it looks great. You can always say, 'this is my place'.

(Kai, Bayer Leverkusen fan)

I mean, I got proud of the place now. You like to talk about it, and I have taken people up there this season when I have tickets, other people in the office, who haven't been Chelsea fans, because I like to impress them, really . . . So, I do have an attachment to Stamford Bridge and I am quite protective of it in a way. I don't like it to be criticized.

(Dan, Chelsea fan)

Similarly, Norman describes DC United's home, RFK Stadium, an ageing multi-function arena:

It's fun. RFK Stadium rocks. I was there with 47,000 other fans for the MLS cup two years ago which United won.

(Norman, DC United fan)

Despite, or – with respect to my earlier claim concerning the self-reflective nature of fandom based upon semiotically emptied texts – because of their a priori placelessness, football stadia have become places of meaning, referentiality and history for their regular attendants, and have in turn become places of human interaction ('I was there with 47,000 other fans'). This is Louise, a 47-year-old Chelsea fan, describing the particular significance Stamford Bridge has for her:

Question: Do you have an emotional attachment to Stamford Bridge?
Louise: I do. I suppose in some respect, because I used to go there with my father, now my father is dead. And it gives me, I feel, as if I have some contact with him still.
Question: So do you have something like a sense of home there?
Louise: Yes, you feel safe, *Geborgenheit*? I would be very much against the fact if next year they were in the Champions League and we were forced to move to Wembley. I wouldn't enjoy that at all.

(Louise, Chelsea fan)

In all these accounts the places of professional football are identified as central dimensions in fans' everyday lives. Some interviewees even referred to football stadia as their 'home' or 'living room'. While the football industry has become increasingly rationalized in its modes of production, consumers have appropriated such standardized products and environments to their own socio-cultural positioning and filled the semiotic vacuum arising from placeless stadia and spaces of consumption on television with human interaction, culture and history. Bearing in mind that fandom is based upon the textual openness of football clubs, it seems that the placelessness and contentlessness reinforce rather than undermine football fandom. To some extent this is certainly true. Under the impact of rationalization, football clubs – increasingly lacking cultural, social or historical referents – have become universal and global phenomena.

However, there is an equally valid, more critical perspective on the interrelation between fandom, rationalization and television. Despite, as Bale puts it, the 'place-making quality of people as sports spectators', despite the ability of consumers to construct signification value from the most plain and featureless products ranging from Big Macs to theme-parkesque football grounds, television has had a fundamental impact on football fandom and its everyday-life context. When fans describe football grounds as their 'home' or 'living room' they also make a choice between and among spaces and places. As I have argued in Chapter 4, all human life is territorially manifested in one place or another. However, whereas in premodern times there was a fixed relation between places and their inhabitants, now the choice of home – much like group membership – is voluntary. As the interconnection between place and fans has become a matter of choice, football clubs and the communities behind them are no longer defined and represented by places, but places are defined by football clubs and fan communities. This is a female pensioner living in Radevormwald, 25 miles east of Leverkusen:

> I would move to Leverkusen because of the football alone. I like the stadium, the manager, Rudi Völler[27] and everything about and around it.
>
> (Gerlinde, Bayer Leverkusen fan)

Other fans in my study living outside Leverkusen or south-west London, respectively, expressed their desire to move to the locales they associated with their object of fandom. Such accounts verify the constructed rather than organic relationship between place and community:

> *Tina*: I live in Remscheid [20 miles east of Leverkusen], but I will move back to Leverkusen.
> *Anna*: I want to move to Leverkusen as well.
> *Chris*: We, too, all because of Bayer. I have a car now so I will just drive to work in Cologne.
>
> (Anna, Chris, Tina, Bayer Leverkusen fans)

> *Gary*: I can't imagine Chelsea playing anywhere else. I think Chelsea are extremely lucky where they are and where the ground is, and I can't think of any other football ground where you have so much choice of places to live, places to drink, smart area, safe area. When I think about going to Arsenal, going to Tottenham, going to West Ham, it is no comparison. I think, Chelsea is in a great area . . . I'd like to live there myself, I'd like to live in Fulham, that would be my ideal place to live. But, my wife doesn't want to live in London.
>
> *Question*: Is Chelsea a place you would have ever come to, if it wasn't for football?
>
> *Gary*: No. Because of where Chelsea is, and what's around it, that would be my favourite place to live.
>
> (Gary, Chelsea fan)

What I am arguing, then, is that football fans, much in the same way that they choose the communities they are part of, choose spaces in which they develop a perception of home and belonging. However, fans select between different landscapes as much as between space and place. The landscapes of international football ranging from Manchester's Old Trafford to Yokohama's International Stadium therefore reflect not only their socio-territorial position but the deterritorialized communities, who experience them televisually. In addition to its position as modus operandi of deterritorialized fan consumption, television thus emerges as the driving force behind the transformation of place itself, based on the technological trinity of televisual representation, rationalization and hyperreality. I now want to turn to the social and cultural consequences of this trinity.

Chapter 7

Television, football and hyperreality

Television, in its unique capacity to distribute visual content across vast distances nearly simultaneously, has radically shaped the premises of football consumption and fandom on a number of levels. However, as demonstrated above, electronic mass media and television in particular must not be understood as an external corruption of the game because its proliferation is rooted in the same historical configuration as spectator sports. Moreover, in the symbiosis of spectator sports and television, arising out of their common socio-economic framing, each has grown into an innate aspect of the other. However, television – which to many theorists constituted the quintessential cultural form of postmodernity – has propelled aspects and articulations of formal rationality in contemporary football to a degree that forces a shift of our focus from the analysis of television in its consequential nature to an analysis of television as social, cultural and technological form in the postmodern realm.

There are two important observations we must bear in mind in our analysis of football fandom and television. Firstly, most professional football is indeed consumed through television rather than *in situ*. Fans in the ground will hardly ever outnumber those following a game on television screens. Similarly, many fans will rarely or never attend live games:

> I wouldn't make any effort to go to a football match in London . . . the atmosphere at most of the London clubs I have been to is nasty and threatening . . . I am a television football fan generally speaking, and I read the newspapers, *Guardian*, and then I have a circle of friends whom I watch with.
>
> (Logan, Greenock Morton fan)

Similarly, even those fans who regularly attend matches at the ground engaged in extensive televisual consumption:

> When Leverkusen are not playing [at home] then I will stay here at home . . . and at half past three I turn on the radio. That usually takes till quarter past five, then I turn the radio off. At six o'clock it is *SAT.1* [highlights

programme] and at ten o'clock the *Aktuelle Sportstudio* [highlights and discussion programme on a public service channel]. It is about all on Saturdays then really, it is all about football.

(Gerlinde, Bayer Leverkusen fan)

Secondly, those fans watching football on television engage in a practice in line with the cultural and social framing of televisual consumption. This is a female Manchester United and Crystal Palace supporter from London:

[Football] is entertaining. I usually watch it on TV, so you tend to see a sort of an overview of the game. Sometimes it is a bit like watching ballet or something. I heard that sort of analogy used by the people. The movements are very graceful sometimes and you can actually see the moves on the pitch. But then also, there is the drama, what is going to happen, is your side going to make it, the really tense moments. It is very rarely boring, unlike some sports which can be. My husband is quite keen on cricket, but I can't sit down and watch cricket for five days, whereas a football match, it is two or three hours, so it is quick and fast and you usually get an outcome . . . There is also the personalities of the players. I suppose there is a sort of slight, sort of element to like, to see the attractive male body, although I am not really into that, but you know, obviously it is nice to see athletic bodies moving around. And also the colours, things like the World Cup, you see all the colourful gear, the dress of the spectators and everything else. It is a quite colourful event sometimes, like a fairground scene or something.

(Doris, Crystal Palace and Manchester United fan)

Football then fulfils desires of the audience classically associated with other forms of televisual entertainment. It is home-centred, fitting neatly into the rhythm of daily life ('it is two or three hours, so it is quick and fast and you usually get an outcome'); it transports an ongoing narrative and a sense of drama not dissimilar to popular soap operas or other television series; it is visually pleasing and colourful ('like ballet', 'like a fairground scene'). It even allows an erotic 'gaze' at the competitor, which psychoanalytical film critique has described as 'scopophilic' (Mulvey 1975). In brief, television football is first of all television with all its related everyday practices and conventions.

Identifying the televisual element of television football as central has far-reaching implications for its further analysis. As a medium of 'mobile privatization' (Williams 1974), television contributes to the rationalized organization of (suburban) modern living. Television is part of the formal rational system of modern living. Surprisingly, the literature on contemporary phenomena of rationalization has hitherto paid little or no attention to television. In contrast the study of football audiences suggests that television is an important force in the rationalization of the lifeworld of television football audiences. As television provides the framework of consumption to millions of fans, it is important to understand why television football enjoys such popularity. I asked fans what they considered to be the advantages of television football, as opposed to attending games at the ground, and under what circumstances they preferred to follow games on television. A number of fans, especially those who generally attended a considerable number of *in situ* games, singled out television's capacity to over- come territorial place and thus offer decentralized, almost universal access to games:

> The good thing about television is that you can watch games you can't attend in person, such as the European Cup.
>
> (Sandro, Bayer Leverkusen fan)

> You can see games when you are not at the ground. You also have the op- portunity to inform yourself about things that are going on elsewhere. Of course, it is not possible to be everywhere.
>
> (Marco, MSV Duisburg and AC Milan fan)

In relation to the rationalization of place on television, other fans emphasized the time-saving capacity of television, underlining the predictability of football con- sumption:

> [If you] watch it on TV . . . you don't have to queue 20 minutes to get in Fulham Broadway station at the end of the game.
>
> (Jarrett, Chelsea fan)

> The advantage is that you don't have to commute to the stadium.
>
> (Norman, DC United fan)

> I would save the hour's drive, if I watched the game at home.
>
> (Herbert, DC United fan)

> It is a completely different amount of time you have [to dedicate to attend- ing games in the stadium]. It is not only the 90 minutes of football. It is a full three to four hours and then maybe more in the evening.
>
> (Christoph, Bayer Leverkusen fan)

> The main advantage is that you don't have to go there, it takes quite a long time. A game lasts for about two hours, but including going there and coming back, you are on the road for three and a half hours.
>
> (Julia, 1.FC Köln fan)

> The advantage is, the only advantage is, if I can't afford to go to, say, Middlesbrough mid-week.
>
> (Will, Chelsea fan)

I clearly haven't gone to Blackburn or wherever, it is a hell of a long way and particularly on a week night it is impossible . . . If I was really pressed with exams, then I might be more inclined to watch it on TV, just because I haven't got the time to go through the whole thing and whatever.

(Emil, Chelsea fan)

These accounts underline how the rationalization of time and place in the tele-visual representation of football has become part of the lifeworld of fans. As in McLuhan's analysis (1964) of the mass media, time and space have 'imploded' in fans' media-bound consumption. Whereas television football is universally available, its consumption is nevertheless firmly situated within the domestic sphere. A third group of fans emphasized the comforts television offers through its homebound consumption:

Watching football at home is much, much cosier.

(Manfred, Bayer Leverkusen fan)

Well, it [television football] is less hassle, it is very convenient.

(Dinh, Liverpool FC fan)

Watching it on TV, it is the comfort of your own home.

(Rudolfo, Colo-Colo fan)

Watching football on television, I am at home, I sit in my warm living room and not outside, while it is raining . . . Just comfort in general.

(Mr Perschul, Bayer Leverkusen fan)

First of all, it is about comfort. It really makes a difference to sit at home, nice and warm during the winter.

(Pascal, football fan)

To some fans, the consumption of football was also intrinsically intertwined with other domestic activities that could not be as easily adopted as *in situ* attendance of matches:

Football and drinking beer and so on really belong together in my eyes . . . Travelling all the way to the ground, drinking something, having to get home – that's a problem, I really can't be asked to do that.

(Moritz, Bayern München fan)

Well, I think it is more comfortable, because you just watch it at home and you move around and come and go.

(Doris, Manchester United and Crystal Palace fan)

A fourth dimension of the rationalization capacity of television football has traditionally been its comparatively low cost. Thus many fans employed notions of efficiency in arguing the financial advantages of the televisual consumption of football:

> It is cheaper, a lot cheaper.
>
> (Catherine, Chelsea fan)

> Travelling up from Sussex, there is always an expense element to it . . . I suppose the disadvantages are the expense and the time that it takes up.
>
> (Dan, Chelsea fan)

> You haven't got the expense, it is a lot cheaper to watch it at home. So that's important to us, because we don't have a big income.
>
> (Doris, Manchester United and Crystal Palace fan)

Although the arrival of new technologies such as digital television and pay-per-view is set to raise the cost of television football substantially, to some viewers – especially those whose life is particularly homebound – the financial advantages of televisual consumption prevail:

> *Question*: Would you subscribe to pay-TV or pay-per-view to watch football?
> *Manfred*: Yes, I say to myself, I have got three children, I rarely get to go to the cinema or to go out at all. I don't go to any pubs, I don't drink, so I say, 'all right, I will spend some money on this'.
>
> (Manfred, Bayer Leverkusen fan)

These quotes confirm that formal rational considerations of efficiency (in terms of access, time, money and comfort) are the main reasons for choosing television over *in situ* attendance. Television allows fans to consume the maximum number of games with the least effort and at the smallest cost. To most fans television is not the preferred, but is the most formally rational, mode of the consumption of football. In the same way consumers might prefer to eat in five-star restaurants but choose McDonald's for its seeming efficiency in terms of time, availability and money, fans consume football on television because its emphasis on home-centred consumption makes it easier to integrate into the structure of industrial and post-industrial everyday life. *En passant*, television football, reflecting the patterns of a rationalized lifeworld, thereby sets the pace for the transformation not only of football at large but also of its *in situ* consumption.

The impact of television on the consumption of spectator football has thus been far-reaching. Television has fundamentally transformed the ways games are viewed and experienced by viewers. Many of these changes can be summarized as a rationalization of vision. On television the image has become both selective

LIVERPOOL JOHN MOORES UNIVERSITY
LEARNING SERVICES

and repeatable and thus seemingly efficient. Nowell-Smith (1978: 46), in his canonical essay on the televisual representation of the 1978 World Cup in Argentina, argues that unlike

> sound transmission . . . which can be almost neutral in respect of the event recorded . . . television is a process with effects: the television picture is always different from the event of which it is a picture – or, put another way, it is a different picturing from the one that one would obtain in the presence of the event itself. Even where one can legitimately talk about events, the television picture is never exactly a reproduction of one: it is always, in some way or other, a *representation* . . . The television picture . . . is always *somewhere*, and always presents an 'angle' – a point of view coming from somewhere and directed somewhere.
>
> (Nowell-Smith 1978: 46–7)

As football is televisually represented it allows for an increased efficiency in the viewing of games. The camera generally focuses on the ball, with only a fraction of the playing field visible, with alternating shots and close-ups of single players during breaks in play. Television privileges certain angles and shots, constantly following the action. Therefore television seeks to make the most efficient use of the limited space it provides. Rather than showing the whole pitch, of which some parts are empty and others only of indirect relevance to the momentary action on the field, television selects what is conceived to be crucial to the consumption of football by those in charge of the transmission of games, ranging from camera operators to directors. Like other rationalized and McDonaldized services, television offers viewers its own 'no-nonsense' approach to a football game, cut down to the 'beef' of the game, the action on the ball. To some fans I interviewed, this efficiency of vision was television's crucial advantage:

> The advantages are, you get to see everything, every a bit dodgy decision.
> (Nick, Chelsea fan)

> You can see the replays straight away, if there is anything . . . a stuffy goal, I missed a penalty decision, any controversial decision. The advantage is that you can . . . have a good look.
> (Vicky, Chelsea fan)

> Well the advantage of watching it on television, there is no obstruction of your view. You can see most angles and they show you replays and all that.
> (Brendon, Chelsea fan)

> You get the replays, you get the slow motion replays and you get extra coverage . . . If a goal is scored, you are not sure how it went in, there was

an incident, so it is not till you come home and you see it on the news, see a re-run. So you do miss that.

(Jack, Chelsea fan)

You can see the game more as a whole on TV, there are some advantages, because the camera that shows you the whole pitch, you can't always see that well when you are in a football ground, you can't always see over the people in front of you. That's what I found, I couldn't always see what is happening.

(Doris, Manchester United and Crystal Palace fan)

To these fans, television has maximized the efficiency in viewing a football game by offering maximal vision within a minimal space. While television's small screen technology per se implies a tendency towards a rationalized, 'action efficient' narrowing of the game, the ever faster cutting patterns and the increasing employment of close-ups from various angles by many broadcasters underline the effort by television professionals to heighten the efficiency and calculablity of their product.[1]

There are two immediate concerns that arise out of the televisual representation of football. The first one – which can be classified as largely modernist in nature – arises out of the growing divide between unmediated and mediated event and ultimately of the authenticity of the latter. In his investigation of the influence of television news programmes on the perception of representation of the events taking place in the British miners' strike in 1984 Philo concludes

that direct experience can have a crucial influence on how new information from the media is understood. Such direct contacts together with political culture, class experience, process of logic, and comparisons made between accounts, were the most important factor in relations between perception and belief.

(Philo 1990: 154)

Much as the participants in Philo's study with direct experience of the actual event had a significantly different relation to their televisual representation, football fans who regularly witness matches *in situ* are generally more critical of the televisual representation of football:

I remember a game, Köln versus Leverkusen, 3–3, after Bayer was up 3–1. That was the last match day of the season, nothing was at stake but their rivalry. Everybody in the stadium was raving, only a draw, but who cares. I watched the game with my father on television and he said, 'what a boring game, only plenty of blunders by the goalkeepers'. I said it was a great game and was rather angry that it was all lost in the summary.

(Sandro, Bayer Leverkusen fan)

Another fan contrasts his direct experiences at the ground with the media texts he encountered thereafter following the previously discussed clash between Graeme Le Saux and Robbie Fowler:

> It [being in the ground] is more authentic. A good example of that is the Robbie Fowler incident against Graeme Le Saux. Having been to the ground, we saw the whole thing, from where we got the free kick and the nasty tackle. I did actually see that on the telly that night. And they showed a split second of him bending over and all other people's opinions were based upon that one flick. They didn't see the rest of what was going on for two or three minutes, so in that case it did distort it.
>
> (Jeff, Chelsea fan)

Many other fans voiced their impression that the stadium experience often differed significantly from what they see in television highlights. However, at the heart of the implicit notion of authenticity employed by these fans is the assumption that mediated and unmediated events are still separate and that the latter arises out of the former. Having identified television as the driving force in the transformation of *in situ* football, such a premise is increasingly questionable. This leads me to a second concern, largely rooted in postmodern conceptualizations of social and cultural change: the increasingly simulated nature of football, acknowledging the merging between television and its object of representation. Or, as Jean Baudrillard puts it (1983: 55), 'the dissolution of TV into life, the dissolution of life into TV'.

Television football has rationalized the consumption of matches by prioritizing vision over other forms of perception such as sound (which television, of course, dramatically reconstructs) and the absent dimensions of smell, feel and touch. Following football's televisual representation, fans do not consume the game, but an image of the game. This is further verified by the privileging of vision over sound.[2] Many television viewers felt little need for the commentary or the acoustic level of television. This Chelsea fan explains his dislike of television commentary:

> I would rather not have it, really rather not have it. I find it obtrusive, I find it boring, sometimes unintelligent, they say too much . . . I think television commentaries are hangovers from radio. Then they had to fill the air space, you got to keep going. On television you don't need to do that. You can let the pictures tell the story.
>
> (Samuel, Chelsea fan)

This account verifies the predominantly visual character of television. According to Baudrillard the dominance of vision in the televisual image is in itself rationalizing, as vision is the most time-efficient form of (inter-)action:

We will be looking for something faster than communication: challenge, the duel. Communication is too slow; it is an effect of slowness, working through contact and speech. Looking is much faster; it is the medium of the media, the most rapid one. Everything must come into play instantaneously.

(Baudrillard 1990: 8)

Baudrillard's claims also apply to the consumption of contemporary football. The *in situ* consumption of matches manifests a form of communication, as spectators interact with the action on the pitch and thus actively contribute to the construction of the event. Television football, in contrast, has no room for such communication. It only allows for the quick gaze, the rapid vision of the game. The one-dimensionality of the perception of televisual texts is thus based on television's rationalization potential. In turn television football leads to a standardization in fans' vision and therefore consumption of football games. As Bale argues,

Television sport produces a landscape of sameness. Drawing on the writing of Virilio . . . we can note the difference between spectating at a sports event and watching it on television (Virilio 1991). At a football game no two people see the same event (because no two people can occupy exactly the same place) whereas the game on television is exactly what the camera saw. Spectators see this wherever they sit. Television re-places the spectator.

(Bale 1998: 273)

Bale's observations are crucial to the understanding of the cultural impact of television football. Bale emphasizes the interrelation between the standardization of vision and the relocation of spectators. Both emerge as central aspects of what Virilio calls (1998: 134) the 'industrialization of vision', which in fact is a rationalization of vision. The re-placement of spectators is verified in fans' viewing contexts:

Most of the time I watch [football] at home, of course. And usually I am alone when I am at home.

(Ricky, Fortuna Düsseldorf fan)

I almost always watch the games at home.

(Wojtek, Bayern München fan)

I watch it at home, but if it is a big game, then I will go to the pub. If it is like Arsenal v. United, United v. Chelsea, Chelsea v. Arsenal, internationals, I watch in the pub or at someone's house but in a social surrounding.

(Constantine, Queens Park Rangers fan)

Although these quotes indicate that television might be recontextualized into a communal framing by viewing with friends and family or in pubs or bars (see also Williams 1994b), they also point to the fact that the majority of television football is consumed in domestic settings and often alone. To take Bale's argument further, television football has substituted an individual perspective in a collective environment (the football stadium) with a collective perspective in an individual environment. Hence television dramatically reverses the perspective of football games. Fans' consumption of football on television has been both decentred and standardized by the experience of watching the game on television.

With this changing perspective the event itself undergoes fundamental transformations, which I want to investigate further drawing on Baudrillard's concepts of hyperreality and simulation. While Baudrillard applies the notion of hyperreality to a whole range of contemporary cultural (and technological) phenomena, television football appears to fit neatly into what Baudrillard describes as hyperreality and simulation. For Baudrillard, they are based upon – what Genosko (1994) has called – the 'exaggeration of reality' and the eventual elimination of the actual sign value and referentiality to reality:

> If we were able to take as the finest allegory of simulation the Borges tale where the cartographers of the Empire draw up a map so detailed that it ends up exactly covering the territory . . . then this fable has come full circle for us, and now has nothing but the discrete charm of second-order simulacra . . . Simulation is no longer that of a territory, a referential being or a substance. It is the generation by models of a real without origin or reality: a hyperreal.
>
> (Baudrillard 1983: 1–2)

This hyperreal, simulated condition is partially manifested in the single and collective perspective of television football. As television represents the game event with ever more varying shots, angles, positions and the fragmentation of time through replays and slow motions, it constructs a new event in itself. The televisual representation of football has become so detailed and all-encompassing that this representation – much like the map of the empire – threatens to cover the game in its entirety. Consequently, television football shifts from representation to simulation – and thereby eliminates the game as its actual referent. Moreover, the game itself is defined by its own simulation, becoming its shadow rather than point of reference. To return to Baudrillard's analogy:

> The territory no longer precedes the map, nor survives it. Henceforth, it is the map that precedes the territory – PRECESSION OF SIMULACRA – it is the map that engenders the territory whose shreds are slowly rotting across the map. It is the real, and not the map, whose vestiges subsist here and there, in the deserts which are no longer those of the empire, but our own. *The desert of the real itself.*
>
> (Baudrillard 1983: 2, original emphasis)

Today the simulacra of television football rather than the actual *in situ* attendance of football constitute the point of reference to fans. To many fans television has become the '(hyper-)real thing':

> If they broadcast live games, they are much better than being there. You can see much more on television, more than you could see in the stadium.
>
> (Wojtek, Bayern München fan)

Television offers the viewer the chance to see more than is actually visible to the human eye alone. As Baudrillard argues (1990: 11), 'the real does not efface itself in favour of the imaginary; it effaces itself in favour of the more real than real: the hyperreal. The truer than true: this is simulation'. The accounts of various fans further verify the hyperreal nature of television football:

> You see more of a game on television
>
> (Stephen, Chelsea fan)

> I see more of a football game on television, because they replay all the crucial situations.
>
> (Bengt, Bayern München fan)

> I think you get more of an overall view [of the game] on television.
>
> (Doris, Manchester United and Crystal Palace fan)

The collective, yet ultimately hyperreal, perspective of television has become an integrated part of the simulated experience of watching television football:

> If this is the pitch and you are sitting here and things are passing up in that corner you are looking over there, whereas with the cameras on your TV, you have close-ups, so I am sure you get a better view on television, you do.
>
> (Brendon, Chelsea fan)

To many fans, including a share of those attending games at the stadium, television football rather than the actual game event is the point of reference from which reality is defined. During my participant observations with groups of fans who had previously attended the game itself, the match was renegotiated in the light of the televisual representation. Goals and plays were discussed based on the multi-angle perspective of television. Similarly, many fans underline the crucial role television plays in their understanding of the game:

> Being at the ground I often think I would like to see that again now: 'what do you think, was that a penalty?'
>
> (Thilo, Preußen Köln fan)

Quite often I say, 'come on, let's go home quickly, I have taped the game and let's see whether the referee was right'.

(Chris, Bayer Leverkusen fan)

I like to see everything on television, it is also worth having it on tape . . . You want to see whether it was really a foul or not.

(Gerlinde, Bayer Leverkusen fan)

I go to the games at about 14:15 and I am back at 18:00. And from that moment onwards I am in front of the telly and watch *ran* [highlights programme] and then I watch ZDF at 10 o'clock. That kind of continues throughout the day, I watch and check out how Bayer has played. And then I also watch the repeat from *ran* during the night or early in the morning, 5 or 6 o'clock.

(Mr Schmidt, Bayer Leverkusen fan)

It should be noted that Mr Schmidt had attended the actual game only hours before. In all these accounts it is television rather than the actual *in situ* game event that is credited as the ultimate authority. Although I accept much of the substantial critique directed at Baudrillard's theoretical framework, which suffers from generalization and technological determinism (Kellner 1989), my own empirical findings support Baudrillard's notion of hyperreality in the consumption of contemporary professional football.

Far from enjoying a peaceful coexistence with reality, hyperreality and simulation erode – for their very claim of heightened reality – reality itself. This accords with Umberto Eco's analysis of the Palace of Living Arts in Los Angeles: '[The] philosophy is not, "We are giving you the reproduction so that you will want the original," but rather, "We are giving you the reproduction so you will feel no longer any need for the original"' (Eco 1986: 19).

The relation of the copies displayed in the palace to their originals, mirrors the relationship between football on television and the original game event in the stadium. Television in its early years actively employed the conventions of filmic realism in an attempt to represent the game as realistically as possible:

It may well be that some of the principles of a visual style were merely derived from the well-established conventions of realist cinema. Certainly television merely took over a lot of standard realist conventions from film-making – the 180-degree rule, the principle of complementary angles and so on . . . These conventions aimed at transparency, strengthening the claim of television to reflect events and minimizing its own active construction of representations.

(Whannel 1992: 32)

Following the emergence of new technological means of televisual representation ranging from zoom lenses to video recorders and computer animations,[3] television football has become hyperreal. In recent years, for example, 'reverse action replays' have been introduced, breaching the 180-degree rule as a main convention of representational realism. Consequently, in the hyperrealization of the game on television, the copy overshadows the original. The game event in the stadium seeks to reproduce the copy rather than vice versa. In an attempt to catch up with the hyperreal simulation of football matches on television, clubs have introduced giant video screens to their grounds to provide spectators with the same time- and perspective-fragmenting images they are accustomed to from television.[4] Bale (1998: 274) identifies such jumbotron video screens as marking 'a postmodern condition where the image is superior to reality'. To some spectators such screens offer a much-desired addition to the singular perspective at the ground:

> Highbury is excellent, nice and sharp. At Villa Park the other week, they had the whole match live, which was unusual. I haven't seen that before. So, I thought that was great.
>
> (Jack, Chelsea fan)

> When I went to Highbury recently, there was a screen. It was quite good, because you could see a lot of replays and things and you could see what happened. Sometimes in football, you look away for a second, and you look at the [screen] so it is good.
>
> (Catherine, Chelsea fan)

As the simulation of hyperreality undermines the original in these examples, the life of its own developed by the 'copy' is its simultaneous undoing. Much as according to Baudrillard (1994) music has been dissolved and disappeared in high-fidelity, the televisual representation threatens to erode the actual referents of what is meant to be represented. In approaching a hyperreal, simulated state, the event that television football means to represent becomes less and less recognizable. As Baudrillard argues,

> 'Virtual reality' is at the antipodes of the real world. As for 'high definition', it is synonymous with the *highest dilution* of reality. The highest definition of the medium corresponds to the lowest definition of the message. The highest definition of information corresponds to the lowest definition of the event.
>
> (Baudrillard 1997: 26)

Television has rewritten the narrative of football to the small screen, constantly introduced new angles, moving camera perspectives and super slow motions.[5] Thus television's emphasis has shifted from realist re-presentation towards a more spectacular dramatizing simulation, deepening the gulf between the experience of *in situ* and television football. The higher the definition of the game on television, the lower its actual relation to the event. As 'the highest definition of information corresponds to the lowest definition of the event', information is privileged over participation. As one fan observes,

> The advantage of watching it live [*in situ*] is that you are part of it.
>
> (Jarrett, Chelsea fan)

Rather than participating in the game event, mass media audiences are situated on the receiving end of a one-way communication process. On television, information has replaced participation. For fans not able to attend games *in situ*, the experience of a football game is substituted by information:

> *Samuel*: I don't enjoy watching games on television, no, or listen to them on the radio. It is just going to the game which I enjoy.
> *Question*: Are the media more like something you have to do?
> *Samuel*: Yeah, because I want to know the score.
>
> (Samuel, Chelsea fan)

The simulation of television football has divorced vision – the perceptual dimension within which television football as the copy of the game event is assessed – from experience. The degree to which the fan text, and hence the object of fandom, is reduced to semiotically minimal codes is further highlighted in the case of North American soccer fans. With Major League Soccer available mainly on cable television channels, many fans follow games through updates on the Internet, reducing the game event to its key statistics:

> When the games are away, I usually need to log onto the Internet to get coverage, since we do not have cable.
>
> (Jamie, DC United fan)

> The media coverage of soccer in the US in pathetic. ESPN claim to make an effort, and they have provided some measure of additional coverage, but my soccer news comes from the Internet.
>
> (Donald, DC United fan)

Yet, whether matches are consumed through the World Wide Web or televisually, the consumption of mediated football constitutes a dramatically different experience to live attendance. This is a fan explaining the different levels of experience between televisual and *in situ* consumption:

> I guess if you are watching one of the live games, you are seeing the full game from first to last kick and all the commentary and expert analysis, but you are not getting the experience. You are not getting the overall experience, that you get from going to the match. And the buzz from the crowd,

the journey to the match, the smell of the hot dogs, the whole feel of the
event. Obviously you don't get any of that on television.

(Dan, Chelsea fan)

To rephrase Baudrillard, in this account the 'highest definition' of television
football is synonymous with the 'highest dilution' of experience. The comparison between the experiences of watching a game on television and in the ground
confirms such claims:

I hate watching on television, well, I hate it with Chelsea in particular. I
hate not being there. I feel like I lost something, when I can't go to a
game.

(Karen, Chelsea fan)

Oh, the disadvantage is you don't get the atmosphere . . . I would much
rather be there.

(Vanessa, Manchester United fan)

[On television] there is not the atmosphere, it is not as exciting.

(Catherine, Chelsea fan)

Jim: You get all the atmosphere at the ground, you are actually there.
Matt: People smell the grass, that is one thing I like, going in, sit down.

(Matt and Jim, Chelsea fans)

In the ground . . . the atmosphere is very good. You live it much more
closely. You feel that you are there. And for some irrational reason being
there, plays a very big part in it.

(Manuel, Real Madrid fan)

The disadvantage at home is that you don't have the atmosphere. You are
not there and you look at them and, 'oh, I am not there'.

(Vicky, Chelsea fan)

I think the problem with pay-per-view and TV is, that it is no fun to watch
it . . . Sometimes, the ground is full and . . . the definite advantage of going
to a game is the atmosphere and the day out.

(Gary, Chelsea fan)

You miss out on the atmosphere and the buzz.

(Jack, Chelsea fan)

These accounts depart from the conceptualizations of hyperreality developed by
Baudrillard, and to a lesser degree also Eco, in the actual capacity of consumers –

at least of those who have experienced both original and copy – to recognize and confront the transformations of experience in the face of simulation. Nevertheless, they confirm the dramatic transformations of content and context that football undergoes in its televisual representation. This Chelsea fan links the loss of experience in televisual consumption with the collective, simulated perspective of television:

> They are two different experiences, mostly based on your point of view. If you are in a football ground and you are sitting next to somebody who watches a completely different angle, you not only get the crowd noise and the experience of being there and the feeling of being there live, but you get it from a particular point of view . . . That creates a lot of the impetus football has. And the stories and the mess, the experience of football is that you've seen it, but you haven't seen all of it . . . When you watch it on TV, the most important thing is everyone is seeing the same thing . . . And this is gradually when people, more and more, watch football on television it ceases to be a spectacle. It becomes just something on TV and it is hard to get passionate about it. European games you can't afford to travel to, you just watch them on TV, but the games you actually watch are gonna have a more profound effect on you.
>
> (John, Chelsea fan)

The loss of experience, the dominance of the image over participation and the absence of 'atmosphere' in television football, which are mirrored in the above accounts, also form the basis for Baudrillard's dystopian view on the future of the televisual representation of football:

> In September 1987, in Madrid, a Real Madrid–Naples European Cup match took place at night in a completely empty stadium without a single spectator, as a consequence of disciplinary action taken by the International Federation in response to the excess of the Madrid supporters at an earlier game. Thousands of fans besieged the stadium, but no one got in. The match was relayed in its entirety on television. A ban of this kind could never do away with the chauvinistic passions surrounding soccer, but it does perfectly exemplify the terroristic hyperrealism of our world, a world where a 'real' event occurs in a vacuum, stripped of its context and visible only from afar, televisually. Here we have a sort of surgically accurate prefigurement of the events of our future: events so minimal that they might well not need to take place at all – along with their maximal enlargement on screens. No one will have directly experienced the actual course of such happenings, but everyone will have received an image of them. A pure event, in other words, devoid of any reference to nature, and readily susceptible to replacement by synthetic images.
>
> (Baudrillard 1993: 79–80)

Baudrillard's vision of future events summons up the experience of the consumption of television football by the participants in my study: the simulation of football on television is increasingly non-referential. The event has been stripped of its context ('the atmosphere') and 'occurs in a vacuum'. In its televisual representation football becomes 'minimal' or, in other words, contentless. The simulation of football is intrinsically interrelated with the rationalization imperative of the football industry and industrial capitalism at large. Similarly, Ritzer argues (1998: 121) that new rationalized means of consumption are characterized by simulacra and simulation, referring to examples of McDonaldization that bear interesting parallels to televised football:

> Any given credit card is a simulation of all other cards of the same brand; there was no 'original' card from which all other cards are copied; there is no 'real' credit card from which all others are copied. . . Then there are completely invented foods, for example the millions, perhaps billions, of virtually identical (and simulated) chicken McNuggets, which fit perfectly Baudrillard's (1983) idea of a simulacrum as an identical copy for which no original ever existed. The original, the chicken, had the temerity to be created with bones, skin and gristle.
>
> (Ritzer 1998: 121–2)

Like televised football, Ritzer's example of rationalized simulacra, chicken McNuggets, has lost its original referent to its standardized and therefore ultimately simulated structure. To both there is no original. The resemblance of the actual event in television football is reminiscent of that between nugget and chicken. Television football parallels the easy accessibility, consumability and digestibility of finger food. The televisual representation has been carefully stripped of the 'bones, skin and gristle' of football. Thus television football equals the standardized neutrality of other rationalized and hyperreal means of consumption Ritzer describes. Having said this, the postmodern tendency towards simulation inherent in television must not be misread as a sudden or new phenomenon. Rather it constitutes a continuation of inherent forces within industrial capitalist societies. Horkheimer and Adorno's critique (1997) of the culture industry powerfully illustrates that rationalization and simulation, both intertwined with standardization, preceded contemporary phenomena such as McDonaldization and post-Fordism. Writing in 1942 they argue,

> The striking unity of microcosm and macrocosm presents men [sic] with a model of their culture: the false identity of the general and the particular. Under the monopoly all mass culture is identical . . . No mention is made of the fact that the basis on which technology acquires power over society is the power of those whose economic hold over society is greatest. A technological rationale is the rationale of domination itself . . . It has made the technology of the culture industry no more than the achievement of

standardization and mass production, sacrificing whatever involved a distinction between the logic of the work and of the social system.

(Horkheimer and Adorno 1972: 120–1)

We may disagree with Horkheimer and Adorno's assessment of the degree to which mass culture leads to an economically based *Gleichschaltung* of the individual, but their observations nevertheless illustrate the tendency towards standardization and simulation that articulates wider forces of capitalism, modernity and industrialism, that we find in contemporary (televised) football. Television, as I have argued previously, constitutes an articulation of modernity in its structure as much as in its need to target mass audiences. It has done so through principles of standardization and pasteurization which in turn are manifested in the practice of televisual representation.

Television football aims to reach viewers across divisions of age, class and gender as well as geographical frontiers. Ratings for the Bundesliga highlights programme *ran* confirm that the programme enjoyed comparable popularity throughout all 16 German states (see Table 7.1). Despite the often heavily male and chauvinistic connotations of television football, females still account for approximately a third of the audience.[6] Television's universality and inoffensiveness is based upon the visual modes of representation. The elimination of the game's context through its multi-angle representation on television has transformed football into a standardized, universally accessible spectacle. The traditional visual conventions in the televisual representation of football further confirm television's bid for textual neutrality. Nowell-Smith has argued (1978: 51–2) that the positioning of a lead camera on the halfway line is designed to 'reaffirm impartiality' and hence to construct authority through a seemingly neutral capturing of the events on the field. The fixed positioning of the lead camera has also standardized televisual representation and contributed to the elimination of contextual differences.

The audio level of commentary also furthers the referentlessness and neutrality of the televisual representation of football. The study of a college audience watching a televised ice hockey game by Comisky *et al.* (1977) indicates the significance of commentary in constructing the sporting narrative.[7] They conclude that 'there can be no doubt . . . that commentary can substantially alter perception of play' (Comisky *et al.* 1977: 152). While I witnessed how television viewers negotiate the commentary on television football during my fieldwork, commentators, presenters and panellists nevertheless set the framework of the discourses surrounding the consumption of television football. These frameworks are increasingly hyperreal and referentless in themselves, as they tend to ignore the often specific (geographical) context of clashes between certain teams and substitute for it standardized, universally applicable polarities. This point is also evident in the broadcasts fans consumed during my study. During a broadcast of the German television highlights programme *ran* on 21 November 1998, the commentary on the game between VfL Bochum and Bayer Leverkusen

Table 7.1 Ratings for *SAT.1* Bundesliga *ran*, 7 November 1998, 18:00–20:00

Target audience	TV population		Audience			
	Basis		Reach		Market share	Structure
	millions	structure %	millions	%	%	%
FRG viewers total	71.37	100.0	6.83	10	29.2	100.0
Viewers FRG West	56.71	79.5	5.35	9	30.2	78.4
Viewers FRG East	14.66	20.5	1.48	10	26.1	21.6
Hamburg	1.37	1.9	0.15	11	37.3	2.2
Bremen	0.57	0.8	0.06	10	25.6	0.8
Schleswig-Holstein	2.48	3.5	0.23	9	30.2	2.2
Niedersachsen	6.99	9.8	0.60	9	26.7	8.8
Nordrhein-Westfalen	15.26	21.4	1.55	10	31.0	22.6
Hessen	5.03	7.0	0.51	10	27.3	7.5
Rheinland-Pfalz	3.51	4.9	0.30	9	31.7	4.4
Saarland	0.96	1.3	0.06	7	22.7	0.9
Baden-Württemberg	8.47	11.9	0.80	9	32.7	11.7
Bayern	10.36	154.5	1.00	10	32.5	14.6
Mecklenburg-Vorpommern	1.76	2.5	0.20	11	30.2	2.9
Brandenburg	2.40	3.4	0.18	7	20.2	2.6
Sachsen-Anhalt	2.58	3.6	0.30	11	27.7	4.3
Thüringen	2.42	2.4	0.32	13	31.8	4.7
Sachsen	4.33	6.1	0.40	9	24.7	5.8
Berlin	2.88	4.0	0.20	7	19.7	2.9

Source: GfK/PC # TV/ *SAT.1* Medienforschung.

largely ignored the local and regional roots of the two clubs – a single visual reference was made to the actual place of the event by showing the sunset over the Ruhr Stadium. Although there has been a long-standing rivalry between teams from Northrhine-Westfalia's two main regions, Rhine and Ruhr, this was not taken up in the representation of the game. Instead the commentary focused on particular players,[8] and the performance gap between the two teams that resulted in a 5–1 Bayer win. Bayer's team was described as 'commanding' and 'skilful' and as a 'goal machine'. In contrast the commentary referred to Bochum as 'young and over-determined'. The duel between the Brazilian international Zé

Roberto and Bochum defender Schindizielorz was characterized as 'the 10 million DM man against the amateur'. The polarities employed throughout the broadcast drew on dominant cultural and social distinctions and discourses, which largely ignored the local origin of the two clubs involved. This supports John Goldlust's summary (1987: 94) of the most frequently employed polarities in sports commentary:

- strength versus skill
- favourite versus outsider
- youth (enthusiasm, vitality) versus age (experience, craftiness)
- natural ability versus dogged determination
- temperament/volatility versus coolness/rationality
- innovation/unpredictability versus mechanistic discipline/rigidity
- friendship/affection versus hatred/traditional rivalry

This indicates that football commentary does not amplify geographical and regional dimensions of the competition as is often assumed in the analysis of commentary, but replaces them with wider social and cultural discourses. Day-to-day commentary on football, infrequent exceptions such as the World Cup aside, ignores territorial discourses in an attempt to offer points of identification to its heterogeneous and geographically diverse audience. Commentary is thus also 'placeless' in that it substitutes football clubs' geographical context with alternative lines of identification for its territorially diverse audience.

In conclusion, both visual and audio levels of televised football contribute to its standardization and increasing referentlessness. The standardized nature of televisual football texts and the formal rational regimes of contemporary football production are in turn rooted in the social, cultural and economic transformations reflecting processes of rationalization and globalization. On the one hand these transformations and their accompanying phenomena such as placelessness and hyperreality form the premises of fandom by leading to the production of semiotically open and emptied football texts, which allow fans to project themselves onto the club of their choice. On the other hand the rationalization potential of television and the dominance of vision in the televisual representation of football have resulted in the loss of spaces of experience and participation for fans.

Postmodern football and the limits of appropriation

The fans cited in this chapter illustrate that the preference for the televisual consumption of football is often motivated by formal rational considerations concerning variables such as time and money. Moreover, many fans rely on the televisual hyperrealization as reference point for their negotiation of texts. Yet, as the above examples demonstrate, fans are aware of the profound shifts of experience and participation in the consumption of increasingly rationalized football. In reaction to the loss of experience through the hyperreal, collective perspective and individualized consumption of television, a large number of football fans seek to recontextualize the rationalized texts of television football in communal acts of consumption:

> Most of the games we watch together. If it is a live transmission of a Lever-kusen game or the German national team or other important games, then we watch them together.
>
> (Axel, Bayer Leverkusen fan)

> Usually, whatever game really, we meet up on a Saturday afternoon. Nor-mally three to five people come here to my place to watch football. If it is an attractive game even more people come over, we watch football and then we discuss what we are doing later that night.
>
> (Bengt, Bayern München fan)

This demonstrates that however global, rationalized and hyperreal television foot-ball may be, it is consumed in a local social and cultural setting. The televisual representation of the game is reintegrated into a manifestly local and social con-text. In other words, while television football might well have been stripped of its referents, the appropriation of the televisual images by fans has the partial capacity to overcome the contentlessness of such postmodern texts. This social and cul-tural recontextualization often takes place in public spaces such as clubs or pubs:[9]

> I always watch with friends at a pub . . . I definitely won't sit at home and watch all the games by myself.
>
> (Sabine, Borussia Mönchengladbach fan)

> I started to get some idea of some notion of atmosphere when I was coming down to the pub to watch football. Which is one reason why Sky has been very good, because suddenly you start coming to the pub and you are sitting with your mates and drinking beer during the game, which you can't do when you are going to the ground. And you can stand, shout and other people shout and that is something of getting the atmosphere back to the extent that I go down to the pub to watch Chelsea play, even when they are on terrestrial TV . . . So we get some atmosphere back.
>
> (John, Chelsea fan)

Within the context of communal consumption fans recreate the modes of *in situ* consumption by breaking the formal rationalism of television through seemingly irrational patterns of reading and consumption:

> *Richard*: There have been times when we organized real television nights . . . we turned them into a real occasion.

Thorsten: Always with other people.

Richard: I can remember some games, when we decorated the television and the living room . . .

Thorsten: . . . and put up scarves . . .

Richard: Once we couldn't watch the game because the car was broke, so we decorated the car and listened to the game.

(Thorsten and Richard, Bayer Leverkusen fans)

This example reminds us of the capacity – often overlooked in the postmodern and neo-Weberian literature – of audiences and consumers to appropriate and recontextualize standardized and massified cultural texts and practices. When fans gather in large groups to watch football on television, shout and yell at the screen, discuss the action on the field and voice their support or even go as far as to decorate the television and to wear their club shirts, they subvert the formal rationalized conventions of the medium and create new forms of participation.[10] To return to my distinction between space and place, the rationalized space of television is appropriated in and to the everyday life of fans and, hence, filled with human interaction and participation. The appropriation of rationalized and standardized (and simulated) products is by no means unique to football. Fast food restaurants, for instance, which have been my point of reference in the discussion of rationalization here, are equally subject to unanticipated uses that run counter to their formal rational structure. Kellner (1999), for example, observes that McDonald's restaurants outside the USA are often put to distinctively different uses by their customers. In Thailand, for instance, McDonald's is utilized as a coffee house-style meeting place by young people as somewhere to study and socialize. Kellner (1999: 193) concludes:

> While on one level, McDonald's helps standardize and homogenize a global consumer culture, on another level it brings variety, diversity and novelty to many parts of the world, thus contributing to the creation of a hybridized global popular culture.

The same argument can be made for rationalized television football. Football fans appropriate the televisual representation to their everyday life context. In their reading of the televisual text – as the many examples ranging from the group of Norwegian Chelsea fans to the local enthusiasts in Leverkusen demonstrate – they reflect their socio-economic and cultural positioning. On the other hand, Kellner also points to the fact that McDonald's nevertheless standardizes and homogenizes. Indeed, even if many McDonald's customers in, for instance, Thailand subvert McDonald's formal rational regimes, many of its irrationalities still apply, as customers, for example, still consume ecologically unsustainable food of little nutritional value. Similarly, while we have seen how some television audiences reconstruct the communal context of *in situ* consumption, these audiences still read and appropriate the simulated hyperreal images of the televisual copy rather than the original. While fans might be able to overcome the divide between viewing and participating in the televisual representation of football, they do not participate in the 'game event', but in the 'medium event' (Goldlust 1987). As Adams remarks (1992: 127), 'throwing a brick through a TV screen has no effect on what is seen on any other screen' – although it should be noted that it does have a very profound impact on its local setting. In this sense, my argument is that the rationalized, standardized and increasingly hyperreal state of television does not eliminate participation and experience in the consumption of football, yet television football has indeed divorced the original event from experience, its referents from participation. Theorists taking perspectives as different as Debord (1994) and Bauman (1992) have all observed how (post-)modern systems have privileged the rise of spectacles, which are spectacles *in* and *of* themselves. Similarly, television football constitutes a self-contained, autarkic system of signs that is appropriated by fans to new systems of referentiality, largely unrelated to the actual game and stadium event.

In conclusion, however, this also means that the copy, in other words television football, as it takes on a 'life' of its own, is intrinsically unable to overcome the original in terms of both text and context. As the consumption context of television, even if it is communal, differs from the *in situ* consumption, fans distinguish between the original (the game in the stadium) and the copy (the televisual broadcast):

> Going to football – that's the best bit about it, when you actually go. You walk towards the stadium, with your friends and whoever, maybe have a couple of pints, having a chat, just reading, buying a programme, it is a whole experience, it is a ritual.
>
> (Constantine, Queens Park Rangers fan)

Even to the vast majority of those fans following football exclusively on television the attendance of the game event remains the ideal case of football consumption:

> The stadium, well, if you have the chance to see a top game, I would want to stand in the supporters' end and experience all the atmosphere . . . Leverkusen is the club closest to here, at least in terms of playing on an international level, Champions League and so on, and it is very difficult to get tickets there. But otherwise I would absolutely go there.
>
> (Pascal, football fan)

> You can't really get any feel for the game at home. You are talking to yourself. You are talking to the television. But at the ground, you can get so much more involved. It is quite sad, that I haven't seen a live game for years, I am just dying to get up there.
>
> (Brendon, Chelsea fan)

As these extracts demonstrate, the copy – the televisual representation of football

– is intrinsically unable to replace the game event, as there is no realizable end to its tendency towards hyperreal simulation. Like places and non-places, neither representation nor simulation can be reached in their entirety. When Baudrillard describes television football as hyperreal, I believe he does not actually claim the total disappearance of all referents in television football but identifies the process of a growing elimination of referents in the face of technological progress and new cultural needs. Yet the final stage of total simulation and hyperreality will never be reached. As Baudrillard himself argues,

> Everywhere high definition corresponds to a world where referential substance is scarcely to be found any more . . . The illusion of the world, . . . the wild illusion of passion, of thinking, the aesthetic illusion of the scene, the psychic and moral illusion of the other, of good and evil . . . all this volatilized in psychosensorial telereality, in all these sophisticated technologies which transfer us to the virtual, to the contrary of illusion: to radical disillusion. Fortunately, all this is impossible. High definition is 'virtually' unrealizable, in its attempt to produce images, sounds, information, bodies in microvision, in stereoscopy, as you have never seen them, as you will never see them . . . It will never succeed, fortunately. Not that we trust in human nature or in a future enlightenment, but because there is in fact no place for both the illusion of the world and a virtual programming of the world. There is no place for both the world and its double.
>
> (Baudrillard 1997: 27)

We are left with a world which is marked by increasing degrees of hyperreality and simulation that will never reach their conclusion. In between the varying degrees of hyperreality, simulacra and formal rationality, the cultural and social transformations of football are appropriated, endorsed or resisted by fans.

Modernist studies of rationalization and postmodernist approaches to hyperreality and simulation share a common dystopian theme regarding their consequences and implications, ranging from Weber's notion of the iron cage to Baudrillard's angst of disappearance and terroristic hyperrealism. In its reductionist focus on isolated subsystems, such as the profit maximization of one enterprise, formal rationality runs counter to what Weber has termed 'substantive rationality', as it triggers a number of unacknowledged irrational micro and macro implications. As for McDonald's, Ritzer claims,

> Contrary to McDonald's propaganda and the widespread belief in it, fast food restaurants and their rational clones are not reasonable, or even truly rational, systems. They spawn problems for the health of their customers and the well-being of the environment; they are dehumanizing and, therefore, unreasonable; and they often lead to the opposite of what they are supposed to create, for example, inefficiency rather than increased efficiency.
>
> (Ritzer 1996: 142)

The irrational implications of formal rational systems also mark the boundaries of spaces of appropriation and decoding of rationalized products by consumers in industrial consumer societies. While consumers might put formal rational regimes such as McDonald's restaurants to rather different uses than intended by the creators of these system, their irrational consequences, as I have pointed out previously, prevail in that their employees continue to be exploited, forests are cleared and the health of consumers is endangered. Similarly, as football has become standardized and increasingly isolated from any pre-given referents and signification value – particularly so on television, but also within the increasingly placeless landscapes of football – the texts through which football fandom is constructed have become ever more interchangeable and contentless. Since foot-ball fandom is based upon forms of self-reflection, in other words upon fans' ability to project themselves onto the club they support, this polysemy bordering textual neutrality has provided fans with the ability to integrate their values and socio-cultural positioning in the reading of these texts and to employ them as an extension of self. Because Manchester United has largely eliminated any a priori meaning, fans around the world are able to construct a categorized 'we' between themselves and the club. They read Manchester United according to, quite liter-ally, their *Weltanschauung*. However, as non-places are never fully reached, as hyperreality cannot be completed, football is inherently unable to produce texts fully freed from semiotic referents, not least since the rationalized neutrality and contentlessness of contemporary football texts constitute messages in themselves. If the plain neutral texts of contemporary football have no other sig-nification value, they are still signifiers of rigid industrial rationality, hyperreality and simulation:

> And now all this Mickey Mouse stuff. I read in the newspaper that Bayer has agreed a cooperation scheme with Disney.[11] They turn everything into something like Disneyland here. We really ridicule ourselves in front of all the other fans.
>
> (Achim, Bayer Leverkusen fan)

> *Thomas*: All those people that sit around and do nothing. Maybe they will applaud from time to time. They shouldn't be in our end.
> *Harald*: That is all rubbish. Also like 'Family Street', 'Kids and Teens Tick-ets' – what is that all about, all this amcricanization [. . .]?[12]
> *Thomas*: All this has nothing to do with football, all this commercialization and merchandizing. And it is the Americans that lead the way.
>
> (Harald and Thomas, Bayer Leverkusen fans)

In these accounts 'americanization' and 'Disney' are used almost synonymously with what I have described as rationalization, McDonaldization and hyperreality. Thus, in the face of the commercialization, rationalization and placelessness, a growing number of fans find it difficult to maintain the common ground of self-reflection and identification with their object of fandom. As football embodies and expresses tendencies of rationalized and hyperreal production, fans opposing such change are confronted with landscapes they cannot integrate into their construction of fandom:

> It is Chelsea Village, the hotel, it's a leisure complex and behind it is somewhere the football team. The aim of Chelsea Village is to make the football team unimportant to the income stream of Chelsea Village . . . If you drive to Stamford Bridge now, you can't see a football ground, you can only see hotels and restaurants.
>
> (John, Chelsea fan)

> And now there is the new hotel and at some stage all this doesn't look like a stadium but like a small town and, I think, that's really negative. Because a stadium should be recognizable as a stadium and not look like a shopping centre.
>
> (Hilmar, Bayer Leverkusen fan)

The rationalization and simulation in the televisual representation of football were equally resented by some fans:

> While people gradually more and more watch it on television, it ceases to be a spectacle, it becomes just something on TV and it is hard to get passionate about it.
>
> (John, Chelsea fan)

Further accounts confirm the profound shift of fans' experiences as football environments, whether experienced directly or televisually, have become standardized and increasingly placeless. In the following two Bayer fans discusses the loss of creativity and participation in contemporary football:

> *Richard*: I think all the modernization of the ground and the introduction of an all-seater policy is negative. It has contributed to the fact that the entire feeling isn't there any more. I really have a sense of artificiality there now. What they market as 'Bayer 04 feeling'[13] is absolutely synthetic. Even if other fans always try to insult us as when calling us 'test tube fans', to some extent they have a point.
> *Simon*: The feeling has been sold out.
>
> (Richard and Simon, Bayer Leverkusen fans)

These fans blame the profound shift of experience, of 'feeling', in the *in situ* consumption of football predominantly on the rationalization and McDonaldization of their object of fandom:

At home games we have absolutely no *Kurvenfeeling*[14] any more. Before, I remember my first game, you came onto the terrace and the first people were singing their songs 45 minutes before the game started. When the teams came out to warm up there was already a sense of atmosphere. Now everyone goes there, gets themselves a Cola before the game, walks around and goes in five minutes before kick off, because they know they have their seat secure anyway. And so it is almost asking too much to stand up again and applaud the teams when they come out of the tunnel.

(Richard, Bayer Leverkusen fan)

What these accounts verify is that the transformations of the context of football consumption have profoundly changed the way fans read, appropriate and experience football: new standardized stadia with regulated seating arrangements offering global fast food products (notice the reference to Cola in the above account), shops and even hotels as well as the hyperrealization of football on television with its multi-angle perspectives and replays, all have affected the reading of football texts by fans. Not surprisingly, fans who attend a great many home and often also away games have been most affected by such change, as their fandom is more dependent on football's context and their own participation and fan activity. The rationalized means of televisual consumption fail the needs of *in situ* fans, whose fandom is integrated in social networks and set everyday-life rituals:

I rarely ever see a game. On away trips I hardly see anything of a game, 15 minutes at most. You just stand underneath the terraces and you talk to all the people you only see once a week. I have thought about it, it is more the scene, and that's also my circle of friends and everything goes together.

(Dominik, Bayer Leverkusen fan)

It is one of the irrational consequences of the application of formal rational principles in professional football that such systems are intrinsically unable to take account of substantive aspects in the construction of fandom. They focus on the maximal enlargement of the product which is understood as the game rather than the context of football. As the rationalization and hyperrealization of football progress, and football clubs become signifiers of the transformations of industrial (post-)modernity, some fans are unable to sustain the categorized 'we' between themselves and the fan text (the club, its landscape and its televisual representation).

I realize that by now, if everything continues as it is, then one day a bus will pick me up two kilometres away from the ground, because I drive through a theme-park to the stadium – and I feel how I distance myself from that.

(Dominik, Bayer Leverkusen fan)

As football clubs take on a semiotic meaning that is opposed by fans and that cannot be negotiated and appropriated, their fandom is undermined, because fans are no longer able to project themselves onto the club. As football clubs increasingly embody messages of rationalization and standardization, more and more fans are unable to appropriate these messages within their fandom. Thus their fandom is ultimately eroded. Dominik indicates how his fandom is drawing to a close due to the current transformations of football:

> I always wonder who actually wants this, who the people are who want football vacuum-packed like other products . . . I have already said that there are more and more problems, especially going to home games. And I can definitely imagine that, well, currently it has reached the threshold of pain. But I can imagine it goes beyond that. It is mainly about all the social contacts. And if all this commercialization, etc., progresses further, and me and the guys look for something else we could do together on a regular basis, then that would be an alternative. For a time we followed Bayer's amateur team. I don't do it any more because I don't have enough time, but that was still an intact world.
>
> (Dominik, Bayer Leverkusen fan, emphasis added)

As the rationalization of 'super-clubs' continues, a growing number of fans have deliberately sought to escape its implications by supporting smaller, local teams in the lower divisions. Thilo, for example, supports the fourth division side Preußen Köln, where he is 'closer to things' and still has the freedom to live out different forms of fan participation. Similarly fans of FC St Pauli traditionally interact with the Hamburg house-squatting and anarchist scene and have increasingly supported their club's amateur team in a deliberate escape from the commercialized and rationalized nature of professional football. While the support of small, local teams indicates one path of resistance for fans who seek to conserve the social and cultural ground of their fandom, the more common response to the transformations of football among fans seems to be a continuous distanciation from the object of fandom, that eventually results in a dissolution of the fixed consumption patterns that football fandom is based upon. This is a former Chelsea season-ticket holder who used to attend home and away games:

> Now I identify more with my fellow supporters than the club. I am not a season-ticket holder now, I am not a member . . . I did enjoy it back then far more than now. The football wasn't as good, nowhere near as good, but the actual, the day out, the experience around it was better . . . This season I did probably about seven games, seven or eight, that's about it . . . At least I have been here for thirty years. If I stop going now, I can still say I have been around the world with Chelsea . . . I guess, I will still pick one or two games.
>
> (Michael, Chelsea fan)

The above accounts summarize the inner ambiguity of football fandom in the age of mass production and consumerism. While the rationalization and hyperrealization of *in situ* and television football contribute to the textual openness and accessibility of football clubs, and therefore constitute the premises for the construction of a fan-relation between club and spectator, they, in turn, undermine the basis of fandom. This is the inherent dialectic of football fandom.

Summary to Part III

The condition of football fandom reflects the deep-running ambiguities of industrial rationality. The transformations of football production, whether *in situ* or in the televisual representation of football, confirm a tendency towards the growing contentlessness of football texts and the progressive elimination of social and cultural referents within the production of football. Instead 'super-clubs' that are televisually accessible around the globe strive to offer a semiotic vacuum, which in turn constituted the ground of the diverse, reflective readings of these texts. As the super-clubs are freed of any pre-given meaning, they constitute ideal spaces of self-reflection and projection. Hence football clubs become increasingly universally accessible and form suitable objects of fandom across different socio-demographic and cultural groups. Football clubs and their landscapes become spaces of consumption which are selected upon individual and voluntary grounds, further eroding the interconnection between place, locally coherent communities and fandom.

The key to the increasing contentlessness of football clubs lies in the standardization and hyperrealization of football. The application of formal rational principles has resulted in a standardization of both football and its context, which itself reflects the logic of capitalist exchange. Such standardization, as reflected in the analogy of McDonaldization, has made football texts interchangeable and largely lacking in any local differentiation. The rationalization of football is crucially advanced in the televisual hyperrealization of the game. Overcoming time, space and a singular perspective, television increasingly hyperrealizes and simulates rather than represents football. The simulation of football on television in turn reflects the rationalization of the lifeworld in industrial modernity. In other words, while the cultural implications of the growing consumption of television football are postmodern, they are based upon regimes of modernist, formal rational production.

The accounts of fans in this chapter highlight the substantially irrational consequences of the rationalization of football. I have demonstrated the profound impact of rationalization and hyperreality on the erosion of place. Moreover, McDonaldized stadia and the televisual representation of football have privileged vision over participation, information over experience. This loss of experience and participation is a growing concern to fans which has given rise to active resistance to contemporary changes in spectator football. At the same time, however, the accounts of fans who are driven out of stadia and into the televisual consumption of football on economic grounds demonstrate that the forces of rationalization and interrelated cultural phenomena such as McDonaldization, placelessness and hyperreality are socially, culturally and economically manifest in the everyday life of fans and may ultimately be inescapable.

Chapter 8

Conclusion

Concluding my examination of the micro mechanisms of football fandom and the macro structural foundations of these practices, a dialectical position emerges: the macro structures which have given rise to football fandom and constitute its ground as mass phenomenon simultaneously threaten to erode its very basis. Football texts are appropriated by fans as spaces of self-reflection and its pleasures, yet at the same time they are a realm dominated by rationalized forms of production. Football fandom is based upon the affection for an external object, yet the object of fandom is foremost a mirror of self. Football as a modern cultural phenomenon in this sense reflects the dialectic of industrial modernity.

Football fandom, as the various accounts of fans in this book demonstrate, is constituted through a series of fixed consumption patterns. On the basis of such consumption practices fans construct a categorized 'we' between themselves and a given club by projecting themselves onto the club (or an alternative object of fandom such as a league). Understanding football fandom as a form of self-projection and subsequent reflection elucidates the intense emotional involvement of fans. The fortunes of 11 strangers on a football field, with whom most fans have hardly any demographic factors in common, matter to fans because the team or club is experienced as an extension of self. Hence, the fundamental attraction of football fandom is narcissistic in that, as McLuhan has observed (1964: 42), 'men at once become fascinated by any extensions of themselves'. The narcissistic images at the heart of football fandom combined with the imminent thrill of victory or defeat help to explain why fans around the world passionately follow their teams and clubs and take up the rigid consumption patterns of football fandom. It needs, however, to be explained why it is especially through the leisure practice of spectator football that such narcissistic self-reflections become possible, and what the economic, social and cultural preconditions for the projection and articulation of the self in fandom are.

Following Pierre Bourdieu's analysis (1984) of taste I have illustrated how football fandom – like other forms of consumption – functions as a form of communication and articulation. Thus the consumption of football becomes a crucial tool of distinction and of the articulation of identity in everyday life.

Many fans carefully plan their leisure time and even work in order to accommodate the changing and ever busier schedules of professional football. The examples of the young Leverkusen fans dropping out of a school trip to travel with the club, the father of three planning his holidays according to the fixture list of Bayer matches and the Chelsea fan delaying the birthday party of his daughter to be able to attend Chelsea's home and away games illustrate the fixed patterns that structure the everyday life of football fans. While the degree to which football fandom defines the structure of everyday consumption varies among different fan groups, fandom for all fans functions as a focal point in the organization of leisure time, often forming rigid patterns strikingly reminiscent of the formal rational organization of labour in industrial capitalism. Through such regular fan practices, fans construct their own life stories in light of their fandom and interpret and illustrate their personal history through the fortunes of their object of fandom.

As part of this pivotal role in everyday life, football fandom serves as an interface between fans and the macro structures of their social, cultural and economic environment. Football fandom functions as an agent and representative to the outside world. Fandom as an extension of self thus constitutes a two-way channel of communication through which the fan communicates with the world and vice versa. In the first case, fans seek to position and articulate themselves through their fandom. Fans communicate numerous demographic variables, their cultural preferences and tastes by participating in the consumption of spectator football. Similarly, football fans participate in ongoing discourses covering a vast range of everyday issues concerning politics, religion, class, race, gender and sexuality. Thus fandom constitutes a form of participation in public life and the public sphere. As the case study of the Le Saux–Fowler incident in Chapter 4 illustrates, fans contribute to debates concerning everyday politics in their own negotiation of football texts. Spectator football therefore plays an increasingly prominent role within this public sphere, blurring the boundaries between football and other media-bound entertainment genres (ranging from music to comedy) as well as between football and other areas of public life. Football fandom thus creates spaces in which identity and citizenship are constituted through everyday political participation. The political discourse in which fans participate may have little in common with Habermas's normative notion of the public sphere; however, given football's growing universality, it enables forms of political participation in which fans position themselves in cultural and political debates in relation to their own values and beliefs. In this sense football allows for what Hartley (1999) labels 'DIY citizenship', in that audiences construct their own citizenship through the reading and appropriation of mediated texts. The accounts of fans discussing issues ranging from drug abuse to racism and from party politics to xenophobia in their reading of professional football verify how football fandom has opened up spaces of interaction and participation. While this engagement of fans in political discourses remains largely unrelated to the institutions of contemporary parliamentary democracy, its cultural, social and political impact must not be underrated. While parliamentary channels of political participation are often de facto discriminative, the practices of mass consumption in football fandom – although fans themselves are often highly discriminatory with regard to, for instance, gender – provide spaces of political participation for those who are underprivileged and disenfranchised by concepts of traditional liberal political participation. If we were to follow Fiske's radical claims (1989: 25) this serves as 'the empowerment of the disempowered'.

Similarly, football fandom functions as an interface between fans and social, cultural and economic macro transformations, most notably globalization. Drawing on my interviews with football fans from different quarters of the world, I have illustrated how football fandom serves as an agent of the fan in an increasingly global environment. Fans position themselves within a proliferating global system through their support of particular teams or leagues. The consumption of, for instance, Italian Serie A football in England or of Chelsea matches in South Africa exemplifies how fans situate themselves through their fandom locally and globally. The 'local', which thus grows increasingly phantasmagoric, as well as notions of *Heimat*, is constructed through the negotiation and appropriation of global resources. The integration of football fandom into the global–local dialectic is based upon the televisual representation of professional football, which has dissolved the correlation between place and time and has put fans in touch with a large variety of football from various localities around the world. It is through the indigenization of such football texts that the locale and the lifeworld of the fan are constructed. In this context I have demonstrated how Chelsea FC has different connotations in Norway than in London. As the example of the tight social network of the Norwegian Chelsea fan club illustrates, the consumption of global texts is locally anchored and sometimes even strengthens local social networks. However, while my research confirms the inherent interrelation between globalization and localization Miller (1992) and Morley (1991) observe, it also indicates that such physical localities are increasingly divorced from a sense of home and *Heimat*. In other words, in the face of globalization the automatism between locale and lifeworld and between place and community is eroded. Similar to the locale itself, a sense of belonging, community and *Heimat* is negotiated through the consumption of global resources. This sense of belonging is directly articulated through football fandom, which is based upon the imagined bond between the fan and the object of fandom. Given the increasing geographical diffusion of fans of large-scale professional football clubs, fandom increasingly lacks territorial referentiality; it becomes 'deterritorialized'. This is not to argue that the deterritorialized audiences of football do not constitute actual communities, as their consumption of the texts of contemporary football is marked by 'something shareable and particular' which communities are based upon (Silverstone 1999: 97). The opposite is the case. Contrasting the accounts of fans living outside the locale of the team they support with fans supporting a local team, we can conclude that the membership of deterritorialized communities and the fandom of physically distant objects is reflected in clearly defined patterns of everyday life which are as time-consuming, as rigid and as significant to the formation of identities as the fandom of local fans. To the Bayern München fan living in London or the Chelsea FC fan living in South Africa, their membership of an imagined fan community is nevertheless real in its consequences, in that their fandom is reflected in the structure of their everyday life and constitutes a tool in communicating a projection of themselves.

In light of such findings it would be tempting to celebrate football fandom as a liberating vehicle of self-positioning and identity construction, bridging geographical, social and cultural divides, and as a channel of participation and potential resistance. Indeed, many scholars, such as the above-quoted John Fiske, have chosen to eulogize the potential of self-determination and resistance resulting from the audience's capacity to read and appropriate mediated texts to their particular social, cultural and economic needs. Many such studies focusing on the capacity of audiences to construct distinct and autonomous meanings are, I believe, of tremendous benefit to the analysis of (media) consumption and its implications. However, at the same time such approaches tell only one side of the story. What is neglected in such accounts are the macro structural, economic conditions of the production of cultural texts and commodities. The impact of such macro structures on patterns of consumption and consumers' capacity for appropriation is an important aspect of the analysis of football fandom. Many facets of professional football have been subjected to an increasing number of formal rational considerations. In an attempt to emulate rational regimes of production, which Ritzer has summarized under the term 'McDonaldization', football clubs have begun to match fast food restaurants in their search for maximal efficiency, calculability, predictability and control. Such efforts have resulted in increasingly predictable, plain and interchangeable products that are available well beyond regional or national frontiers. Here my analysis of football fandom and consumption departs from Bourdieu's earlier (1984) findings concerning consumption and taste. On the one hand, Bourdieu emphasizes that identical activities are pursued by different socio-demographic groups, yet that the practices in exercising such activities – such as sports, watching films or eating habits – are markedly different. On the other hand, Bourdieu identifies particular cultural commodities that signify certain groups within his multi-dimensional class spectrum. In the McDonaldized universe of contemporary spectator football the link between signifier and signified has become increasingly blurred. It is no longer possible to identify universally recognized links between teams or clubs – at least those located in the core regions of global consumerism – and particular classes or other demographic groups, the still dominantly male following of all football clubs aside. Processes based on the rationalization of contemporary football such as the universalization and the standardization of football clubs have made distinction a matter of individual rather than collective definitions. In this context it is worth bearing in mind, however, that – as I have demonstrated in Chapter 1 – rationalization and football have been intertwined from the outset of the game. The arrival of industrial modernity accompanied by fundamental transformations of everyday life constituted the *conditio sine qua non* of modern sports.

While accounting for the first mass audiences inside stadia, football's inherent, formal rational imperative was taken to a different plane by the arrival of electronic mass media, particularly television. Television, both historically and in the everyday construction of fandom, is a milestone in the rationalization of the production of football. Like spectator football the rise of televisual consumption is interconnected with the proliferation of consumerism in industrial-rational societies. Television is embedded in a process of 'mobile privatization' (Williams 1974), articulating rationalization, mass production and consumption. Like spectator football, television fits neatly into the structures of modern, clock-regulated work and leisure. This structural congruity forms the ground for the symbiosis between television and professional football. The accounts of interviewees in this study have almost univocally emphasized the degree to which the televisual consumption of football forms a means of rationalization. Its pivotal role in the construction of football fandom is underlined by the fact that even fans who consume football matches *in situ* position this consumption within the semiotic systems and spaces they encounter on television. Moreover, the rationalization of time and space in the televisual representation of football has induced far-reaching transformations of football. The landscapes of football that embody clubs' historical heritage are reduced to a bare minimum on the small screen. The action on the field is interpreted in terms of generally accessible and applicable discourses. Different camera angles, replays and slow motion dissolve and reconstruct the game in terms of both space and time. Accessible from millions and sometimes even billions of homes around the globe, television football has replaced *in situ* spectators' individual perspective in a collective environment with a collective perspective in an individual environment. The manifestations of the rationalization of football, largely but not exclusively based upon televisual consumption, run counter to football fandom as the focal point of identity, citizenship and participation. Alongside such empowering notions, football itself becomes the site of postmodern, dystopian visions such as hyperreality, simulation and placelessness.

The televisual representation of football thus threatens to transform into its own simulacrum: a copy, endlessly duplicated, to which there is no original. In this sense, football has entered a postmodern stage. Television has set the pace for the transformation of stadia into placeless environments which seek to emulate the televisual representation of football, not shape it. Consequently, to many fans football on television has replaced the actual game as the point of reference. Hyperreality prevails over the actual event, which becomes defined by its own shadow. Television simulates the game, burying the original under its maximal enlargement in the televisual representation. Like the empire in the Borges tale, the vestiges of *in situ* football are left to decay underneath the all-encompassing televisual representation of the game. Thus football's historical, social and cultural referents, upon which participation and citizenship are exercised in football fandom, are increasingly eliminated and replaced by standardized, universally applicable discourses – in other words simulated connotations. The accounts of fans in Chapter 7 illustrate how the hyperreal and simulated state of contemporary football has minimized the spaces of participation and creativity and thereby fundamentally transformed the experiences of football consumption. As vision acts as the fundamental dimension of perception in contemporary football, other dimensions of experience have been impoverished. In light of the increasingly standardized and pasteurized semiotic structure of contemporary football, DIY citizenship is progressively transformed into 'IKEA citizenship' in which fans merely choose between interchangeable, ever similar, stereotypical messages and discourses, rooted in a pseudo-creative and pseudo-participatory environment. Fans are left to reassemble pre-cut parts with uniform results, from which the only possible digression is complete failure of assembly. Thus a number of fans in my study expressed the fear that the basis of their fandom was eroded in the face of the rationalization and simulation of football.

Herein, I believe, lies the inherent dialectic of football fandom and maybe – although this has to remain speculative given the focus of this book – of contemporary popular culture at large. While on the one hand rationalization and televisual simulation emerge as undoing football fandom, they constitute its premises on the other, since rationalization and standardization are the forces that have been instrumental in the rise of spectator football as a form of modern leisure and in the construction of fandom. As clubs are being overshadowed by their televisual representation, they have eclipsed their own referents and left fans with a semiotic vacuum to be filled through a process of self-reflection. It is, for instance, through televisual consumption outside Spain or Scotland that Real Madrid or Glasgow Rangers are being freed of their historical connotations. The more a club as object of fandom preserves such referents, the narrower and more socio-demographically specific is its appeal: only those fans who can accommodate the club's textual structure within their self-reflection will be able to construct a fan–object relation with the club. The less clubs have a meaning of their own, the better they function as spaces of self-projection to a large number of fans. This self-reflection forms the modus operandi of football fandom. To return to the Narcissus myth, it is on plain water that Narcissus sees his reflection. Precisely such even, semantically empty surfaces are fostered by the application of formal rationality and its postmodern consequences in the realm of football.

Although I have demonstrated the interrelations between various premises and forces within football fandom, this is not to argue that these premises and forces stand any less in opposition to each other. Fandom is constructed between these polarities which reflect the opposition between standardized, rationalized production and creative consumption. Postmodern hyperrealism as well as the model of local, organic authenticity are analytic conceptualizations which do not find their full match in contemporary social and cultural realities.

No football club, I think, will be able to strip itself of all semiotic referents, no football stadium will become entirely placeless. Similarly, television football will continue to bear rudiments of the actual game and the social, cultural, historical and geographical referents that mark the participating teams, even if the hyper-realization of football on television is taken further by digitalization and the computer-based animation of the televisual image. Neither, I think, does football fandom as a form of mass consumption constitute a source of unrestricted creativity, untouched self-reflexivity, self-determined citizenship or authentic and organic identity formation. Having said this, we should bear in mind that the balance between the forces of the macro and micro levels of football fandom is subject to significant shifts. The production and consumption of football do not exist in isolation from each other, but the fundamental changes in the rational, global production of football texts have substantially transformed football fandom over the past decades. The balance between macro systems of production and micro patterns of consumption and appropriation thus constitutes an uneven match. This, I think, is well captured in Michel de Certeau's distinction (1984) between the 'strategies' of texts (and we should add textual and in turn cultural, social and economic systems) and the 'tactics' of the reader and consumer. This asymmetric power relation is illustrated in the globalization of fandom. While the structures of global cultural production provide fans with increasingly polysemic texts, such texts contain a 'second order of meaning' often beyond the negotiation and appropriation abilities of audiences. Football fandom, as I illustrate in the discussion of fandom as a form of narcissism, incorporates the metastructure of the fan text. In other words, like Narcissus, the fan becomes 'the servo-mechanism of his own extended or repeated image' (McLuhan 1964: 41). This image, in turn, is framed by the ideological structure of the space through which the image is reflected. Through its global distribution and redistribution patterns, professional football has become increasingly independent of nation states. At the same time, the nation state appears to be a decreasingly significant focal point in the identity construction of fans, bypassed in the accelerating dynamic between local and global. The various examples of fans regularly following foreign leagues or supporting club teams of supranational composition verify that the 'texts' of professional football have become part of an increasingly global cultural semiotic system. As to whether fans welcome this globalization of football or oppose it, the reading of football texts by the interviewees in my study confirms that the consumption of football inescapably introduces global dimensions and cultures into the lifeworld of fans. The Chelsea fan who is proud of his club's right-wing and racist heritage (Benny) or the Bayern München fan who – although himself of Polish origin – rejects the growing number of 'foreign players' (Wojtek) is as much integrated into the consumption of the global textual resources as those fans enthusiastically following international football. And as in the example of Benny, who eventually finds himself coming to terms with foreign players and who is confronted with his own children admiring Chelsea's black and foreign players, values and beliefs are not constituted in isolation from such global production and consumption patterns. While fans interact and choose between various discourses of the public sphere through their fandom, and thereby articulate and form identity and DIY citizenship, the ground upon which their fandom is constructed is firmly positioned within the ideological apparatus of mass consumerism, rationalization and industrial capitalism.

Football, then, remains an interface between the macro transformations of an increasingly global economic, social and cultural system and individuals and their ability to position themselves in today's world through acts of consumption, negotiation and indigenization. It is, quite simply, a game of two halves.

Method and research

The question of an appropriate methodology for the study of fans and fandom has attracted increased attention in recent years. To some extent this seems surprising, as the answer to the methodological challenge posed by fans is in one sense straightforward: football fans are spectators. Whether inside a football stadium, in front of the television in their local pub, or at home listening to the match commentary on the radio, football fans are audiences. The study of football fans is thus by definition a study of audiences. In this sense the methodological framework of my study is derived from the long tradition of qualitative audience studies in Media and Cultural Studies that has developed following Hall's encoding/decoding model (1980) and Morley's pioneering study (1980) of the *Nationwide* audience. Drawing on recent trends in audience research, my method included different qualitative components such as participant observation and informal and semi-structured interviewing. These qualitative and partly ethnographic research methods enabled me to investigate mundane and recurring aspects of fandom and thus to assess the interaction between individuals and groups and their socio-cultural environment. The issues surrounding ethnographic research have been extensively discussed elsewhere (Clifford and Marcus 1986; Hammersley 1992; Alasuutari 1995) and I will abstain here from reiterating in further depth the various general theoretical debates surrounding ethnography.

However, the study of fans through qualitative and ethnographic methods in particular has recently attracted substantial criticism, based on concerns regarding the degree to which fans are both willing and able to give accurate accounts of their actions and motivations. Hills (1999), drawing on Gripsrud (1995), argues that the consumption of fan texts includes processes beyond the communicable. In other words fans are themselves unable to understand and to articulate the pleasures constituted in their consumption of fan texts. A similar observation is made by Harrington and Bielby in their study of soap fans: 'We were struck repeatedly in our interviews and informal conversations with fans by the strength of their passion for, devotion to, and sheer love of daytime television, to an extent beyond their own comprehension' (Harrington and Bielby 1995: 121, quoted in Hills 1999: 10).

To Hills the inability of participants in qualitative studies of fandom to articulate the pleasures and feelings that underlie their fandom renders interviews with fans highly problematic:

> It cannot be assumed (as so often the case in Cultural Studies) that cult fandom acts as a guarantee of self-presence and transparent self-understanding . . . The fan cannot act, then, as the unproblematic source of the meaning of their own media consumption.
>
> (Hills 1999: 9–12)

At first sight many interviews I conducted confirm Hills's suspicion that fans are intrinsically unable to explain their own fandom. Many interviewees were puzzled when asked why they were football fans. Similarly most fans I interviewed would have been unable to give detailed accounts of how their pleasures are constituted in the consumption of football. To Hills, then, the study of fans requires a psychoanalytical rather than sociological-ethnographic approach. Here two objections are to be made. Firstly, this conclusion is based on the incorrect assumption that the answer to why viewers become fans and what sets them apart from other audiences is to be found in the analysis of how singular pleasures are constituted. Yet it is through the study of the everyday context of fandom, through the accounts of fans positioning their fandom within their everyday lives, that I was able to understand the significance of football fandom, the needs it serves as well as its position in the construction of identity. Fans might not be able to articulate why they are fans, but by describing when and how they engage in football consumption, how they position such activities within the flow of daily life and accounting for what they believe to be the significance of their fandom, I was able to assess the cultural and social foundations of their fan practices. It is through the socio-cultural analysis of football fandom that I demonstrate that football fandom functions as an extension of self. Secondly, my method thus also articulates a different focus. Hills's plea for psychoanalytical approaches to fandom bears particular validity to the analysis of fandom at large, across genres and as a unified phenomenon in modern society. Where the social and cultural context of consumption and fan practices differs significantly, such as between cult films and football, art collectors and slash readers, we naturally turn to a psychological level in explaining their common momentum. While this would be a project worth pursuing elsewhere, this book is not a study of fandom in and for itself but an investigation of the social and cultural phenomenon of football, based upon the interplay between the modern leisure practice of football and its audiences. The key to its analysis and its accompanying macro processes then, I believe, lies in the sociological, qualitative examination of the position of fans and their socio-cultural everyday context.

Research design

On the basis of these theoretical considerations I designed a research strategy drawing on different qualitative methods. The first requirement was to define the field of study. Preparing my fieldwork, I had to define the *cases* as much as the *fields* of study. In the case of football fandom, pointing to the significance of *place* in its analysis, the two coincide. Football clubs (the cases) are located within certain localities, which in turn constitute the field. My fields of study were therefore defined by the cases studied. In Bayer Leverkusen and Chelsea FC I selected two western European clubs for my study and in the Washington-based DC United a further North American club. Both European clubs have a comparable pedigree, having featured as title contenders in their respective leagues over the last five years and now regularly featuring in European competitions. DC United has so far claimed three MLS championships. While the choice of Chelsea and Leverkusen in particular was determined by considerations of time and practicality, they fulfilled basic criteria in that they were regular participants in transnational competitions, yet did not occupy the unique position of their domestic competitors Manchester United or Bayern München. Another advantage of focusing on Bayer Leverkusen was that I had attended a number of games there in the past, was familiar with the club's history and had followed the team over a number of years, which allowed a more autoethnographic perspective (cf. Fiske 1990).

Football clubs are situated in clearly defined places. The regions surrounding the homes of the two clubs my main focus rests on, the south-east of England (Chelsea FC) and the Rheinisch-Bergische Land (Bayer Leverkusen), thus constitute my fields of study. In both cases the majority of the fans regularly attending games of these clubs lived in these regions. The majority of Chelsea fans are found in the southern boroughs of London as well as the counties south of the capital such as Surrey, Kent and Sussex. Most of those who regularly attend Bayer games live on the eastern side of the Rhine valley between Bonn in the south and Düsseldorf in the north as well as in the Bergische Land stretching from Leverkusen in the west to Wuppertal and Remscheid in the east. A third – if less extensive – field of study I included was the Washington Beltway and its surrounding areas in the states of Virginia and Maryland. Given that I decided to study different fan groups including geographically dispersed television audiences, the participants in my study are defined through the field, yet not necessarily situated within the field. I studied and interviewed three different groups of fans in the case of Chelsea and Bayer:

*   Fans following either Chelsea or Bayer and living *within* the field, in other words the south-east of England or the Rheinisch-Bergische Land.
*   Fans following either Chelsea or Bayer and living *outside* the field.
*   Fans living *within* the field, but following *different clubs* from either within or outside the field.

Following this categorization I was able to generate data from various angles without losing a common ground for comparison and analysis. Mainly focusing on the fans of one club within each of the respective fields, I was able to juxtapose the accounts and actions of fans in regard to the same object of fandom. In order to understand the dynamics within the field it was equally important to study fans living within the field who chose to support another club, often located outside the field such as the large domestic competitors including the above-mentioned Manchester United and Bayern München or teams in other divisions or regions ranging from other parts of Europe to Latin America.

Organization and access

I conducted my fieldwork over a 15-month period from August 1998 to October 1999. While long periods of time in the field are necessary in order to familiarize oneself with the environment, discover the rhythms and patterns of everyday life and minimize the obstructing effects of the researcher's presence, financial constraints – let alone an academic system that itself has become increasingly geared towards formal rational targets – naturally limit the time one is able to spend in the field. The final period of 15 months supported by a large number of in-depth interviews formed the methodological compromise this research rests upon.

Access to fans and stadia proved varyingly difficult, with DC United being exceptionally supportive of my research, Chelsea allowing limited access to the ground and information and Bayer Leverkusen rejecting any form of cooperation. Bayer's non-cooperation – which coincidentally, I believe, reflects less the club's general policy than the reluctance of the middle management official assigned to deal with my query – proved less problematic than initially assumed as I was able to secure access to the ground through a season ticket and the local *Fan-Projekt*, a publicly funded meeting place for fans of the club, as well as to a representative of the company controlling the club, Bayer AG, in the person of its head of sports sponsorship, Jürgen von Einem, who proved greatly supportive of my research and provided crucial information and assistance.

Having secured an acceptable degree of access to the field, I began my fieldwork in August 1998. Following the theoretical considerations outlined above I relied on participant observations in order to identify distinctions in the readings of and interactions with the fan text by different fan and audience groups, *in situ* fans as well as television audiences. In addition, participant observation enabled me to gather first-hand experiences of the physical and social context of consumption. These experiences of different environments of football consumption proved crucial in the analysis of the role of space and place in football fandom. In total I conducted 43 participant observations. Thirty times I observed fans inside the stadium during games and 13 times I participated in the viewing of televised matches in both public and domestic settings. During participant observations I recorded data on a systematic observation sheet (SOS), which was based upon categories developed during an earlier study of pub audiences for football matches. In addition to providing interesting insights into the patterns of the everyday consumption of football, my participant observations allowed me to contact and recruit interviewees.

I conducted semi-structured interviews with a total of 98 participants lasting between 45 minutes and four hours. In the Rhineland I interviewed 28 Bayer Leverkusen supporters as well as ten interviewees living within the field but supporting either another or no particular team. I have here quoted the interviews which were conducted in German in their English translation. Similarly, I interviewed 35 Chelsea fans, 13 DC United fans and 12 fans with other allegiances. In all cases I sought to conduct interviews in environments that were the fan's preferred site of football consumption. In the case of stadium fans, I sought to schedule interviews in proximity to the ground on match days. Alternatively, I met interviewees in pubs that were their preferred venue for watching games. Fans who watched football mostly on television in domestic settings I mostly interviewed in their home, although this was, of course, only possible when interviewees agreed to such an invasion of their domestic space. In addition to interviews with football fans and audiences, I interviewed a small number of people professionally concerned with football (fandom): these included local journalists, the police and club officials.

My decision to opt for semi-structured rather than unstructured interviews with fans was based on a number of preliminary observations. In contrast to other ethnographic fields of research in which it is essential that respondents are given room to develop their own reflections and frameworks of discourse, football fans often do not require any incentive to talk about their football fandom. Gossip and banter about their object of fandom are often firmly integrated in the practices of football fans. From beneath the vast material of seemingly banal discourses, such everyday talk produces important assumptions, observations and reflections. In the case of football fandom everyday talk tends to focus on the object of fandom (the team or club). Yet, since I also wanted to explore how fandom and the everyday routines of fans interact, how macro influences such as globalization and rationalization shape fans' consumption habits and how they position their fandom within their own personal history, my approach proved helpful in that I prompted fans to talk about their experiences and personal histories as well as about their object of fandom. By asking fans to narrate their own fan history, for instance, I was then able to identify and analyse the actual importance of seemingly trivial everyday talk about the team or club they supported.

In addition I identified a small number of key questions alongside four areas of discussion I intended to include in the interview. Firstly, I pursued questions alluding to people's own definition of being a fan and encouraged interviewees to give their history of being a fan. I also sought to clarify the reasons behind support of particular teams. Secondly, I asked interviewees how they positioned fandom within everyday life. Thirdly, I discussed different geographical levels (local, national, European, global) of competition and consumption for football viewers, seeking to clarify the shifting notions of place and space in football consumption. Fourthly, I focused upon media usage, exploring how fans appropriated and read football-related texts offered by television and other media and how their experience of watching a game live differed from televisual consumption. While there was no necessary chronological order to such themes, and many questions concerning these areas were initially discussed by interviewees themselves, I made sure to have raised all these themes in the course of an interview.

My recruitment and sampling strategies were interdependent. Despite the qualitative nature of my study a certain degree of stratification of the sample of interviewees was required, since I aimed to study all three groups of fans I had identified a priori on the basis of their media usage: (a) organized fans that followed their team *in situ* home and away, (b) fans that (regularly) attended home games and (c) fans that followed football mainly on television. The recruitment of organized fans proved easy and required no particular strategy, as these groups were easy to identify and to contact. Given the tight social networks of such fans, my research usually quickly became known to a large group of fans, many of whom were happy to be interviewed. Particularly in the case of the rather small group of organized Bayer fans, my initial interviews with a few members of the group seemed to draw in other fans who wanted their opinion to be heard as well. To make my contact details known, I circulated leaflets among these fans. Leaflets were also the main means of recruitment of interviewees who were regular stadium visitors. I handed out a total of 6,000 leaflets before and after Bayer, Chelsea and DC United matches. This proved a useful strategy for recruiting interviewees from diverse backgrounds engaging in different practices – although it should be noted that participants with higher educational capital, as in most voluntary interview-based research, seemed overrepresented within my sample. The recruitment of fans who follow football on television proved more difficult. While this is by far the largest group, there is no appointed (public) place for television audiences. For the dispersed nature of the audience of television football I relied on different recruitment strategies. I was able to recruit a number of fans through snowballing (i.e. made contact with fans following interviews with their friends, family or colleagues). Similarly, I relied on my own network of friends by asking them to make contact with keen followers of television football. Thirdly, I publicized my study through newspaper advertisements, posters and leaflets, which I handed out in public places such as town centres. As these recruitment strategies excluded most fans living outside the fields of study I finally relied on mailing lists of clubs or fan organizations in order to make additional contacts with Chelsea and Bayer fans living outside the respective regions of the club.

Notes

I Introduction: football and modernity

1 Prior to the European Cup final on 29 May 1985, 39 Juventus fans were crushed to death following crowd disturbances initiated by Liverpool fans at the Heysel Stadium, Brussels.

2 Interview with Kevin Payne, CEO of triple US champions DC United, 14 October 1999.

3 Recent exceptions to the criminological perspectives on hooliganism include King's comparison (1997) between hooligan groups and *Freikorps* as spaces of articulation of modernist notions of masculinity. This thesis has itself attracted substantial criticism (Smith 2000).

4 Informal interviews with hooligans during my fieldwork suggest that either they do not have a particular interest in football and engage in violence as part of their gang membership, or their acts of violence exist largely independently of their fandom in that they attend the game and later – regardless of what happened on the pitch – meet for prearranged fights with other hooligan groups. Consequently, violence and football fandom are separate phenomena. This is further confirmed by various Chelsea and Manchester United fans I interviewed who, now in their 30s and 40s, recall having regularly taken part in violence during their adolescence. Yet, while their interest in violence ceased through changing life phases such as marriage and parenthood, their fandom continues.

5 Alongside the perspectives outlined here, football has also attracted attention from other disciplines such as economics (Baimbridge *et al.* 1996; Lehmann and Wiegand 1997; Szymanski and Smith 1997) International Relations and politics (Boniface 1998; Riordan and Krüger 1999).

6 A small number of studies focus on the reading of mediated sport, mainly employing quantitative methods (Gantz 1981, 1985; Gantz and Wenner 1989, 1991). Others (Comisky *et al.* 1977; Schweitzer *et al.* 1992) have investigated isolated aspects of the reading of televised sport such as the impact of commentary on the perception of the game by television audiences or the construction of different forms of viewing pleasures in the consumption of televised sports (Brummett and Duncan 1989, 1990, 1992), but fail to account for fandom as a unified phenomenon of contemporary popular culture. Similarly, studies dedicated to particular fan cultures examine subcultural dynamics rather than analyse football fandom on a wider social basis (Jary *et al.* 1991; Haynes 1995; Redhead 1997; King 1998).

7 Schulze-Marmeling (1992) dates folk football back to the tenth century, Guttmann (1986) places tumultuous folk football in the fourteenth and fifteenth centuries and

Elias and Dunning (1986) refer to reasonably reliable sources from the fourteenth century onwards.

8   Beck (1999) translates *Zweckrationalität* as 'purposive rationality', reflecting the literal meaning of the German *Zweck*, in contrast to the more commonly used English translation 'formal rationality'. Either way, both terms accurately summarize the crucial opposition between micro-production system orientated purposive/formal rationality and universal, substantive rationality.

9   Many sports, however, were cautious about radio coverage, and live commentary remained a minor element in sports broadcasting throughout the 1930s (Brailsford 1991). It was not until the days of the radio reporter and later Arsenal manager George Allison, who realized the potential for expansion arising out of radio technology (Mason 1979; Birley 1995) by marketing the club on a supra-local basis and recruiting players from outside the locale of the club, that mass media started to be considered as a potential source of – rather than threat to – income.

10   In 1950, 34,000 television sets could be found in British living-rooms; this number had grown to three million by 1954, and by 1960, 87 per cent of the population of Great Britain had access to a television set (Whannel 1991: 71).

2 Fan practices and consumption

1   Baseball's rise in popularity in late nineteenth-century North America was partly initiated by the sports goods manufacturer Spalding. Spalding successfully promoted the myth of baseball as an American game rather than an adaptation of the game rounders, which was popular at girls' schools in England throughout the eighteenth and nineteenth centuries.

2   This is a problematic observation in as far as it was the aim of my study to approach viewers who had a keen interest in football. Nevertheless, despite their varying consumption practices, all respondents considered themselves 'fans' rather than 'spectators'. One female interviewee made the limitation that she saw herself as a 'moderate fan' (Doris).

3   Premiere: German pay-TV channel broadcasting live Bundesliga matches.

4   *ran*: German highlights programme, broadcast on Fridays at 22:00 and Saturdays at 18:00.

5   The survey was designed to project the 63.3 million residents in Germany over 14 years old. Respondents were classified by income and education, with the base distribution of the population as follow: 52 per cent graduated from the *Volksschule* (nine years of school), 31 per cent had the *Mittlere Reife* (10 years) and 17 per cent the *Abitur* (13 years). In terms of monthly income, 29 per cent came from a household with less than DM 2,999, 30 per cent from a household with DM 3,000 to DM 4,999 per month and 17 per cent from a monthly household income greater than DM 5,000.

6   Respondents were asked to rank their interest in spectator football on a scale of 1 (very interested), 2 (interested), 3 (less interested) and 4 (not interested at all). On average football was ranked 2.4, the highest among all 29 sports included in the study.

7   My interviewees ranged from unemployed adolescents, factory workers, housewives, middle management executives, to higher-education teachers.

8   The surveys Bourdieu extensively draws upon in his study were conducted in 1963 and 1967–8.

9   This was further confirmed during my participant observation at a Freiburg game. One of the recurring chants among Bayer fans was '*Scheiß Studenten!*'.

10   While 33 per cent of all males in Germany had attended at least one Bundesliga game

in the last 12 months, only 7 per cent of all females had done so. This ratio of approximately 5:1 was confirmed by two ad hoc surveys I conducted before matches at Leverkusen and Chelsea.

3 Fandom, identity and self-reflection

1 Different personality structures and value systems are of course themselves subject to different socio-economic and cultural influences. In this sense the different levels of, for instance, modesty displayed by the two interviewees are in themselves indicative and expressive of varying degrees of economic, social and educational capital.
2 As part of the professionalization of spectator sport and its integration into a global capitalist system, trophies and honours are increasingly the ultimate prize to be gained by the fans, whereas the professional athlete is predominantly rewarded in monetary terms.
3 Between the renaissance of the team in the early 1990s and the time of the interviews few seasons had passed in which the team had failed to win a trophy. On the other hand, despite having one of the most expensive squads in England, Chelsea never succeeded in winning the Premier League and have established a track record of spasmodic under-achievement.
4 Since the so-called 'Bosman Ruling' of the European Court in 1995, which forced football associations within the EU to lift restrictions on players from other EU member states, Chelsea have signed a number of players such as the Italian and French internationals Gianfranco Zola, Gianluca Vialli, Frank Leboeuf and Marcel Desailly. During the 1998/99 season when I conducted my fieldwork Graeme Le Saux and team captain Dennis Wise were the only English players able to claim a regular first-team spot.
5 The distinction between text and icon is of an analytical rather than empirical nature as icons themselves come to function as texts which are read and appropriated by their audiences. However, as is illustrated by the use of third person as opposed to first person pronouns, icons allow for more limited possibilities of an active authorship of the fan text.
6 The Grateful Dead, more than most other bands, have sought to ground their popularity in live concerts. Many of their fans follow the band around on concert tours. They, in contrast to football fans, nevertheless sustain the division between themselves and the band.
7 The Narcissus myth has been frequently employed in the work of psychoanalysts following Freud's (1924) and more recently Lacan's (1989) discussion of narcissism. While I here only draw on the myth in an effort to explain and illustrate processes and mechanisms of football fandom, narcissism has also been at the heart of many theoretical discourses of social and cultural life in modernity at large (Lasch 1980; Sennett 1992; Marcuse 1998).
8 McLuhan's summary of the myth is slightly inaccurate here: Narcissus, once he comes to realize that it is himself whom he desires, starts crying. As his tears fall into the water, distorting his mirror image, Narcissus feels deserted and melts.

4 The politics of football: fandom and the public sphere

1 As well as cooking for celebrities in his west London venue, Ramsey has had his own celebrity status reinforced by the Channel 4 docu-soap *Boiling Point* that revolved

around Ramsay's impulsive character, his dehumanizing treatment of his staff and his subsequent appearances in talk shows or panel quizzes such as BBC 2's *Have I Got News For You?*

2   Thus I am relying – in contrast to Habermas – on an empirical rather than normative conceptualization. Even the most repressive societies still have a public sphere in that texts are made open and public, yet the means of control of the power to publicize are distributed unevenly. Interestingly, totalitarian regimes such as the Third Reich or Mussolini's Italy have actively sought to construct an all-encompassing public sphere as a crucial instrument in their attempt to manifest power. Only anti-modernist movements such as the Khmer Rouge during their rule of Cambodia have attempted to suppress the public sphere altogether.

3   Fiske is more cautious in his use of the analogy, stating that television 'is not quite a do-it-yourself meaning kit but neither is it a box of ready-made meaning for sale. Although it works within cultural determinations, it also offers freedoms and the power to evade, modify, or challenge these limitations and controls' (Fiske 1987: 55).

4   Fowler's alleged drug addiction also played a significant role in another incident later. Following taunts by Everton FC fans, Fowler kneeled down over the six-yard line and pretended to snort the white powder marking the playing field after scoring at Goodison Park.

5   Le Saux was previously involved in a brawl with England international Paul Ince and in an on-field punch-up with his Blackburn Rovers team mate David Batty during a Champions League game in Moscow – allegedly after Batty had called him a 'poof' (*When Saturday Comes*, no. 146, 1999).

6   *The Mirror*, for instance, emphasized the sexual dimension of the incident, with the headline 'Fowler called Le Saux "QUEER"', with the word 'QUEER' taking up more space than the following description of the incident. The *Chelsea Independent* concluded that 'the incident has raised an important issue within the game and one that it will have to address sooner or later. There are gay footballers and if the treatment of Justin Fashanu [who committed suicide in 1998] and, to a lesser extent, Graeme have suffered is anything to go by they will be staying in the closet a while longer.'

7   Martin Lipton, football correspondent of the *Daily Mail*, described Fowler's behaviour as 'crude, unedifying and deeply offensive, another in the long-running, asinine and patently false slurs on Le Saux's sexual orientation' (*Daily Mail*, 1 March 1999). *The Mirror* ran the headline 'Revealed. Taunts that drove Chelsea player into rage.'

8   This divide was also underlined through the analogy between the infamous northern working-class comedian Bernard Manning and his southern and openly gay counterpart Julian Clary.

9   Cumming's translation omits Adorno and Horkheimer's addition that this fictitious character has from the outset marked the individual in the bourgeois era: '*Massenkultur entschleiert damit den fiktiven Charakter, den die Form des Individuums im bürgerlichen Zeitalter seit je aufwies*' (Horkheimer and Adorno 1997: 181–2).

10 Interestingly, sport has traditionally been considered as the most universal and least offensive of all genres by the media industry. As Aaron Baker has pointed out (1997: xiv), 'executives from both ABC and Disney explained the value of sports programming as its "universal appeal" and ability to "offend no political position"'.

5 Football and cultural globalization

1   At the signing of Manchester United's new sponsorship deal with mobile phone operator Vodafone both sides eagerly stressed that the deal would go beyond shirt advertisement and offered each of the partners the opportunity to access new regional markets through their cooperation.

2 For a summary of the link between deregulated television markets, pay-TV and globalization, see Rowe (1996).

3 I use the term 'local' in its social as well as its territorial sense. For example, the local
dimension of the fandom of Moritz does not correlate to an actual geographically
physical locale as he is a Bayern München fan living approximately 400 miles from
Munich. Consequently, we might define locales as either physically manifest or deterritorialized communal spaces.

4 Similarly, the notion of an imploded world is questionable in the sense that the world
has not become smaller but our horizon and our ability to encounter the world has
been dramatically extended through modern communication technologies.

5 For an examination of the interrelation between citizenship and community see
Habermas (1994).

6 Prominent examples include Glasgow Rangers and Glasgow Celtic, Liverpool FC and
Everton FC, and Inter and AC Milan from the same city, as well as Arsenal and Tottenham or Nottingham Forest and Notts County from the same part of a city, but
also fierce regional rivalry between, for instance, Real Madrid and FC Barcelona or
between Dynamo Dresden and Dynamo Berlin in the former GDR.

7 Participants were asked to rank all Bundesliga clubs according to their sympathy on a
scale from plus five to minus five. The same scale was used in a survey of Chelsea fans
who were asked to rank respective Premier League opposition.

8 The contrast emerging from the juxtaposition of such fierce local rivalry with the relatively neutral attitude of most Chelsea fans with regard to their fellow London clubs
requires further explanation. The first reason for the more place-bound nature of the
fandom of Bayer Leverkusen fans lies in the qualitative differences of the socio-cultural
and economic configuration of the respective localities. Globalization, as Tomlinson
has remarked (1999: 131), is 'an uneven process'. Leverkusen still constitutes a
stronghold of German industrial production which Lash and Urry describe (1994) as
largely Fordist. Leverkusen remains an environment of stable, long-term employment
and industrial labour and thus relatively low geographical mobility. The second aspect
that sets the fandom of many Bayer fans in my study apart from more deterritorialized
fan communities is that in the medium-sized town of Leverkusen social networks and
imagined community partly coincided with a less deterritorialized fan community.

9 Such territorial referents continue to exist in symbolic form as clubs bear the names of
towns or cities and still have fixed territorial locations – although this has come under
threat from, for instance, the idea of Juventus Turin's not playing its domestic
home games in the Stadio del Alpi in Turin any more, but across the country in order
to give its fans in all Italian regions the chance to follow the team *in situ*. Yet for
most fans territory is predominantly experienced as a semiotic code of televisual
representation.

10 In the only exception to this, one interviewee referred to two South African teams,
while quickly adding that he 'didn't care much though' (Stephen).

6 Football, formal rationality and standardization

1 Consequently, I do not engage in further objection to Ritzer's McDonaldization
thesis based on its lack of empirical grounding outside the realm of fast food, as this
empirical basis is provided in my own investigation of the McDonaldized dimensions
of contemporary football (and I do not intend to make any claims beyond football).
Other recent work on Ritzer's thesis includes Jary's focus (1999) on the 'McDonaldization of sport and leisure'. Jary develops a complex though only marginally helpful
model of rationalization stages. His basic argument remains that sport 'is not a
unitary process'. While it surely is not and while there are 'counter-tendencies and

contestations' of 'dominant commercial and globalizing tendencies' (Jary 1999: 130–1), the occurrence of such resistance confirms rather than contradicts the increasing rationalization and McDonaldization of modern sports.

2   The BayArena in Leverkusen, for instance, includes a large McDonald's drive-through. Fans have instant access to McDonald's products before, during and after the game. During the period of my participant observation such services were frequented widely and sometimes even enthusiastically by spectators. To many fans McDonald's was an integral part of the experience of *in situ* football consumption. One 14-year-old boy seated near me on a number of occasions left regularly five minutes before half-time in order to avoid the rush at the McDonald's counters during the break, returning minutes later with a plenitude of burgers, fries and soft drinks. Most fans I interviewed said they regularly use the McDonald's branch at the BayArena. ('It is nice, that way you don't have to eat sausages or so', 'I use . . . McDonald's too. I don't know, it is just an automatism that you go there.') McDonald's and other fast food providers are found increasingly within or in the vicinity of sports arenas. At the internationally famous Kop end at Liverpool, supporters can now purchase McDonald's burgers before and during the game (Conn 1997: 160).

3   Ritzer describes (1996) the deskilling of tasks that are performed by the kitchen staff at McDonald's restaurants. Workers receive clear instructions about which lines of burgers are to be turned first, and their preparation of fries is 'aided' by semi-automated machines that control the cooking time.

4   While the link between methods and principles of rationalized industrial production might be less surprising in the case of Bayer AG, which is itself a large-scale industrial manufacturer, a general tendency towards smaller stadia which are regularly filled to near-capacity is evident all over Europe. Officials of Chelsea FC confirmed that the club had decided not to extend the ground beyond its currently planned 44,000 capacity, which – still below the demand for tickets for many matches – guaranteed sell-out crowds for most games during the season.

5   In England league games are played on Saturday at 15:00, Sunday at 14:00 and 16:00 and Monday nights. On various occasions Saturday or Sunday games have even kicked off at 11:00 or 12:00 to accommodate the schedules of Sky Sports, the current Premier League broadcaster. In Germany's Bundesliga, games were played on Friday nights, Saturday at 15:30, and Sunday early evenings. In a recent move the Bundesliga scratched Saturday night games which kicked off at 20:15, after a short trial period in the 2000/01 season alongside Friday night matches.

6   During my fieldwork, for instance, Chelsea's away game at Middlesbrough FC was rescheduled three times and finally played on a Wednesday night, two months after the originally set date. Many fans, who had to purchase the tickets months in advance, were unable to arrange a midweek trip to the north-east and forfeited their tickets.

7   League matches in Italy are traditionally played on Sunday afternoons.

8   It goes without saying that the mathematical nature of football results barely represents the whole reality of a football match, nor is it even generally believed to do so, as demonstrated by the constant discourse of commentators, panellists, managers, players and, of course, fans, insisting that 'the better team lost today' or that 'the score-line did not reflect the game'.

9   Even sports that take artistic and aesthetic aspects of sporting performances into account, such as figure-skating, gymnastics or ski-jumping, seek to measure such dimensions in mathematically quantifiable ways, leading to a paradoxical situation in which 'artistic expression' is believed to be adequately reflected in a numerical mark such as '5.8'.

10   Ritzer points (1996) to the introduction of the shot-clock in basketball, leaving each

team 24 seconds to score, thus speeding up the flow of the game and increasing the number of points scored. In baseball several measures have been taken to satisfy the alleged '(home-)run craze among spectators'. While in some ball parks outfield fences have been moved to narrow the field and the introduction of artificial turf has increased the chance of base hits slipping through the infield defence, the American League has gone even further. The traditionally weak-hitting pitcher is replaced by a designated hitter, hence furthering the specialization and Taylorization of the sport while resulting in a higher number of home runs.

11 New, lighter balls have been developed that promise higher speed and more goals scored. Moreover, rule changes have been implemented to guarantee more goals in the traditionally low-scoring game of football. Goalkeepers have lost their right to pick up back-passes with their hands, thus forcing teams to adopt a more attacking, and therefore formally more productive, style of play. Other sports such as handball have gone as far as to allow the referee to end a period of ball possession if the attacking team's style of game appears too 'passive'. Football's offside rule (http://images.fifa.com/fifa/handbook/laws/2002/LOTG2002_E.pdf) has been changed in the favour of strikers. Now attacking players are allowed to be the same distance from the goal line as the second rearmost player of the opposing team. The number of substitutes allowed has been steadily increased over recent decades to currently three players, allowing teams a higher pace and a more attacking style throughout the game. Further rule changes have been considered by national and international federations, which all aim at a higher number of goals scored. Such suggestions range from fewer players on the field or bigger goals to the complete abolition of the offside rule.

12 However, non-human technologies do play an increasing role in modern football as training, medical surveillance, diet planning and other aspects of footballers' lives are regulated by machines and computer programs.

13 The matter was also discussed in various letters to the club and the local press.

14 With ticket prices starting at £22, the most expensive at any Premier League club, economically weak sections of society – particularly many adolescents who have traditionally been associated with hooliganism – are de facto excluded from matches at Stamford Bridge.

15 Diversification is a well-established pattern of industries of scale and scope in Fordist capitalism (Chandler 1990), including to a certain degree McDonald's and its competitors themselves.

16 Bayer Leverkusen opened a new supermarket-sized Fanshop and integrated a McDonald's drive-through as part of the redeveloped 'Family Street' in 1996 and completed the construction of a further stand, which includes VIP lounges, an underground car park and the BayArena restaurant, the following year. In 1999 the club opened a hotel, which despite fierce opposition from fan groups was integrated into the home-fans' end of the BayArena. The transformations in and around Stamford Bridge, Chelsea's west London home, have been even more dramatic. In a complete reconstruction of three of the four stands the newly formed Chelsea Village plc holding company has added bars, numerous restaurants, night clubs, a hotel including conference centres, car parks, a travel agency, new executive headquarters and a two-storey fan shop, named the Megastore. In addition Chelsea Village plc offers various services to its customers such as car and household insurance.

17 The minimum price for a match-day ticket to Stamford Bridge during the 1998/99 season was £22 compared to DM 15 (approximately £5) at Leverkusen's BayArena. Similarly, restaurants at Stamford Bridge were known for their notoriously high prices and poor quality. *The Observer* described one of the restaurants, Fishnets (the traditional English fast food fish and chips is served at Fishnets for a breathtaking £13.95), as 'shockingly pretentious' and 'insultingly preposterous'.

I.M. MARSH LIBRARY LIVERPOOL L17 8BD
TEL. 0151 231 5216/5299

18   Shares in Chelsea Village plc have continuously underperformed in relation to both FTSE and the sector index, reaching a new low in 2002 at 19p, well under half the flotation price in 1996. While the stock market price alone is not an accurate reflection of a company's performance, the poor financial situation of Chelsea Village plc has been the subject of a growing number of press reports since autumn 2000. For updated details see http://www.hemscott.com/EQUITIES/company/cd 03042.htm.

19   Similarly, King has observed (1998: 160) that Manchester United privileges fans from Ireland in the allocation of tickets as such fans from abroad are willing to spend more on a single trip to Old Trafford than most fans in the Manchester area. Chelsea has limited the number of season tickets sold to about 50 per cent of the total ground capacity in order to vary the audience.

20   Earlier kick-offs are only allowed when games are played in time zones two or more hours ahead of GMT.

21   Broadcasters can interview players and managers only in designated areas and in front of the competition sponsors' logos. The length and frequency of transmissions are regulated in the contracts between networks and UEFA, requiring that broadcasters show highlights of all Champions League matches and guarantee fixed weekly slots for games. Moreover, broadcasters have to continue to broadcast at least one live match per match day, even if all 'national' representatives have been eliminated from the competition.

22   According to Bradley's own – though admittedly very small – sample, Rangers supporters are, at 32 per cent, three times more likely to vote for the Conservatives than supporters of any other Scottish Premier League club.

23   In Spain, Real Madrid and FC Barcelona have historically expressed the opposing poles of Spanish centralism and Catalan separatism. Similarly, clubs such as the Basque Athletic Bilbao have represented national minorities within nation states. In Belgium, clubs have been located within the field of cultural tension between Flemings and Walloons, while in Turkey the three Istanbul clubs Galatasaray, Fenerbahce and Besiktas have traditionally represented different socio-cultural groups in the capital.

24   During the 1998/99 season Glasgow Rangers employed a Dutch manager and players from many European countries including Italy, France, the Netherlands and Germany.

25   See, for example, the cases discussed by Kuper (1994), Del Burgo (1995), Stuart (1995), Wagg (1995a), Bar-On (1997) and Taylor (1998).

26   The Müngerdorfer Stadion is home to 1.FC Köln, and alongside Leverkusen's BayArena is the stadium closest to Bengt and Lukas's home town.

27   Rudi Völler, now Germany's national coach, was part of Bayer's management team at the time of the interview.

7 Television, football and hyperreality

1   The changing nature of the visual representation of football games is particularly evident in the trend away from a more cautious use of close-ups, which break the naturalistic flow of the coverage from a grandstand position. Barr (1975: 47–53) has argued that the coverage of the 1974 World Cup by the public German broadcasters ARD and ZDF relied on longer shots and fewer close-ups than comparable British coverage, therefore pursuing a more naturalistic style, in contrast to the more constructed and mediated representation of football in Britain. Over the last two decades the use of close-ups has intensified on an international scale. In comparison to Charles Barr's analysis (1975) of various broadcasts of the 1974 World Cup, my own analysis

of BBC and ITV broadcasts during the European Championship in 1996 reveals that close-ups were used more frequently, accounting for 8.5 per cent (England v. Scotland) and even 14.9 per cent (Germany v. Croatia) of the air-time during the match. Similarly, observations have been made by Whannel (1992: 101) that have demonstrated that close-ups amounted to around 13 per cent of all shots in the 1966 World Cup Final, but had increased to 20–30 per cent of all shots in selected football broadcasts between 1988 and 1992. In both cases I analysed in 1996, the number of close-up shots outnumbered normal shots (27 to 23 for England v. Scotland, and 29 to 21 for Germany v. Croatia). This tendency has been accompanied by increasingly fast-paced cutting. According to Barr (1975: 47–53), a 50-shot sequence of Scotland v. Brazil in the 1974 World Cup took 10 minutes 20 seconds, and in the case of Holland v. Brazil 12 minutes 15 seconds. BBC's Euro '96 coverage of England v. Scotland used 50 shots in 5 minutes 48 seconds and ITV's coverage of Germany v. Croatia in 5 minutes 21 seconds.

2 Television is often watched without sound. During my participant observations of screenings of football games in pubs it was often impossible to hear the commentary. Similarly, some interviewees remembered how they 'turn off the sound and listen to some music while watching the game' or 'watch a game on television with the sound down and listen to another game on radio'.

3 High-quality zoom lenses allowed uninterrupted alternations between long shots and medium shots (Whannel 1992: 33). Improving transmission quality and the introduction of colour television allowed a brighter, more spectacular representation. The introduction of Ampex video-recorders enabled the fast production of highlight programmes and allowed for immediate action replays.

4 The majority of grounds I visited during the 1998/99 season were equipped with large video installations. The clubs employing such screens include, to name a few, Arsenal, Aston Villa, Bayern München, Werder Bremen and VfB Stuttgart.

5 Some scholars such as Morse (1983), drawing on Laura Mulvey's work (1975), have argued that replays are the crucial element in watching televised football as they construct scopophilic viewing pleasures. Yet my own understanding of watching televised sport is that replays are not valid to the audience in and for themselves but rather in their contextual position within the sporting narrative.

6 In October 2002 an average of 1.55 million female viewers in Germany (34 per cent of all viewers over 14 years) watched the *SAT.1* Bundesliga highlights programme *ran* (Source: *SAT.1* Medienforschung/GfK).

7 Having selected two extracts of a televised ice-hockey game, one which was considered to contain normal action and the other considered to include a great deal of rough play, they overlaid the segments with commentary stressing the opposite in each case. Respondents perceived the normal play segment with the commentary stressing the roughness of the play as rougher than the actual rough play that was underplayed by the commentary as normal.

8 The game was introduced by the presenter in reference to a public row between the two Bayer strikers, Eric Meijer and Paulo Rink, who were both hoping for a regular place in the team. The antagonism between the two strikers was also taken up by the commentator, who described Rink's style of play as typically Brazilian and technically advanced, while the tall Dutchman Meijer was portrayed as tough and determined. Rink was also described as a sensitive player who, because of his disappointment about losing his regular first-team place, 'can't even enjoy his goals'.

9 During my fieldwork in Leverkusen the local fan centre was a particularly popular meeting point for teenage or adolescent enthusiasts who watch television games there in large groups. Similarly, fans frequented bars and pubs where they met to watch football communally.

10 I witnessed all the above examples of fan participation during the viewing of television football. The wearing of replica shirts, which have – especially in Britain – become an item of everyday clothing well beyond situations of actual football consumption, was particularly popular among television viewers watching in groups. Verbal interaction at the 'game event' and 'medium event' (Goldlust 1987) also took place in most of the communal television viewing situations I participated in.

11 Alleged negotiations over cooperation between the Disney Corporation and Bayer Leverkusen were reported by the *Kölner Express* in August 1998. In the interview I conducted with a representative of Bayer AG, he rejected these reports but considered a closer link-up with one of the major international media conglomerates in the future, arguing that 'media companies could become very interesting strategic partners one day'. In January 2003 Bayer entered negotiations with AEG, a subsidiary of Anschutz Entertainment, the owner of the MLS teams Colorado Rapids, Chicago Fire, Los Angeles Galaxy, San Jose Earthquakes and MetroStars as well as hockey franchises in the NHL and Europe. As part of their link with AEG, Leverkusen also entered a partnership agreement with DC United.

12 Rather than using the correct term *Amerikanisierung*, Thomas uses the prefix '*ver-*' and speaks about '*Ver*amerikanisierung', emphasizing the element of dissolution and deconstruction within this process.

13 Both Richard and the advertisement slogan use the English word 'feeling' here rather than the German term *Gefühl*, reflecting the global standardization of experience and languages of leisure.

14 Richard uses the term *Kurve* as synonym for 'supporters' end'.

Bibliography

Abercrombie, N. and Longhurst, B. (1998) *Audiences: A Sociological Theory of Performance and Imagination*, London: Sage.

Adams, P. (1992) 'Television as gathering place', *Annals of the Association of American Geographers*, vol. 82 (1): 117–35.

Alasuutari, P. (1995) *Researching Culture: Qualitative Method and Cultural Studies*, London: Sage.

Alfino, M. (1998) 'Postmodern hamburger: taking a postmodern attitude toward McDonald's', in M. Alfino, J. Caputo and R. Wynyard (eds) *McDonaldization Revisited: Critical Essays on Consumer Culture*, Westport: Praeger Publications.

Anderson, B. (1991) *Imagined Communities*, revised edition, London: Verso.

Appadurai, A. (1990) 'Disjuncture and difference in the global cultural economy', in M. Featherstone (ed.) *Global Culture: Nationalism, Globalization and Modernity*, London: Sage.

Arabena, J. L. (1993) 'International aspects of sport in Latin America: perceptions, prospects and proposals', in E. Dunning, J. Maguire and R. Pearton (eds) *The Sports Process: A Comparative and Developmental Approach*, Champaign, IL: Human Kinetics.

Arnold, T. (1991) 'Rich man, poor man: economic arrangements in the football league', in J. Williams and S. Wagg (eds) *British Football and Social Change: Getting into Europe*, Leicester: Leicester University Press.

Augé, M. (1995) *Non-places: Introduction to an Anthropology of Supermodernity*, London: Verso.

Bacon-Smith, C. (1992) *Enterprising Women: Television Fandom and the Creation of Popular Myth*, Philadelphia: University of Pennsylvania Press.

Baimbridge, M., Cameron, S. and Dawson, P. (1996) 'Satellite television and the demand for football: a whole new ball game?', in *Scottish Journal of Political Economy*, vol. 43 (3): 317–33.

Baker, A. (1997) 'Introduction: sports and the popular', in A. Baker and T. Boyd (eds) *Sports, Media and the Politics of Identity*, Indiana University Press.

Bale, J. (1993) *Sport, Space and the City*, London: Routledge.

Bale, J. (1998) 'Virtual fandoms: futurescapes of football', in A. Brown (ed.) *Fanatics: Power, Identity and Fandom in Football*, London: Routledge.

Bale, J. and Maguire, J. (eds) (1994) *The Global Sporting Arena: Sports Talent Migration in an Interdependent World*, London: Frank Cass.

Barnett, S. (1990) *Games and Sets: The Changing Face of Sport on Television*, London: British Film Institute.

Bar-On, T. (1997) 'The ambiguities of football, politics, culture and social transformation in Latin America', in *Sociological Research Online*, vol. 2 (4). Available <http://www.scores online.org.uk/scoresonline/2/4/2.html> (accessed 15 June 1999).

Barr, C. (1975) 'Comparing styles: England v. Germany', in E. Buscombe (ed.) *Football on Television*, London: British Film Institute.

Baudrillard, J. (1983) *Simulations*, New York: Semiotexte.

Baudrillard, J. (1990) *Fatal Strategies*, edited by Jim Fleming, New York: Semiotexte.

Baudrillard, J. (1993) *The Transparency of Evil: Essays on Extreme Phenomena*, London: Verso.

Baudrillard, J. (1994) *The Illusion of the End*, Oxford: Polity Press.

Baudrillard, J. (1997) 'Aesthetic illusion and virtual reality', in N. Zurbrugg (ed.) *Art and Artefact*, London: Sage.

Bauman, Z. (1992) *Intimations of Postmodernity*, London: Routledge.

Beck, U. (1992) *Risk Society*, London: Sage.

Beck, U. (1999) *World Risk Society*, Cambridge: Polity Press.

Beck, U. (2000) *What is Globalization?*, Cambridge: Polity Press.

Birley, D. (1995) *Playing the Game: Sport and British Society, 1910–45*, Manchester: Manchester University Press.

Blain, N. and O'Donnell, H. (1994) 'The stars and the flags: individuality, collective identities and the national dimension in Italia '90 and Wimbledon '91 and '92', in R. Giulianotti and J. Williams (eds) *Game without Frontiers: Football, Identity and Modernity*, Aldershot: Arena.

Blain, N., Boyle, R. and O'Donnell, H. (1993) *Sport and National Identity in the European Media*, Leicester: Leicester University Press.

Blake, A. (1995) 'Sport and the global media: unofficial citizens', in *New Statesman and Society*, vol. 2, June: 47–9.

Bode, P. (1990) 'Leverkusen/Köln: mehr als Lokalrivalität', in S. Gehrmann (ed.) *Fußballrandale: Hooligans in Deutschland*, Essen: Klartext-Verlag.

Boniface, P. (1998) 'Football as a factor (and a reflection) of international politics', in *International Spectator*, vol. 33 (4): 87–98.

Bourdieu, P. (1984) *Distinction: A Social Critique of the Judgement of Taste*, London: Routledge and Kegan Paul.

Boyle, R. and Haynes, R. (1996) '"The grand old game": football, media and identity in Scotland', in *Media, Culture and Society*, vol. 18 (4): 549–64.

Bradley, J. M. (1995) *Ethnic and Religious Identity in Modern Scotland: Culture, Politics and Football*, Aldershot: Avebury.

Brailsford, D. (1991) *Sport, Time and Society: The British at Play*, London: Routledge.

Brohm, J.-M. (1978) *Sport: A Prison of Measured Time*, Worcester: Pluto Press.

Brummett, B. and Duncan, M. C. (1989) 'Types and sources of spectating pleasure in televised sport', in *Sociology of Sport*, vol. 6 (3): 195–211.

Brummett, B. and Duncan, M. C. (1990) 'Theorizing without totalizing: specularity and televised sports', in *Quarterly Journal of Speech*, vol. 76: 227–46.

Brummett, B. and Duncan, M. C. (1992) 'Toward a discursive ontology of media', in *Critical Studies in Mass Communication*, vol. 9 (3): 229–49.

Bryman, A. (1999) 'Theme parks and McDonaldization', in B. Smart (ed.) *Resisting McDonaldization*, London: Sage.

Calhoun, C. (1993) 'Civil society and the public sphere', in *Public Culture*, vol. 5: 267–80.

Carrington, B. (1998) '"Football's coming home", but whose home? And do we want it? Nation, football and the politics of exclusion', in A. Brown (ed.) *Fanatics: Power, Identity and Fandom in Football*, London: Routledge.

Cashmore, E. (2002) *Beckham*, Cambridge: Polity Press.

Cavicchi, D. (1997) *Tramps like Us; Music and Meaning among Springsteen Fans*, New York and Oxford: Oxford University Press.

Chandler, A. D. (1990) *Scale and Scope: The Dynamics of Industrial Capitalism*, Cambridge, MA: Belknap Press of Harvard University Press.

Clarke, A. and Clarke, J. (1982) 'Highlights and action replays: ideology, sport and the media', in J. Hargreaves (ed.) *Sport, Culture and Ideology*, London: Routledge and Kegan Paul.

Clifford, J. and Marcus, G. (eds) (1986) *Writing Culture: The Poetics and Politics of Ethnography*, Berkeley: University of California Press.

Colley, I. and Davies, G. (1982) 'Kissed by history: football as TV drama', in *Sporting Fictions*, Birmingham: CCCS.

Colombijn, F. (1999) 'View from the periphery: football in Indonesia', in G. Armstrong and R. Giulianotti (eds) *Football Cultures and Identities*, Basingstoke: Macmillan Press.

Comisky, P., Jennings, B. and Zillmann, D. (1977) 'Commentary as a substitute for action', in *Journal of Communication*, vol. 27 (3): 150–3.

Conn, D. (1997) *The Football Business: Fair Game in the '90s?*, Edinburgh: Mainstream.

Couldry, N. (2000) *Inside Culture: Re-imagining the Method of Cultural Studies*, London: Sage.

Crafts, Susan D., Cavicchi, D. and Keil, C. (1993) *My Music*, Hanover: Wesleyan University Press.

Crolley, L., Hand, D. and Jeutter, R. (1998) 'National obsession and identities in football match reports', in A. Brown (ed.) *Fanatics: Power, Identity and Fandom in Football*, London: Routledge.

Cross, G. (1997) 'The suburban weekend: perspectives on a vanishing twentieth-century dream', in R. Silverstone (ed.) *Visions of Suburbia*, London: Routledge.

Cunningham, H. (1980) *Leisure in the Industrial Revolution*, London: Croom Helm.

Curran, J. (1991) 'Rethinking the media as public sphere', in P. Dahlgren and C. Sparks (eds) *Communication and Citizenship: Journalism and the Public Sphere in the New Media Age*, London: Routledge.

Dayan, D. (1998) 'Media and diaspora', in S. Livingstone (ed.) *Television and Common Knowledge*, London: Routledge.

de Certeau, M. (1984) *The Practice of Everyday Life*, Berkeley and Los Angeles: University of California Press.

Debord, G. (1994) *The Society of Spectacle*, New York: Zone Books.

Del Burgo, M. B. (1995) 'Don't stop the carnival: football in the societies of Latin America', in S. Wagg (ed.) *Giving the Game Away: Football, Politics and Culture on Five Continents*, Leicester: Leicester University Press.

DiMaggio, P. (1979) 'Review essay: on Pierre Bourdieu', in *American Journal of Sociology*, vol. 84 (6): 1460–74.

Duke, V. (1995) 'Going to market: football in the societies of Eastern Europe', in S. Wagg (ed.) *Giving the Game Away: Football, Politics and Culture on Five Continents*, Leicester: Leicester University Press.

Duke, V. and Crolley, L. (1996) *Football, Nationality and the State*, Harlow: Longman.

Dunning, E. (1971) 'The development of modern football', in E. Dunning (ed.) *The Sociology of Sport*, London: Cass.

Dunning, E. (1994) 'The social roots of football hooliganism: a reply to the critics of the "Leicester School"', in R. Giulianotti, N. Bonney and M. Hepworth (eds) *Football, Violence and Social Identity*, London: Routledge.

Eco, U. (1986) *Travels in Hyperreality*, London: Picador.

Elias, N. (1986a) 'Introduction', in N. Elias and E. Dunning (eds) *Quest for Excitement: Sport and Leisure in the Civilizing Process*, Oxford: Basil Blackwell.

Elias, N. (1986b) 'An essay on sport', in N. Elias and E. Dunning (eds) *Quest for Excitement: Sport and Leisure in the Civilizing Process*, Oxford: Basil Blackwell.

Elias, N. (1994) *The Civilizing Process*, Oxford: Basil Blackwell.

Elias, N. and Dunning, E. (1986) 'Folk football in medieval and modern Britain', in N. Elias and E. Dunning (eds) *Quest for Excitement: Sport and Leisure in the Civilizing Process*, Oxford: Basil Blackwell.

Erickson, B. (1996) 'Culture, class and connections', in *American Journal of Sociology*, vol. 102 (1): 217–51.

Featherstone, M. (1990) *Global Culture: Nationalism, Globalization and Modernity, Theory, Culture and Society Special*, London: Sage.

Featherstone, M. (1995) *Undoing Culture: Globalization, Postmodernism and Identity*, London: Sage.

Fenster, M. (1991) 'The problem of taste within the problematic of culture', in *Communication Theory*, vol. 1 (2): 87–105.

Fiske, J. (1987) *Television Culture*, London: Routledge.

Fiske, J. (1989a) *Reading the Popular*, Boston: Unwin and Hyman, reprinted 1991, London: Routledge.

Fiske, J. (1989b) *Understanding Popular Culture*, Boston: Unwin and Hyman.

Fiske, J. (1990) 'Ethnosemiotics: some personal and theoretical reflections', in *Cultural Studies*, vol. 4 (1): 85–99.

Fiske, J. (1992) 'The cultural economy of fandom', in L. Lewis (ed.) *The Adoring Audience*, London: Routledge.

Fraser, N. (1990) 'Rethinking the public sphere: a contribution to the critique of actually existing democracy', in *Social Text*, vol. 25/26: 56–80.

Fraser, N. (1992) 'Sex, lies and the public sphere: some reflections of the confirmation of Clarence Thomas', in *Critical Inquiry*, vol. 18 (3): 595–612.

Freud, S. (1924) *Zur Einführung des Narzißmus*, Leipzig: Internationaler Psychoanalytischer Verlag.

Frow, J. (1987) 'Accounting for tastes: some problems in Bourdieu's sociology of culture', in *Cultural Studies*, vol. 1 (1): 59–73.

Gans, H. (1966) 'Popular culture in America: social problem in a mass society or asset in a pluralistic society?', in H. S. Becker (ed.) *Social Problems: A Modern Approach*, New York: Wiley.

Gantz, W. (1981) 'An exploration of viewing motives and behaviours associated with television sport', in *Journal of Broadcasting and Electronic Media*, vol. 29: 263–75.

Gantz, W. (1985) 'Exploring the role of television in married life', in *Journal of Broadcasting and Electronic Media*, vol. 29: 65–78.

Gantz, W. and Wenner, L. A. (1989) 'The audience experience with sport on television', in L. A. Wenner (ed.) *Media, Sport and Society*, Newbury Park: Sage.

Gantz, W. and Wenner, L. A. (1991) 'Men, women, and sports: audience experiences and effects', in *Journal of Broadcasting and Electronic Media*, vol. 35: 233–43.

Garnham, N. (1993) 'The mass media, cultural identity and the public sphere in the media world', in *Public Culture*, vol. 5: 251–65.

Gehrmann, S. (1988) *Fußball – Vereine – Politik: Zur Sportgeschichte des Reviers 1900–1940*, Essen: Bouvier.

Genosko, G. (1994) *Baudrillard and Signs: Signification Ablaze*, London: Routledge.

Giddens, A. (1990) *The Consequences of Modernity*, Cambridge: Polity Press.

Giddens, A. (1991) *Modernity and Self-identity: Self and Society in the Late Modern Age*, Cambridge: Polity Press.

Giddens, A. (1997) 'The globalizing of modernity', in A. Sreberny-Mohammadi, D. Winseck, J. McKenna and O. Boyd-Barret (eds) *Media in Global Context*, London: Arnold.

Giulianotti, R. (2000) *Football: A Sociology of the Global Game*, Cambridge: Polity Press.

Giulianotti, R. and Williams, J. (eds) (1994) *Game without Frontiers: Football, Identity and Modernity*, Aldershot: Arena.

Giulianotti, R., Bonney, N. and Hepworth, M. (1994) *Football, Violence and Social Identity*, London, Routledge.

Goffman, E. (1959) *The Presentation of Self in Everyday Life*, Harmondsworth: Penguin.

Goksøyr, M. (1994) 'Norway and the World Cup: cultural diffusion, sportification and sport as vehicle for nationalism', in J. Sugden and A. Tomlinson (eds) *Hosts and Champions: Soccer Cultures, National Identities and the USA World Cup*, Aldershot: Arena.

Goldlust, J. (1987) *Playing for Keeps: Sport, the Media and Society*, Cambridge: Polity Press.

Gregory, D. (1989) 'The crisis in modernity? Human geography and critical social theory', in R. Peet and N. Thrift (eds) *New Models in Geography*, vol. 2, London: Unwin Hyman.

Gripsrud, J. (1995) *The Dynasty Years: Hollywood Television and Critical Media Studies*, London: Routledge.

Grossberg, L. (1985) 'Critical theory and the politics of empirical research', in M. Gurevitch and M. R. Levy (eds) *Mass Communication Review Yearbook*, Beverly Hills: Sage.

Guttmann, A. (1978) *From Ritual to Record: The Nature of Modern Sport*, New York: Columbia University Press.

Guttmann, A. (1986) *Sports Spectators*, New York: Columbia University Press.

Guttmann, A. (1994) *Games and Empire*, New York: Columbia University Press.

Habermas, J. (1974) *Strukturwandel der Öffentlichkeit*, Neuwied: Luchterhand.

Habermas, J. (1989) 'The public sphere: an encyclopaedic article', in S. E. Bronner and D. Kellner (eds) *Critical Theory and Society: A Reader*, London: Routledge.

Habermas, J. (1992) 'Further reflections on the public sphere', in C. Calhoun (ed.) *Habermas and the Public Sphere*, Cambridge: Polity Press.

Habermas, J. (1994) 'Citizenship and national identity', in B. van Steenbergen (ed.) *The Condition of Citizenship*, London: Sage.

Hall, S. (1979) 'The treatment of football hooliganism in the press', in R. Ingham (ed.) *Football Hooliganism: The Wider Context*, London: Inter-Action Inprint.

Hall, S. (1980) 'Encoding/decoding', in S. Hall, D. Hobson, A. Lowe and P. Willis (eds) *Culture, Media, Language: Working Papers in Cultural Studies, 1972–1979*, London: Hutchinson.

Hammersley, M. (1992) *What's Wrong with Ethnography?*, London: Routledge.

Hannerz, U. (1990) 'Cosmopolitans and locals in world culture', in M. Featherstone (ed.) *Global Culture: Nationalism, Globalization and Modernity*, London: Sage.

Hannerz, U. (1997) 'Notes on the global ecumene', in A. Sreberny-Mohammadi, D. Winseck, J. McKenna and O. Boyd-Barret (eds) *Media in Global Context*, London: Arnold.

Harrington, C. L. and Bielby, D. (1995) *Soap Fans: Pursuing Pleasure and Making Meaning in Everyday Life*, Philadelphia: Temple University Press.

Hartley, J. (1987) 'Invisible fictions', in *Textual Practice*, vol. 2, 121–38.

Hartley, J. (1996) *Popular Reality: Journalism, Modernity, Popular Culture*, London: Arnold.

Hartley, J. (1997) 'The sexualization of suburbia: the diffusion of knowledge in the postmodern public sphere', in R. Silverstone (ed.) *Visions of Suburbia*, London: Routledge.

Hartley, J. (1999) *The Uses of Television*, London: Routledge.

Harvey, D. (1990) *The Condition of Postmodernity: An Inquiry into the Origins of Cultural Change*, Oxford: Basil Blackwell.

Harvey, J. and Houle, F. (1994) 'Sport, world economy, global culture and new social movements', in *Sociology of Sport Journal*, vol. 11: 337–55.

Haynes, R. (1995) *The Football Imagination: The Rise of Football Fanzines Culture*, Aldershot: Arena.

Held, D. (1990) 'An assessment of the Frankfurt School and Habermas', in D. Held (ed.) *Introduction to Critical Theory: Horkheimer to Habermas*, Cambridge: Polity Press.

Hills, M. (1999) 'The dialectic of value: the sociology and psychoanalysis of cult media', unpublished thesis, University of Sussex.

Hills, M. (2002) *Fan Cultures*, London: Routledge.

Hoehn, T. and Szymanski, S. (1999) 'The Americanization of European football', in *Economic Policy*, vol. 28: 205–40.

Holt, R. (1989) *Sport and the British: A Modern History*, Oxford Studies in Social History, Oxford: Oxford University Press.

Holub, R. C. (1992) *Jürgen Habermas: Critic in the Public Sphere*, London: Routledge.

Honneth, A. (1986) 'The fragmented world of symbolic forms: reflections on Pierre Bourdieu's sociology of culture', in *Theory, Culture and Society*, vol. 3 (3): 55–66.

Horak, R. (1994) 'Austrification and modernization: changes in Viennese football culture', in R. Giulianotti and J. Williams (eds) *Game without Frontiers: Football, Identity and Modernity*, Aldershot: Arena.

Horkheimer, M. and Adorno, T. W. (1972) *Dialectic of Enlightenment*, New York: Seabury Press.

Horkheimer, M. and Adorno, T. W. (1997) 'Kulturindustrie: Aufklärung als Massenbetrug', in M. Horkheimer, *Gesammelte Schriften, Band 5: Dialektik der Aufklärung und Schriften 1940–1945*, Frankfurt am Main: Fischer.

Hornby, N. (1992) *Fever Pitch*, London: Victor Gollancz.

Horne, J. (1996) '"Sakka" in Japan', in *Media, Culture and Society*, vol. 18 (4): 527–47.

Houlihan, B. (1994) 'Homogenization, americanization and creolization of sport: varieties of globalization', in *Sociology of Sport Journal*, vol. 11: 356–75.

Ingham, A. and Beamish, R. (1993) 'The Industrialisation of the United States and the bourgeoisification of sport', in E. Dunning, J. Maguire and R. Pearton (eds) *The Sports Process: A Comparative and Developmental Approach*, Champaign, IL: Human Kinetics.

Iser, W. (1978) *The Act of Reading: A Theory of Aesthetic Responses*, London: Routledge and Kegan Paul.

Jameson, F. (1991) *Postmodernism, or, the Cultural Logic of Late Capitalism*, London: Verso.

Jarvie, G. and Maguire, J. (1993) *Sport and Leisure in Social Thought*, London: Routledge.

Jary, D. (1999) 'The McDonaldization of sport and leisure', in B. Smart (ed.) *Resisting McDonaldization*, London: Sage.

Jary, D., Horne, J. and Buckle, T. (1991) 'Football fanzines and football culture: a case of successful cultural contestation', in *Sociological Review*, vol. 39 (3): 581–98.

Jenkins, H. (1992) *Textual Poachers: Television Fans and Participatory Culture*, New York: Routledge.

Jenson, J. (1992) 'Fandom as pathology: the consequences of characterization', in L. Lewis (ed.) *The Adoring Audience*, London: Routledge.

Jhally, S. (1989) 'Cultural studies and the sports/media complex', in L. A. Wenner (ed.) *Media, Sports and Society*, Newbury Park: Sage.

Jones, S. G. (1988) *Sport, Politics and the Working Class*, Manchester: Manchester University Press.

Kellner, D. (1989) *Jean Baudrillard: From Marxism to Postmodernism and Beyond*, Cambridge: Polity Press.

Kellner, D. (1999) 'Theorizing/resisting McDonaldization: a multiperspectivist approach', in B. Smart (ed.) *Resisting McDonaldization*, London: Sage.

Kerr, J. (1994) *Understanding Soccer Hooliganism*, Milton Keynes: Open University Press.

King, A. (1997) 'The postmodernity of football hooliganism', in *British Journal of Sociology*, vol. 48 (4): 576–93.

King, A. (1998) *The End of Terraces: The Transformation of English Football in the 1990s*, London: Leicester University Press.

Klatell, D. and Marcus, N. (1988) *Sports for Sale. Television, Money and the Fans*, New York: Oxford University Press.

Kuper, S. (1994) *Football against the Enemy*, London: Orion.

Lacan, J. (1989) *Ecrits: A Selection*, London: Routledge.

Lanfranchi, P. (1994a) 'Exporting football: notes on the development of football in Europe', in R. Giulianotti and J. Williams (eds) *Game without Frontiers: Football, Identity and Modernity*, Aldershot: Arena.

Lanfranchi, P. (1994b) 'Italy and the World Cup: the impact of football in Italy and the example of Italia '90', in J. Sugden and A. Tomlinson (eds) *Hosts and Champions: Soccer Cultures, National Identities and the USA World Cup*, Aldershot: Arena.

Lanfranchi, P. (1995) 'Cathedrals in concrete: football in southern European societies', in S. Wagg (ed.) *Giving the Game Away: Football, Politics and Culture on Five Continents*, Leicester: Leicester University Press.

Lasch, C. (1980) *The Culture of Narcissism: American Life in an Age of Diminishing Expectations*, London: Abacus Press.

Lash, S. and Urry, J. (1994) *Economies of Signs and Space*, London: Sage.

Lee, S. (1998) 'Grey shirts to grey suits: the political economy of English football in the 1990s', in A. Brown (ed.) *Fanatics: Power, Identity and Fandom in Football*, London: Routledge.

Lehmann, E. and Wiegand, J. (1997) 'Money makes the ball go round: Fußball als ökonomisches Phänomen', in *IFO Studien Zeitschrift für Empirische Wirtschaftsforschung*, vol. 43: 381–409.

Leite Lopes, J. S. (1997) 'Success and contradictions in multiracial Brazilian football', in G. Armstrong and R. Giulianotti (eds) (1997) *Entering the Field: New Perspectives on World Football*, Oxford: Berg.

Lever, J. and Wheeler, S. (1993) 'Mass media and the experience of sport', in *Communication Research*, vol. 20 (1): 125–45.

Lewis, G. H. (1987) 'Patterns of meaning and choice', in J. Lull (ed.) *Popular Music and Communication*, Beverly Hills: Sage.

Livingstone, S. (1998) *Making Sense of Television*, second edition, London and New York: Routledge.

McLaughlin, L. (1993) 'Feminism, the public sphere, media and democracy', in *Media, Culture and Society*, vol. 15 (4): 599–620.

McLuhan, M. (1964) *Understanding Media: The Extension of Man*, London: Routledge.

Maguire, J. (1992) 'Towards a sociological theory of sport and the emotions: a process-sociological perspective', in E. Dunning and C. Rojek (eds) *Sport and Leisure in the Civilising Process*, Basingstoke: Macmillan.

Maguire, J. (1993) 'Globalisation, sport and national identities: the empire strikes back?', in *Society and Leisure*, vol. 16 (2): 293–322.

Maguire, J. (1994) 'Sport, identity politics, and globalization: diminishing contrasts and increasing varieties', in *Sociology of Sport Journal*, vol. 11: 398–427.

Maguire, J. and Jarvie, G. (1993) *Leisure and Sport in Social Thought*, London: Routledge.

Maguire, J., Poulton, E. and Possamai, C. (1999) 'The war of the words?: Identity politics in Anglo-German press coverage of Euro 96', in *European Journal of Communication*, vol. 14 (1): 61–89.

Marcuse, H. (1998) *Eros and Civilization: A Philosophical Inquiry into Freud*, London: Routledge.

Marples, M. (1954) *A History of Football*, London: Secker and Warburg.

Marsh, M. (1990) *Suburban Lives*, New Brunswick: Rutgers University Press.

Marx, K. and Engels, F. (1952) *The Communist Manifesto*, Moscow.

Mason, T. (1979) *Association Football and English Society*, Brighton: Harvester Press.

Mason, T. (1995) *Passion of the People: Football in South America*, London: Verso.

Meyrowitz, J. (1985) *No Sense of Place: The Impact of Electronic Media on Social Behaviour*, New York: Oxford University Press.

Miles, S. (1998) 'McDonaldization and the global sports store: constructing consumer meanings in a rationalized society', in M. Alfino, J. Caputo and R. Wynyard (eds) *McDonaldization Revisited: Critical Essays on Consumer Culture*, Westport: Praeger Publications.

Miller, D. (1987) *Material Culture and Mass Consumption*, Oxford: Basil Blackwell.

Miller, D. (1992) '*The Young and the Restless* in Trinidad: a case of the local and the global in mass communication', in R. Silverstone and E. Hirsch (eds) *Consuming Technologies: Media and Information in Domestic Spaces*, London: Routledge.

Miller, T. and McHoul, A. (1998) *Popular Culture and Everyday Life*, London: Sage.

Miller, T., Lawrence, G., McKay, J. and Rowe, D. (2001) *Globalization and Sport*, London: Sage.

Moorhouse, H. F. (1991) 'On the periphery: Scotland, Scottish football and the New Europe', in J. Williams and S. Wagg (eds) *British Football and Social Change: Getting into Europe*, Leicester: Leicester University Press.

Morley, D. (1980) *The 'Nationwide' Audience*, London: British Film Institute.

Morley, D. (1991) 'Where the global meets the local: notes from the sitting room', in *Screen*, vol. 32 (1): 1–15.

Morley, D. and Robins, K. (1995) *Spaces of Identity: Global Media, Electronic Landscapes and Cultural Boundaries*, London: Routledge.

Morse, M. (1983) 'Sport on television: replay and display', in A. Kaplan (ed.) *Regarding Television*, Los Angeles: University Publications of America and The American Film Institute.

Mulvey, L. (1975) 'Visual pleasures and narrative cinema', in *Screen*, vol. 16 (3): 6–19.

Murphy, P., Williams, J. and Dunning, E. (1990) *Football on Trial: Spectator Violence and Development in the Football World*, London: Routledge.

Nkwi, P. N. and Vidacs, B. (1997) 'Football: politics and power in Cameroon', in G. Armstrong and R. Giulianotti (eds) *Entering the Field: New Perspectives on World Football*, Oxford: Berg.

Nowell-Smith, G. (1978) 'Television – football – the world', in *Screen*, vol. 19 (4): 45–59.

O'Connor, B. and Boyle, R. (1993) 'Dallas with balls: televised sport, soap opera and male and female pleasures', in *Leisure Studies*, vol. 12 (2): 107–19.

O'Donnell, H. (1994) 'Mapping the mythical: a geopolitics of national sporting stereo-types', in *Discourse and Society*, vol. 5 (3): 345–80.

O'Neill, J. (1999) 'Have you had your theory today?', in B. Smart (ed.) *Resisting McDonaldization*, London: Sage.

Overman, S. J. (1997) *The Influence of the Protestant Ethic on Sport and Recreation*, Aldershot: Avebury.

Parker, M. (1998) 'Nostalgia and mass culture: McDonaldization and cultural elitism', in M. Alfino, J. Caputo and R. Wynyard (eds) *McDonaldization Revisited: Critical Essays on Consumer Culture*, Westport: Praeger Publications.

Perry, N. (1998) *Hyperreality and Global Culture*, London: Routledge.

Peterson, R. and Kern, R. M. (1996) 'Changing highbrow taste: from snob to omnivore', in *American Sociological Review*, vol. 61: 900–7.

Philo, G. (1990) *Seeing and Believing: The Influence of Television*, London: Routledge.

Pohl, H. (1989) *Aufbruch der Weltwirtschaft: Geschicht der Weltwirstchaft von der Mitte des 19. Jahrhundert bis zum Ersten Weltkrieg*, Stuttgart: Steiner Verlag.

Real, M. R. (1998) 'Media sport: technology and commodification of postmodern sport', in L. A. Wenner (ed.) *Media Sport*, London: Routledge.

Redhead, S. (1991) *Football with Attitude*. Manchester: Wordsmith.

Redhead, S. (ed.) (1993) *The Passion and the Fashion: Football Fandom in the New Europe*, Aldershot: Avebury.

Redhead, S. (1997) *Post-Fandom and the Millennial Blues: The Transformation of Soccer Culture*, London: Routledge.

Relph, E. (1976) *Place and Placelessness*, London: Pion Limited.

Riordan, J. (1993) 'Sport in capitalist and socialist countries: a western perspective', in E. Dunning, J. Maguire and R. Pearton (eds) *The Sports Process: A Comparative and Developmental Approach*, Champaign, IL: Human Kinetics.

Riordan, J. and Krüger, A. (eds) (1999) *The International Politics of Sport in the 20th Century*, London: E. and F. N. Spon.

Ritzer, G. (1996) *The McDonaldization of Society*, Newbury Park: Pine Forge Press.

Ritzer, G. (1998) *The McDonaldization Thesis: Explorations and Extensions*, London: Sage.

Robertson, R. (1990) 'Mapping the global condition: globalization as the central concept', in M. Featherstone (ed.) *Global Culture: Nationalism, Globalization and Modernity*, London: Sage.

Rojek, C. (1995) *Decentring Leisure*, London: Sage.

Rose, A. and Friedman, J. (1994) 'Television sport as mas(s)culine cult of distraction', in *Screen*, vol. 35 (1): 22–35.

Roversi, A. (1994) 'The birth of the ultras: the rise of football hooliganism in Italy', in R. Giulianotti and J. Williams (eds) *Game without Frontiers: Football, Identity and Modernity*, Aldershot: Arena.

Rowe, D. (1996) 'The global love-match: sport and television', in *Media, Culture and Society*, vol. 18 (4): 565–82.

Rowe, D. (1999) *Sport, Culture and the Media*, Buckingham: Open University Press.

Rowe, D., Lawrence, G., Miller, T. and McKay, J. (1994) 'Global sport? Core concern and peripheral vision', in *Media, Culture and Society*, vol. 13 (3): 297–308.

Sacks, H. (1995) *Lectures on Conversation Volume I*, edited by G. Jefferson, Oxford: Basil Blackwell.

Schulze-Marmeling, D. (1992) *Gezähmter Fußball: Die Geschichte eines subversiven Sports*, Köln: Die Werkstatt.

Schweitzer, K., Zillmann, D., Weaver, J. B. and Luttrell, E. S. (1992) 'Perception of threatening events in the emotional aftermath of a televised college football game', in *Journal of Broadcasting and Electronic Media*, vol. 36 (1): 75–82.

Sennett, R. (1992) *The Fall of Public Man*, New York and London: W. W. Norton.

Shaw, M. (1997) 'The theoretical challenge of global society', in A. Sreberny-Mohammadi, D. Winseck, J. McKenna and O. Boyd-Barret (eds) *Media in Global Context*, London: Arnold.

Silverstone, R. (1994) *Television and Everyday Life*, London: Routledge.

Silverstone, R. (1999) *Why Study the Media?*, London: Sage.

Simpson, L. C. (1995) *Technology, Time, and the Conversations of Modernity*, New York and London: Routledge.

Sklair, L. (1995) *Sociology of the Global System*, second edition, London: Prentice Hall Harvester Wheatsheaf.

Smith, T. (2000) 'Bataille's boys: postmodernity, fascists and football fans', in *British Journal of Sociology*, vol. 51 (3): 442–60.

Spigel, L. (1992) *Make Room for TV: Television and the Family Ideal in Postwar America*, Chicago: Chicago University Press.

Stacey, J. (1994) *Stargazing: Hollywood Cinema and Female Spectatorship*, London: Routledge.

Stuart, O. (1995) 'The lions stir: football in African society', in S. Wagg (ed.) *Giving the Game Away: Football, Politics and Culture on Five Continents*, Leicester: Leicester University Press.

Sugden, J. and Tomlinson, A. (1998) *FIFA and the Contest for World Football*, Cambridge: Polity Press.

Szymanski, S. and Smith, R. (1997) 'The English football industry: profit, performance and industrial structure', in *International Review of Applied Economics*, vol. 11 (1): 135–54.

Taylor, C. (1998) *The Beautiful Game: A Journey through Latin American Football*, London: Victor Gollancz.

Taylor, I. (1971) 'Football mad: a speculative sociology of football hooliganism', in E. Dunning (ed.) *The Sociology of Sport*, London: Cass.

Taylor, R. (1992) *Football and its Fans: Supporters and their Relation with the Game, 1885–1985*, Leicester: Leicester University Press.

Thompson, E. P. (1974) *Patrician Society, Plebeian Culture*, in *Journal of Social History*, vol. 7: 382–485.

Thompson, J. B. (1993) 'The theory of the public sphere', in *Theory, Culture and Society*, vol. 10: 173–89.

Thompson, J. B. (1995) *The Media and Modernity: A Social Theory of the Media*, Cambridge: Polity Press.

Thornton, S. (1995) *Club Cultures: Music, Media and Subcultural Capital*, Cambridge: Polity Press.

Tomlinson, A. (1991) 'North and south: the rivalry of the Football League and the Football Association', in J. Williams and S. Wagg (eds) *British Football and Social Change: Getting into Europe*, Leicester: Leicester University Press.

Tomlinson, A. (1996) 'Olympic spectacle: opening ceremonies and some paradoxes of globalisation', in *Media, Culture and Society*, vol. 18 (4): 583–602.

Tomlinson, J. (1991) *Cultural Imperialism: A Critical Introduction*, London: Pinter.

Tomlinson, J. (1998) 'Review essay: unfinished business – varieties of retrospection in the analysis of global communications', in *European Journal of Communication*, vol. 13 (2): 235–44.

Tomlinson, J. (1999) *Globalization and Culture*, Cambridge: Polity Press.

Tuastad, D. (1997) 'The political role of football for Palestinians in Jordan', in G. Armstrong and R. Giulianotti (eds) *Entering the Field: New Perspectives on World Football*, Oxford: Berg.

UFA (1998) *UFA Fußballstudie: Marketinginformationen für Vereine, Medien und Werbung*, UFA Sports GmbH: Hamburg.

Vamplew, W. (1987) 'Sport and industrialisation: an economic interpretation of the changes in popular sport in nineteenth-century England', in J. A. Magan (ed.) *Pleasure, Profit and Proselytism: British Sport at Home and Abroad 1700–1914*, London: Cass.

Vamplew, W. (1994) 'Wogball: ethnicity and violence in Australian soccer', in R. Giulianotti and J. Williams (eds) *Game without Frontiers: Football, Identity and Modernity*, Aldershot: Arena.

Virilio, P. (1991) *The Lost Dimension*, New York: Semiotexte.

Virilio, P. (1998) *The Virilio Reader*, edited by J. Der Derian, Malden: Blackwell.

Wagg, S. (1995a) 'The missionary position: football in the societies of Britain and Ireland', in S. Wagg (ed.) *Giving the Game Away: Football, Politics and Culture on Five Continents*, Leicester: Leicester University Press.

Wagg, S. (1995b) 'On the continent: football in the societies of north west Europe', in S. Wagg (ed.) *Giving the Game Away: Football, Politics and Culture on Five Continents*, Leicester: Leicester University Press.

Waldstein, D. and Wagg, S. (1995) 'UnAmerican activity? Football in the US and Canadian society', in S. Wagg (ed.) *Giving the Game Away: Football, Politics and Culture on Five Continents*, Leicester: Leicester University Press.

Wann, D. L., Melnick, M. L., Russel, G. W. and Pease, D. G. (2001) *Sport Fans: The Psychology and Social Impact of Spectators*, New York: Routledge.

Ward, A. and Taylor, R. (1995) *Kicking and Screaming: An Oral History of Football in England*, London: Robson.

Weber, M. (1921) *Wirtschaft und Gesellschaft*, Tübingen, reprinted in W. Nippel (2000)

Max Weber: Wirtschaft und Gesellschaft. Die Wirtschaft und die gesellschaftlichen Ordnungen und Mächte. Die Stadt, Tübingen: Mohr.

Weeks, J. (1990) 'The value of difference', in J. Rutherford (ed.) *Identity: Community, Culture, Difference*, London: Lawrence and Wishart.

Whannel, G. (1991) '"Grandstand", the sports fan and the family audience', in J. Corner (ed.) *Popular Television in Britain: Studies in Cultural History*, London: British Film Institute.

Whannel, G. (1992) *Fields in Vision: Television Sport and Cultural Transformation*, London: Routledge.

Williams, J. (1994a) 'Sport, postmodernism and global TV', in S. Earnshaw (ed.) *Postmodern Surroundings*, Amsterdam: Ropodi.

Williams, J. (1994b) 'The local and the global in British football and the rise of BSkyB', in *Sociology of Sport*, vol. 11: 376–97.

Williams, R. (1974) *Television: Technology and Cultural Form*, London: Fontana.

Wynyard, R. (1998) 'The bunless burger', in M. Alfino, J. Caputo and R. Wynyard (eds) *McDonaldization Revisited: Critical Essays on Consumer Culture*, Westport: Praeger Publications.

Index

I.M. MARSH LIBRARY LIVERPOOL L17 6BD
TEL. 0151 231 5216/5299